This book is dedicated to 1. [illegible] [illegible].

Tracey, whose remarkable and unfailing generosity ensures that we still have a roof over our heads. There are not enough words to express our gratitude. It is *only* because of you that we are able to go on.

My ever loving parents, who have always been there for us and have caught us when we have fallen... so many more times than parents should have to. "Thank you" hardly seems adequate.

We would like to offer our grateful thanks to those others who have provided invaluable support and assistance along this journey: Colleen and Diane, without whose generous intervention, 'Some Dogs' would never have begun to see the light of day; our best-in-the-world neighbours, Scott and Shannon who support without question and have *never* let us down – you guys rock! Chris who gives without question and is learning to put up with the madness of our household; Christine and Andi who keep pushing us when we need it and never give up on us, even when we're being lame. Thank you all.

To Ingrid and the team at Eastern Slopes. Thank you so much for looking after our extended animal family. Ingrid, we are very grateful for your skill, sensitivity and understanding, both of our dogs and of us!

Last, but not least, Cheryl at Stonehaven Kennels. We're not quite sure where we'd be now without your support when we needed it. Your unquestioning acceptance and love of our dogs meant the world to us. Thank you.

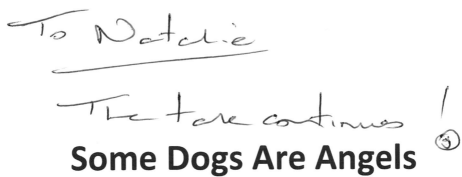

Some Dogs Are Angels

TAILS

AND

TRIBULATIONS

Foreword

'Some Dogs Are Angels' was published in September 2009; or to be more accurate, it was printed then. Somehow, it didn't capture the imagination of either agents or those limited few publishing houses that will accept direct submissions from authors. The fact that I was a previously published author meant nothing. That was in the field of business books, and my existing publisher wouldn't have dreamed of touching this one! The two publishers that did want to publish it quoted two year publication times. This was not acceptable to the etheric.

By the beginning of August, I had begun to lose faith in how it would make it to the bookshelves. In the world order of things, there are literally millions of books that never make it to 'the public eye' so just one more seemed pretty insignificant. However, I had been told by an Archangel that the book *must* be made available. After all, so much of it was channelled, he had a vested interest in it! Nevertheless, it seemed that no opportunity to get it out there existed.

If the etheric wants something to happen, it will happen. So I guess I shouldn't have been surprised when a dear friend of ours called Colleen announced one day that not only *must* the book be published but that she would also pay for it.

Colleen was one of around a dozen people to whom I had given the manuscript to see what 'the public' response might be, without suspecting for one moment that this is where it would lead me. In fact, to be honest, I was very reluctant to accept her offer at first. I had long ago concluded that self-published books were those that had a content or writing style that rendered them unworthy of being on a bookshelf. Simply having a book printed is known as 'vanity publishing' and having a desire to demonstrate this form of conceit is not something you could really accuse me of. It's not that I didn't think the book was good enough; I was just prepared to bow down to the judgement of those more knowledgeable in the world of books. Archangel Michael however, was not!

I am never rebuked by the etheric for my thoughts or errors of judgement; they do offer 'helpful' advice where necessary. In this instance, the feedback was quite forthright. The message contained within the book and its availability to all was of far more significance than whether or not I deemed it to have been 'published'. The views of those who might assess it would be based upon their commercial assumptions that caused them to judge without knowledge or understanding of the content of this work or its higher purpose. Paraphrase for this "stop whining and get it printed".

At this point, another lady, also a 'trial reader' voiced her concurrence with Colleen. She suggested a more commercial contract wherein they would become investors in the book for a percentage return, and on this basis we agreed that five hundred copies would be printed.

Thus it was that on the first day of the Body, Soul, Spirit Expo that is held bi-annually in Calgary, 'Some Dogs Are Angels' went on sale to an unsuspecting public! We sold sixty six copies in three days which wasn't a bad start. A month later, during the same show in Vancouver, we sold only twenty three. Not so good. We advertised the book on our newly created website, although that didn't really bring any benefit. (We have actually only ever sold three copies via this route.) Perhaps the book wasn't going to be the barnstorming success I had hoped, and Archangel Michael had promised.

Of course, I found it necessary to ask Michael what on earth was going on and he counselled that I "not be concerned". Easier said than done; but I should have known that promises from the etheric are not idly made.

Around December time, a friend suggested to us that we see if 'Angela's Attic', one of the stores in the tiny hamlet of Bragg Creek would be interested in stocking it. The proprietor (funnily enough, called Angela) agreed to give it a try with a few copies. Enthused by this acceptance of it, Sharon asked Michelle, the owner of 'One Of A Kind', also in the hamlet, if she might be interested, and happily, she agreed. Over the Christmas period, quite a number of copies were sold and both we and the store owners were very pleased with the result. However, the pleasure with this limited success did little to prepare us for what would happen next.

It would be safe to say that based on what Michael had told me, I was expecting that 'Some Dogs' would be received reasonably well by those who read it. After all, I was instructed to write the book. A large percentage of its content was channelled and those aspects that weren't being reported verbatim, I was specifically told to include. Even so, I was unprepared for the responses that the story elicited from others. From February onwards we were veritably inundated with the most wonderful and supportive emails from people who'd received the messages within the book and wished to share their enjoyment and pleasure. I was particularly surprised at the number of people who read it multiple times. I was astonished that even my parents read it three times each! I was bowled over at the number of people who explained what the story had meant to them and their reports of how it had changed their outlook, or even their lives. I was positively taken aback by the number who now wanted to know more and asked when the 'next instalment' would be coming out.

At the same time demand, on a relative basis, skyrocketed. Then in March, yet another store in the hamlet, 'Belcourt Pet Spa', agreed to stock the book. There was a further surge in demand. Many readers seemed to be coming back to buy another copy for a friend or relative; some bought as many as ten additional copies! We received orders from as far afield as Florida in the US and got feedback from people who had come from Europe as tourists and bought the book. By the end of summer, our five hundred copy print run had vanished.

In both its reception by its readership, and in the demand for it, 'Some Dogs' has done just as Michael promised. I was incredulous that so many copies had been sold when the book had not been on sale in a single bookstore, and there had been no publicity, write-up or review by professional critic. Word of mouth is a powerful thing.

However, Michael was not satisfied.

Increasingly I began to receive reminders that not only was a second instalment required, but that the market we had established thus far was way too small for his intentions for the book and its messages. He was absolutely insistent that the book be available globally. Again, easier said than done. So at this point I will just have to trust that somehow, someone is out there who is going to read the book who has the contact and will make the connection that will facilitate this happening.

So as I write this, the second print run of 'Some Dogs' is just about to come off the presses and we already have a list of backorders. And here you are with a copy of the next instalment!

I guess that many of you reading this now are a part of the success that 'Some Dogs' has had. Both Sharon and I thank you from the bottom of our hearts for your support. Your purchase(s) of the book is helping us to get through what are, as you will see, the most difficult times we have ever experienced. But there I go again, getting ahead of myself.

A Brief Recap!

I suppose that I should really begin with a brief recap of what happened in 'Some Dogs Are Angels' in case you're new to this or have forgotten(!). So here's a 270 word summary of a 270 page book.

- Whilst living in the UK I was a successful international businessman. At one point in my life I became curious about angels and decided to attend an unusual seminar about them.
- Two months later, the voice of another being came out of my mouth and told my wife Sharon that I was 'meant' to be a channel, a mouthpiece for beings that exist in the etheric (a parallel dimension type thing) who wish to help us upon our Ascension Pathway (a term that describes the purpose, if not the meaning of life).
- I was somewhat reluctant at first but eventually gave in and was taught by various angels how to let their messages be delivered through me. Apparently, my destiny was inescapable.
- In the process I learned that angels sometimes visit earth in the bodies of animals so that they may experience a (very rare) chance to know what it is like to be physical, that they may better assist us upon our Ascension Pathway. When they do this they're called 'avatars'. NB. This has absolutely nothing to do with movies about big blue people with tails.
- I subsequently discovered that we already had not one, but two of these beings living in our house who my family had hereto believed were just Kaiti and Dougal, two of our dogs.
- We were then 'encouraged' to seek out and rescue other avatars (and some 'normal' dogs) who, for various reasons, had fallen upon hard times.
- In the process we ended up being guided to emigrate to Canada and owning eighteen dogs.
- Then a nineteenth being arrived that is something altogether different...

And on that cliff-hanging note, let's pick up the story!

A Spirit Dog Foretold

There are many things about our lives that the reader may find unusual, somewhat strange, or even downright bizarre. It all depends upon your relative perspective. When you live it, all of the events in your life eventually become perfectly normal. So the fact that Sharon had been woken up in the early hours of the morning by the booming voice of an extremely mighty angelic being called Asrael emanating from the body of her still sleeping husband lying beside her, did not strike her as anything too out of the ordinary.

What was unique was the exact wording of the message that he gave her. Up until that point all of those messages that we had received from the etheric regarding our extended pack had been gentle suggestions. They had always been phrased with terms like "you may wish to consider..." or "it would be of benefit if you..." The difference was that in the past they had all come from an Archangel, and Asrael is a 'Power'.

What is a 'Power'?

Angels have a hierarchy. I often refer to it, in explaining their existence and purpose, as a management structure. That is a very third dimensional way of describing it because it has nothing to do with status. It is simply a way of understanding a delineation of responsibility.

I don't profess to fully understand the nature of the different roles, particularly as those at the most senior levels (Seraphim and Cherubim) have responsibilities that are, I am told, almost inconceivable to us. Also, the levels as described to me are moderately different from religious texts that cover the same subject matter.

However, Asrael has what is best described as an inter or trans-dimensional level of responsibility. His concerns are with different forms of evolving reality and parallel dimensions.

At this point, my mind starts to get blown; I am unable to fully grasp the broader concepts due to my woeful lack of ability to understand quantum physics, so it is seldom explained to me in any more detail!

On this occasion there were few subtleties, just a basic command.

"You are already familiar with the nature and being of the avatars that live amongst you. You are cognoscent of the differences between their essence and those of the other creatures whom you would think of as dogs. One type may be regarded as of the earth and the third dimensional planes; the others as visitors from our realms.

You have sought to make others aware of this as you have been directed but as yet you are ignorant of another type of being that walks the planet.

This may be described as a being of pure spirit or, if you will, a spirit dog.

It is a trans-dimensional creature and as such, it is of interest to myself.

You have already been directed to a source where you may obtain one of these creatures.

I wish you to obtain it as it will be of service to you in your understanding of the knowledge that I have to impart.

It will accompany you in those activities that I have asked you to perform and will request of you in the future.

It will bridge the gap of understanding and fear that exists between third dimensional beings and that which is.

I am Asrael."

The "it" that was being referred to was a dog that our friend Jean and I had been corresponding about for a few days. It was a breed of dog I'd never heard of called a Native American Indian Dog, but since Michael had told me that it wasn't an avatar, I'd pretty much ignored it other than to be fascinated by a breed I'd not come across before.

When I woke up in response to Sharon's insistent shaking, she was equally commanding. "Go and contact Jean and tell her we'll take the dog she was talking to you about." She then gave a brief explanation of what Asrael had said, and blearily, I started to get out of bed. As soon as I tried to do so, I was overwhelmed with a very uncomfortable sensation at the base of my spine. It was rather dull aching that felt as if there was something lodged under my skin. I decided to have a bath before contacting Jean, but as soon as I got in the water, Asrael was back.

The bath is always a good place for channelling because of the fact that my body is surrounded by water. However, it can be a little tricky doing full body channelling lying down! So I was fortunate that on this occasion, I was allowed to simply relay the information he gave me.

Why is water a good place for channelling?

Water is often explained to me and others as something akin to a 'golden thread' that runs through everything. It connects all things on our planet in one way or another.

As our bodies are seventy percent water, immersing myself in it gives me a broader level of connection and therefore greatly enhances the clarity of channelling.

The ultimate best place for channelling I have found is in our hot tub. However, since it is outdoors and the temperature is kept quite high, it can also prove to be an uncomfortable experience. This is because my body temperature often rises during a channelling session as energy from the etheric is run through me. Several times I have finished a session and found it necessary to get out quickly because I am massively overheating, almost to the point of passing out!

Asrael revealed that the sensation that I was being 'allowed' to experience was that of a dog's tail chakra. He explained that whilst humans have seven chakras and conventional diagrams indicate that a dog also has seven, they in fact have eight.

What is a chakra?

A chakra may be regarded as an energy centre within the body which acts as both a generator and a relay centre for the vibrations that emanate throughout our bodies. Each of the seven human chakras performs a particular function or may be said to be a regulator of an aspect of our being.

If you were to do an internet search, you would find numerous colourful diagrams illustrating them as having associated colours and symbols. The colours are a reflection of their vibration (since every colour has a vibrational emanation) and the symbols are simply the names they are given. For instance, the lowest (always shown as red) is known as the base chakra and the highest (usually shown as purple), the crown.

If you are then wondering why in x-ray or MRI these energetic spheres do not make for very pretty pictures, it is simply because they vibrate at a level that is above the density of a third dimensional body, effectively rendering them invisible. They are far more apparent within the etheric where their presence and functionality is very evident.

Chakras may become unbalanced. This means that the vibration of one or more is out of synchronisation with the others, or that it is vibrating (often envisaged as a spinning action) at an unintended frequency. This may be caused by our responses to the external world around us; equally, it may result from that which we create within ourselves. For instance, intense feelings of anger are said to distort the balance of the base chakra.

Chakras may be balanced or restored to their proper functionality with relative ease. Perhaps most powerfully, this is achieved through the use of sound. By using a frequency that is compatible with the intended vibration of the chakra, its proper resonance may be restored by entraining one vibration with the other.

Prolonged imbalance of the chakras often results in disease because it goes against the nature of the way in which an individual's state of being should exist. In the etheric, disease is always referred to as dis-ease. In

14

other words, it describes a lack of congruity between the chakras that makes them not at ease with one another.

Asrael went on to explain that the eighth chakra in all beings relates to the ability to communicate telepathically. For me, this immediately put into context the fact that many who have studied canis lupus familiaris in its purest original form (canis lupus, i.e. wolf) have remarked upon apparent levels of extrasensory perception that the animals seem to have. This, he revealed, is because they are using the inherent ability that comes from the eighth chakra. However, in most domesticated dogs the eighth chakra has fallen into a state of relative disuse, much like the appendix in the human body.

<u>Why has the eighth chakra fallen into disuse?</u>

Unlike the lower level chakras, effective functioning of both the seventh and eighth chakras is not strictly required for physiological existence. In fact, the eighth has become almost completely unusable by most humans.

Within domesticated dogs, isolation from a pack environment, which is the lot of so many, means that the eighth chakra is not utilized on a moment by moment basis. Like an unused muscle, it wanes in strength. Its functionality is replaced by the most powerful physical sense, which is that of smell. But even this within a dog is different from within a human. A dog's sense of smell is linked to its visual perception and actually helps to form pictures or images within the brain and adds an additional dimension to their sight which, as any dog owner will tell you, they seldom rely on.

The fact that it is absent within humans almost suggests that animals are a spiritually higher form of being. This is not so. It is simply the case that since we have more complex ability with our vocal cords when used in conjunction with our tongues, we have evolved reliance upon these more physical attributes.

There is no doubt that our forbearers would have enjoyed a fully integrated eighth chakra. However, in times gone by, its utilisation became frowned upon and seen as inferior to language (which it is most certainly not) and thus, its use was discouraged. So we have evolved by societal habit, although not form, into beings without an eighth chakra.

In fact, humans are actually born with a full ability to use the eighth chakra; regrettably, because it is all we know, our manner of developing children has us teaching them from earliest childhood to use language as a means of communication, and thus it is discarded. Our eighth chakra may be thought of as sitting above our heads, waiting to be reintegrated, if we but realize that we have the power to incorporate it into our being once more.

The seventh or crown chakra is somewhat different. Within both humans and dogs it provides an 'uplink' to the etheric. At the moment of birth, we are incarnating as physical beings and leaving an environment of pure light. The shock of this experience is never overcome, no matter how many times we reincarnate. To give us reassurance and ease our transmutation, the uplink that the seventh chakra provides allows us to receive comfort and support from the etheric. When babies in their cribs suddenly smile and laugh, quite intent on something that cannot be seen, their mothers may muse that they are talking with angels. They are!

In all likelihood, their earthbound families have already lost their ability to communicate with them through the eighth chakra, so they talk to the etheric via the seventh. It makes a potentially highly disorientating and highly stressful experience a whole lot more bearable. The link may be maintained permanently throughout a lifetime, or it may be shut down completely at a very early age due to the feedback our families give us. Many invisible childhood 'friends' are in fact beings from the etheric with whom children maintain a relationship but are discouraged from doing so by parents who become convinced that their offspring are merely seeing things.

Alternatively, the action of the crown chakra may be all but closed, only to be re-opened again at a later stage in life when it is required. (This is a very usual phenomenon for old souls.) Its purpose is in allowing us to receive information from the etheric that will assist us on our ascension pathways. We are not alone!

The crown chakra is the gateway to the etheric that I use for all of my channelling. However, its utilisation is not without risk or effect.

These matters will be addressed later in the book.

The utilisation of an eighth chakra would give us far more in common with beings of the etheric, who exist as purest vibrations of light (or as what we might refer to as 'spirit') rather than physical form. So when Asrael talked about a spirit dog, he meant a being that was still very connected to not only its higher self in the etheric but also capable of communicating with other beings who were able to maintain a functional eighth chakra.

Almost as a casual aside, he added that not only would I be able to communicate with the dog but that my connection with it was beyond my current level of knowledge. Asrael then proceeded to blow my mind with a download of information. He gave a full account of why he referred to the dog as a trans-dimensional being and went into considerable detail regarding her purpose for coming to us. He outlined her true nature and what we would perceive as the history of spirit dogs such as her. Then he told me some facts about myself, the implications of which I am still reeling from.

At this point I consider what was revealed as way too strange for the average reader. I am still having difficulty coming to terms with all of it myself. Thankfully, I am also told that it is not necessary for me to reveal this knowledge now. So you'll just have to wait for the third book if you want to go even further down the rabbit hole than this one will take you!

The Spirit Dog Cometh

Since the writing of 'Some Dogs' I have received many serious and off-the-cuff comments from people that they would like an avatar in their household. My response is always an astounded "Why?" because I am only too well aware of the issues that they bring with them and their difficulty in the management of their energies. Put simply, they are way too powerful for their own bodies and basically they are trouble. This is not in any normal doggy type way. They are seldom Marley-like in their behaviours, although they could easily be. Instead they are disruptive in ways that are unseen and may be described in Star Wars terms as 'disturbances in the force'. So being told that we were supposed to get a 'spirit dog', which would presumably be even worse, caused me some concerns.

Nevertheless, after my very revealing bath, I contacted Jean who had told me about the Native American Indian Dog in the first place. Apparently, the dog was now with a lady we had not come across called Karen, in another State, who I now needed to contact. In the meantime, Jean was able to fill me in on some background.

The dog had been owned by a man who had thought that having such a breed was quite fashionable, or had some cachet attached to it. The dog had been in a fenced yard in an urban environment, and most often chained. It sought to escape wherever possible. When it did so, it would go missing for days without really knowing where to go. We were later to learn that in its attempts to find some form of home, it would be stoned by local children. When it was eventually caught and returned to its owner, it would be severely beaten. This did not dissuade it from making many more escapes and eventually, complaints from neighbours drew the attention of animal welfare services who came and took the dog away with complete assent from the owner.

The dog then found itself in a kill shelter, fortunately being rescued by Jean before its allotted time was up. However, the animal proved too much even for this well-seasoned rescuer, so she moved it on to Karen who, like us, had a facility with seven foot fencing. Karen adored the dog but it did not cease its escape artist tendencies. Instead, it either jumped or scaled the fence with apparent ease and by the time we came to know of it, the dog had already cost Karen many hours and a great deal of stress in trying to recover it. Although it never strayed far, it was very reluctant to return to the safety her compound offered, most likely afraid of the beating it now anticipated as a result of its experiences before it came to Karen. In desperation she had used drugged meat to secure its return; thereafter it was too clever to be fooled again by this ruse and only lucky chance brought her back to safety a third time. Much against her wishes to give the dog a happy and free life, Karen had to resort to keeping the dog attached to a 'skywire', a leash suspended on a long cable above the ground that gave the dog a free run, but still restricted her movement to backwards and forwards along the raised cable.

With great sadness, Karen realised that there was something about this dog that needed more than she was able to offer. Clearly it needed major rehabilitation of some kind. The question was would it stay with us? It was suggested that we would need an eight foot fence to cope with the athleticism of this creature, and we would possibly need to electrify that fence to dissuade this canine Houdini from breaking out.

From our perspective, this was obviously going to be an issue. Nonetheless, Asrael was undeterred and his guidance was quite clear. "The dog will not escape." So without further ado, we arranged that we would meet Karen at a point on the US border a few days hence.

Karen had named the dog Kenani Breeze, dispensing with a ridiculously inappropriate moniker her previous owner had given her. However, following a piece of guidance given to us by a First Nations Ascended Master about the importance of names, we thought that we might call her 'Kachina' instead. This is the Hopi Indian word for a doll that actually means 'spirit dancer'. Bearing in mind all of the information that Asrael had given us, this seemed a far more appropriate name. We decided to reserve judgement until we actually saw the dog to see if the name would suit her.

<u>What was the advice regarding the importance of names?</u>

There is a great deal more to a name than meets the eye.

We choose our earthbound names in the etheric before we incarnate, not because we like the name but because of the vibration that it carries.

Our 'true' names are utterly unique. There is not a single being in existence that has the same name because it is an expression of the unique individual vibration that each one carries.

In consideration of the inconceivable number of beings that exist, you might well appreciate that the name is then also long and complex, made up of many syllables, and from a third dimensional perspective, highly unusual and difficult to pronounce. Nevertheless, it carries with it the essence of our distinct individuality; and despite the fact that we are regularly reminded that we are all part of the great oneness, it is important.

Thus we chose our earthbound names to be a reflection of the essence of our being and to serve as a reminder to us of that which we really are. Our parents are actually informed of our choices (in a manner that will be explained later on) and although they may ignore the guidance they receive (!) the majority of people end up with the name of their choice.

For an animal, the name given to it by a human owner is of less consequence. When I think of some of the names I have come across by which people call their dogs, I believe that this is probably a good thing.

However, for the spirit dog, it apparently *did* matter. This is what the First Nations Ascended Master explained, along with advice as to what a more appropriate name would be.

During the five hour drive to collect Kenani Breeze, we gave precious little consideration to what we were about to do. Despite all of the knowledge we had been given regarding the 'spirit' dog, we did not expect her to be all that different from the others. When we looked at the photos we had been sent, we saw an attractive animal that, whilst bearing very little resemblance to any dog we already had, was nonetheless perfectly 'normal'. After all, how different could it be?

We had arranged to meet Karen and collect the dog at a Starbucks with a large parking lot. We arrived first and when her truck turned into the lot, we instantly knew that it was her. It was like connecting with a kindred spirit and we spent a couple of hours over coffee discussing our experiences in rescue. She was far more experienced than we were and acted as a half-way house for dogs (that would otherwise have been put to sleep) on their way to their (hopefully) forever homes. She is a remarkable lady and features more in our story later on.

Then it came time for us to meet the dog. Sitting warily in the back of the truck was the most gorgeous but very wary creature, quite unlike any that we had encountered before. She was big and leggy, almost the height of Indy (our enormous Leonberger), with a fan shaped section of yellow fur just below her shoulder blades. Her coat was short, thick and lush. Behind a long and magnificent muzzle was set a pair of the most unimaginably knowing and bright yellow eyes.

Kenani Breeze eyed us warily for a few seconds and then after gentle encouragement from Karen, got out of the truck. Her custodian was in floods of tears by now, so attached to the dog had she become. There was a great knowing within the creature and she jumped into the back of our SUV with precious little concern. Karen said her final goodbyes to Kenani Breeze and we parted company, without realising that our paths would cross again many times in the future.

The five hour return journey would have passed without any indication that we even had an animal in the back, apart from the fact that Sharon suggested that I try to communicate with the dog as Asrael had promised I could. Instantly, at the mere instigation of the suggestion, I experienced an odd and somewhat alarming sensation that can best be described as a pulsing band all around the back of my head. I had an overwhelming awareness of there being another presence with whom I could communicate, quite unlike anything I experienced when communicating with the etheric. All at once, the Native American Indian Dog in the back was expressing shock and alarm that someone was communicating with her in this way! She got up and wide eyed, stared at me through the dog grill that separated her from the main body of the car. We made eye contact in the rear view mirror, and although I don't remember her exact words, I can tell you that her response to being contacted in this way used some colourful language!

Unfortunately, after only a few moments, the pulsing turned into an uncomfortable throbbing, so I stopped. Clearly, my eighth chakra was a much depleted muscle and using it was a strain. The last thing she said to me was that she didn't want to be called Kenani Breeze; and we took that to be more than a happy coincidence. Kachina was on her way home!

Upon our arrival back at our house, we opened the tailgate and were met with those piercing yellow eyes that seemed to look into our very souls. It is somewhat embarrassing looking back now, to note that in spite of all we saw and the evidence before our eyes, not for a single moment did it cross our minds that we were face-to-face with a wolf.

You think *that's* a dog? : Kachina's tale

If we had assumptions about what would happen next, they were highly flawed.

The first one was that Kachina would continue to be an escape artist. For days we kept her on a thirty foot long leash but when we finally plucked up the courage to release her, she showed not the slightest interest in leaving the compound. She didn't dig, she didn't look for weak spots in the fence line, and she certainly didn't jump. Instead, she appeared to be totally relaxed and happy with her new surroundings.

The second assumption was that (since we still believed she was a dog at this stage) she would behave like a dog. This was very far from the truth. She didn't even move like a dog, let alone act like one. Most surprising to us was that she acted like a creature of the wild. Her days were spent gazing at the house from a safe distance, ever watchful for any attempt to trap her. She was obviously interested in the comings and goings of the other dogs, but showed precious little inclination to form relationships with them. For their part, they seemed to respect her choice and kept their distance. As for the human members of the pack, they were to be avoided at all costs. Even bad weather couldn't persuade her to come in during the daytime.

Nights were a different story. In common with most dog owners, we have a routine that last thing at night, the dogs go out for their final 'bathroom break'. When they're done, all of ours rush back inside, anxious to ensure their place on their favourite bed of choice. Those who are less concerned might linger longer outdoors, and the whole process of getting everyone to bed can take upwards of thirty minutes.

During this activity, Kachina would be invisible. The light of our porch only extends twenty feet or so away from the house and the trees beyond this point afforded ample opportunity for concealment. After the last dog had found their way back indoors, I would remain with the door open, calling to her; my efforts were in vain and for weeks, Kachina lived her life exclusively outdoors.

Then one night, for no apparent reason, my patience was rewarded. Just as I was turning to go indoors, a svelte and shadowy figure brushed past me, immediately disappearing in the darkness of the interior. Amazingly, she defied all my attempts to find where she had gone and managed to either secrete herself totally, or move just one step ahead of me as I searched the open-plan house. So where she spent that night was something of a mystery. When the doors were flung open in the morning to release the rampaging hordes, Kachina slipped out with them.

Thereafter, it became her preference to be indoors at night. Whether it was the cold or some other factor playing upon her mind, she developed a routine of being last dog in. However, if she thought that her route was blocked, she would stay away. So after all of the others were in, we would leave the door ajar and stand away from the door. After a few moments wait, there would be a flash of fur and a rush of energy like a gust of wind and Kachina would have made her grand entrance. She didn't do it every night, but by the fifth month it was the exception rather than the rule that she spent the night outdoors.

After a little while, she came to realize that rushing outdoors in the morning was not such a sensible thing to do. On several days of the week, the dogs are fed an 'indoor' meal in their bowls, rather than the bones they have outdoors on other days. On these occasions she would miss out on the action and have to wait a lot longer to get her food. Only after all of the others had eaten would her bowl be taken to a place on the deck outside. She would then cautiously approach it when her confidence got strong enough. Sometimes she was getting her food an hour after the rest of the dogs; nevertheless, she was the archetypal hungry wolf. Something had to change.

Thus began her new routine. Dash in last thing at night. Slip out with the others in the morning. Try to slip in unseen if it's an indoor food day. Make a break for it afterwards. In between, don't let anyone touch you and if they look at you, move away quickly. Above all else, don't EVER let yourself be cornered.

For our part, we were happy to go along with her routine and allowed her the space she needed. We were just pleased that at least she was making some progress. Whilst the rest of the pack crammed into the kitchen she would remain in the lounge which, because of the open plan nature of the house, still allowed her access to the food when it came, but also allowed her to keep a safe distance from us.

Once the others had eaten, one by one, they would go out until only a few of the more passive dogs remained. Then we would put down Kachina's food near to the lounge and she would creep carefully up to it, crouching down as she did so. Her startling yellow eyes would constantly dart around, looking for signs of danger; and if you looked at her, she'd stare right back at you. There was never any menace or threat in her eyes; just a deep seated fear of what might happen if she let down her guard.

More in keeping with our assumptions was her response to humans generally. She was extremely fearful of newcomers, and although over the months she began to accept Sharon and I if we maintained a discreet distance, she was hugely wary of Tristan and would sometimes greet his return from school with angry barking, albeit from a distance. I decided to question her about this one day, and feeling the same uncomfortable pulsing in my head, was rather shocked by the rather profane response. In this curious manner, we came to know of the unpleasant experiences she had before coming to us. She explained the chasing and stoning by unkind children and it became obvious that she now associated him with them. For the first time, I understood the advantage of being able to talk with her in this way, since I was able to explain that he was not one of them and that he would not repeat their actions. This mollified her slightly and since that time there have been very few occasions on which she has barked at him.

The first glimmers of recognition of the fact that she might not actually be a Native American Indian Dog came fairly early on. Our neighbour Scott's reaction on seeing her went something like "Jeez. You got a wolf there." We brushed his comment aside and assured him that no, she was in fact a pure bred Native American Indian Dog. "Yeah, right", was his grinning response. I was only mildly curious at his fascination with watching her move. "I could watch that all day", he said.

In keeping with our practice of taking newly acquired dogs to the vet, we had taken Kachina to the clinic and been greeted in the foyer by our friend Murray who at that time operated a dog grooming service there. He eyed the dog with considerable interest and asked us what breed it was. When we responded with 'Native American Indian Dog' his "Hmmm" response seemed to conceal that he knew differently, although he said nothing further.

Shortly after she arrived, a friend visited who was enthralled by Kachina, even though she only allowed herself to be glimpsed from a considerable distance. She had just lost a dog and was looking for a replacement, so we told her the breed and she began detailed research, eventually getting a lovely dog from one of their accredited breeders. However, we were perplexed that her Native American Indian Dog bore not even so much as a passing resemblance to Kachina.

Then a few months later Murray told us that one of his clients had three wolves that he was bringing in for grooming next week. He suggested that we drop in and see them if we were passing. I was very excited at the prospect of seeing such exotic creatures. Ever since coming to Canada, I had harboured a desire to visit the wolf sanctuary in Golden, BC, but had never gotten around to it. Now I made it a point to be 'passing' on the day of their visit.

So I was shocked and even a little disappointed that when we encountered the wolves, the two females were almost exact replicas of Kachina. They could have been sisters they were all so much alike. As we drove away, Sharon and I discussed the remarkable similarity and joked that perhaps Kachina was a wolf. Although initially funny, the joking soon turned serious. Was she in fact a wolf? "Ask Michael" demanded Sharon. As usual the response was totally matter of fact. "Oh yes."

We felt rather dumb. How could we not have known?

How could we not have known that Kachina was a wolf?

At the time that we took Kachina, we were as ignorant of the true nature of wolves as the next person. We had been told that wolf hybrids could be highly unreliable as pets. We were also aware of how fashionable they had become at one point. As part of this, we were also very aware of the danger they posed. We had heard nightmare stories of their potential for 'going bad'.

Conversely, as you may recall, we had already encountered wolf hybrids (which I now believe to have been full-blooded wolves) when we acquired Cinnda and Ktuu. They were intense, but not threatening in the slightest. It is commonly accepted (and within our experience very true), that any animal tends to become the product of its environment. Yet in spite of all of this, we still would have said "No" if Asrael had asked us to take a wolf. It would definitely have been a case of "Thanks, but no thanks" irrespective of how big an angel you are. We still value our freedom of choice.

So were we deceived by Jean or Karen or even the etheric to serve their own ends?

Well, not really.

I certainly do not believe that either Jean or Karen knew for one moment that Kachina was a wolf. They would *never* have sought to deceive us. Her labelling as a Native American Indian Dog was essential so as to allow for her safe transit across the border. In the eyes of all of those who assisted her passage, including ourselves, the wolf was invisible. Instead we all simply saw the being that required help.

In those moments, our perception of reality was almost certainly somewhat distorted. It was for Kachina's highest good, our highest good and the highest good of all. This type of distortion is a technique discussed in 'Some Dogs' and may only be carried out if the 'highest good' criteria apply. When it occurs, there is a guarantee that no harm will come from it. And even amidst the distortion, our freedom of choice may still prevail. How it is brought about is fully explained later.

When I look at her photos now, the very same photos we were sent at the time, it is blindingly obvious that she is a wolf. We just couldn't see it and that was our choice.

Michael filled in the gaps and instantly everything became much clearer.

Kachina had been first 'taken' as a cub by a hunter. Although killing wolves is illegal in some States (as it is in all of Canada), due to their endangered nature and the need to protect them, Kachina came from a State where killing wolves *is* legal. The hunter shot her mother and then discovered a cub. His actions in keeping her suggest that he thought having a captive wolf was 'cool' and his subsequent abusive behaviour towards her was probably intended to knock all the spirit out of her and ensure that in later life, she would betray no wolf-like behaviours (although for the large part these expectations are a nonsense).

Why are our expectations of wolves a nonsense?

Wolves are the stuff of legend for all sorts of reasons. The origins of their mythology goes back even before our commonly held beliefs about them and relates in large part to the information Asrael had shared with me regarding the true nature of spirit dogs. Put simply, they are portrayed as creatures of which we should be fearful.

The reasons for the evolution of this foolish mindset are many and complex. In large part, on an historical basis, it is due to the practicalities of humans and wolves competing for food sources. Inevitably, one set of needs must prevail over another. In their need to achieve dominance, humans are cruel and selfish. To justify actions, it becomes a matter of convenience for the supressed to be vilified, and thus it is with wolves. It actually serves our interests for them to be branded as some of nature's worst villains.

Some see this and recognize the imbalance between ourselves and other creatures. As any knowledgeable naturalist will tell you, wolves are massively misunderstood, mostly as a result of hundreds of years of ingrained preconceptions and assumptions that come from story rather than fact. Prevalent amongst these is the fear of attack. Yet relative to their size as a predator, there are far fewer recorded incidents of fatalities from wolf contacts than from any other major predator. Indeed, most are shy and fearful of human contact. As with all creatures, they will defend their young and protect food. Treated with respect, they are far less threatening than other species. According to the definitive National Audubon Field Guide to North American Mammals, there have only been three recorded attacks by a wolf upon a human, in history. None were fatal.

Several respected naturalists have concluded that the response of a wolf to a human is based upon that which it has learned i.e. it has developed a fear response because of its own persecution; a feature of its existence that has pushed it almost to the point of extinction.

Yet everyone knows the extent of their reputation as monsters, and as such they are harbingers of the most fearful responses with precious little justification. Anyone who has spent time in the company of wolves will be aware of the intensity of their presence and will also have become aware of how benign that presence can ultimately prove to be.

When she escaped from the hunter's yard, the local children behaved as children in fairy tales do: with fear. Their reaction towards her merely served to exacerbate Kachina's fears and make her even more skittish. This, coupled with the harsh treatment she received at her owner's hands, had engendered a deep sense of mistrust and fear of humans that probably went far beyond that which is normally encountered, even in a truly wild animal.

Of course, as the hunter lived in a state where killing wolves was legal, it was correspondingly illegal to have one as a pet! It was wildlife control that had been called in, not animal welfare. Kachina had been removed to a facility for termination, and it was 'luck' that the adjacent State had a far more progressive policy with regard to the species. To have her taken there simply removed the burden of her destruction from her State of origin.

So now the truth was out, what difference would it make to us?

None of course. Our shock was momentary and Michael's explanations rapidly calmed any concerns we might have had. If anything, we were quite amused to discover the wolf in our midst and it made understanding Kachina's many quirks and foibles much easier. We were careful about whom we told because of the reactions we feared they might have, and some who we did tell doubted her provenance anyway: A friend and her husband had come to drop off a package at our house one day and the husband, unaware of what we did, was asking about the dogs that frequently passed the gateway as we talked outside. We explained that we had a large number of dogs and a wolf. He smiled indulgently and explained that in the course of his daily working life, he had seen many full blooded wolves. Did we know that many people had what they thought were wolves or wolf hybrids, but they were just Alaskan Malamutes crossed with German Shepherds? As he continued in full flow to dispel our erroneous belief about what we had behind the gates, Kachina trotted past with her unique gait. He stopped mid-sentence, his jaw dropping. "But that's a wolf", he stuttered.

Over time we began to recognize more and more of her wolf characteristics and her dissimilarity with the rest of the pack, despite their common heritage. I read a great deal about wolves and gained a deeper understanding and respect for them.

Most marked amongst her behavioural traits was her selection of Indy as her mate. This was both amusing and sad to see. Her fondness for him, which developed within the first few weeks of coming to us, soon developed into full blown adoration. As soon as he appeared outside, she would rush towards him with the closest thing to a smile on her face that you can possibly imagine. The shy retiring wolf became the playful coquette, flirting outrageously and running in circles round and round him. Her invitations to play were obvious and excited. If he came out on a hike with us, as he frequently did, she would be waiting anxiously at the gate upon our return, whimpering with evident joy at the return of her paramour.

For his part, Indy was at best indifferent. Her attempts at closeness were met with aggressive rebuffs and he would repeatedly chase her away. Her passion was totally unreciprocated and we feared that she would be disillusioned by her unrequited love. We were quickly to learn wolves are made of sterner stuff than that. To this day she remains unabated in her enthusiasm for the big Leonberger, and despite his best resolution to remain aloof, he now tolerates her devoted attentions. Even though he is not a playful dog, she teases him mercilessly, provoking him, in spite of himself, into games of chase and bringing him out of his otherwise serious persona. She will creep up behind him and pat his hindquarters with her paw, and he will turn and give pursuit, never able to match her speed or agility. When he sleeps, she will get as close to him as possible. When he wakes, she is there to wash his face, unquestionable pleasure written all over hers. And if he leaves, she never fails to be on unrelenting watch for his return.

Female wolves are fiercely loyal creatures and tend to mate for life. If the mate dies, they may pine terribly, and particularly in captivity, a female that loses her mate will often starve herself to death or just die, seemingly of a broken heart. When she came to us, Kachina was two years old, with a life expectancy of more than eighteen years. Indy was three with a life expectancy of eight. Although the rarefied energies of our household seem to ensure a much greater degree of longevity amongst our dogs than would be normal, we still fear for what may face her in the future.

Since this account is chronological, I will not get ahead of myself in explaining why and how Kachina's relationship with us changed. We will leave her as a moody and recalcitrant creature who still eschews human contact and lives in our midst as a truly wild being. Certainly, it would take many months and a most alarming turn of events before she would begin to transform.

Growing Pains

By this time, our little brood of Husky avatars had started to come into their own. Each had already developed their own unique personalities that gave a clear indicator of the dogs they have become today.

Idaho, the only male, is big, strong and quite leggy. He has grown to be the tallest of our Huskies and his thin face gives him a vaguely coyote-like appearance. He takes great delight in sampling everyone he meets by biting them gently on their hands and chewing, so as to get their full flavour. I spent a great deal of time training him not to do this to me, and he was either a slow learner or simply enjoyed it too much to stop. However, he did eventually, but now insists on licking me instead. It can be very annoying! Idaho obviously fancies himself as alpha male at some point (although with Indy to compete with, he has very little chance).

Aura always was, and still is very feisty. She is endearingly crazy and prone to moments of extreme madness. Of the four puppies, she seems to have the greatest zest for life, and also the greatest propensity for getting herself into trouble with the other dogs. In her play, she doesn't always know when to stop. She is adventurous to the point of being fool hardy and this has resulted in experiences for her that we will come back to as the book progresses.

Zoe is sweet and gentle and the mildest of the four. She has grown into a petite dog with a slightly longer than normal silver coat (that gives her a 'fluffy' appearance) and a delicate foxy face with perfectly proportioned features. If a dog may be so, she is demure, and in her dealing with humans, takes treats from our hands in a delightfully gentle way. She is the only one of our dogs who has, with no instruction, learned to beg, she does this quite spontaneously by sitting back on her haunches and waving her front paws in the air. It's very cute and quite irresistible. Her general appearance is very appealing and she just looks like a cuddly little dog. She could easily be a role model for a soft toy. Although she has moments of puppy madness, she is generally calm. Moreover, Zoe has some unique attributes which will be discussed in another chapter later on.

Inara, the first born, is deceptively angelic. She has a beautiful pale apricot and white coat and amber eyes. To look at, you would think butter wouldn't melt in her mouth. She has a fixation with wanting to be a lap dog and as soon as you sit upon a sofa, she will be up there with you wanting to be cosseted. She will force her face into yours no matter how many times you try to push her away, and like brother Idaho, she's a real licker. Her desire to be cuddled has earned her the nickname 'Teddy Bear'. When Zoe saw Inara getting this kind of attention, she wanted some too, so they began to vie for our attentions. If Inara was on Sharon's lap, Zoe would come to mine, or vice versa. Consequently, Zoe earned herself the nickname 'Teddy Bear Two'. Or as they are collectively known, the Teddy Bears. These two are alike in many respects.

They all get along famously and play together well. As a family of siblings, they are very well adjusted and accepting of one another. But let's go back again to three months after they were born, just as 'Some Dogs' was being finished...

It was fascinating for us to experience the family structure at work. As we had never had a litter of puppies before, we were enthralled by the interaction of the babies with their parents. Totally contrary to our expectations, both Lara and Timba were very active in sharing responsibilities for bringing them up. As soon as they were able to leave the whelping box, they would take it in turns to escort them around the compound, and although the more unpleasant tasks, such as cleaning them, fell exclusively to Lara, we watched in awe as Timba took an ever larger role in their socialisation.

It was slightly heartbreaking to observe Molly's role in their development. We had her spayed when she was a puppy and now, in her behaviour towards the pups, it became clear that the Grand Bassett Griffon Vendeen might have liked a litter of her own. She was the only dog that Lara ever allowed in the whelping box and she was almost as much of a participant in their bathing and care as Lara herself.

The remainder of the pack accepted them totally too. They were born in their midst and their assimilation was instant. As in all dog society, a pack order has to be established. Very rapidly, the puppies began to push back boundaries. They very quickly learned who they could play with, and who to leave alone. Kaiti, for example, treated them with her usual disdain; Indy prowled around like a lion, emitting a roar-like growl if they tried to mess with him; Molly was an active playmate; Daisy ran from them as if they were carriers of the plague. Sometimes, in their antics, they would push another dog too far and earn themselves a snapping, but harmless, rebuke. As the weeks passed, they developed a strong interest in Kachina who, in the early days, would always remain at a discreet distance in her outdoor world. Curiosity may have killed the cat, but this was a lesson the pups were not aware of; so at one point, they seemed to decide that they would chase her, as a group. Bad move. Kachina is a large and powerful animal and she did not respond well to what must have appeared, from her perspective, as an unprovoked attack. She became all raised hackles, flashing teeth and snarling predator, and was more than a match for all four puppies put together. Then from out of nowhere, Timba and Lara appeared, responding in kind, and as a pack of six Huskies, they gave chase to a now whimpering and very frightened wolf.

Because I had seen the whole thing, which was over in no more than a few seconds, I was able to intercede. My position as pack leader commanded enough respect from them all to break off their pursuit with one bawled command. Within seconds, they were all relaxed with one another again and the incident has not repeated itself. Whilst I was amazed at their instantaneous re-establishment of friendly relations, Michael explained that it was merely an aspect of their ability to live in the moment.

What did Michael mean: "Live in the moment"?

As humans, we spend inordinate amounts of time looking forward to the future or looking back on the past. Although these experiences may bring us pleasure, they are a complete waste of the moment. Indeed, dwelling upon either the past or the future has a great deal to do with how rapidly our lives seem to pass us by.

Were we to be living in the moment, we would be unencumbered by concerns with things that have happened and can't be changed, and untroubled by those things that have happened that we have not yet accepted as being for our highest good. We would also not spend time conjecturing as to future outcomes of things that may be out of our control. Even manifesting which, by its nature, involves thoughts of the future can be achieved in moments.

Living in the moment involves simply that. A focus on the present that let's go of the past and accepts the inevitability of the future. To a dog, this is apparently second nature. They may not forget, but they certainly forgive, almost instantaneously. Therefore they are able to move on from the majority of experiences that are unpleasant and are perceptibly able to enjoy their lives more without anguish about the future either.

Of course, the past may be scarring and difficult to let go of. Our experience with rescue dogs like Kachina has indicated that continuous repetitive experience can form habits of emotion, attitude and behaviour. (Fear is the most usual amongst these.) Even these are habits that a dog can get over and we can learn from the relative ease with which they do this, when compared with humans.

There is great danger for us in hanging on to past hurts, or trying to escape the present by constantly imagining ourselves in the future.

The parameters of the acceptable had obviously been established between them that day. Perhaps fortunately, as we still thought Kachina was a dog at this point, we weren't too worried by these confrontations. In hindsight, had we thought of her as a wolf, our own flawed expectations might have caused us to respond very differently and affected her ultimately easy assimilation into the pack.

It would be fair to say that the only harm the Husky puppies have actually suffered is from each other. In the full throes of their rough and tumble games, they occasionally get carried away and all have suffered a bloody ear or bitten paw. Yet even within their own puppy interactions, their parents have been very active in controlling their energies. At first, this was quite alarming to see, since it involved one puppy being singled out by the parents for a 'roughing up'. The offending pack member would be rolled onto their back and held down by one parent (usually Timba) whilst the other appeared to be savagely biting them. The squeals and screams from the infant brought us racing to their rescue on many occasions, until we finally realized that no-one ever got hurt. The 'bites' did no damage, and it was all part of the socialisation process. No puppy was immune from the process, although we noticed that Zoe and Inara, as the calmest, got beaten up far less frequently than their siblings. Aura, on the other hand, got taken to task on an almost daily basis!

Finally we got to understand that this was all part of their own parenting technique and became inured to our own knee-jerk responses upon hearing puppy screams. However, this did little to stop the alarm of visitors who did not understand what was going on when the cries for help would start. "Oh yes, that's just Timba and Lara killing their puppies" we would say, wickedly amused by the momentary horror on their faces.

Throughout, Lara and Timba worked very obviously as a team. In fact sometimes, they were like a pair of tag-team wrestlers. When one parent tired of perfecting their pin-down technique upon their infant, the other would step in; only to allow their 'spouse' to return to the fray if they got bored or the pup was being too submissive in the face of their latest stranglehold. As a couple, they are not 'bonded' in the way that Kachina regards herself with Indy; yet they show each other great respect and have none of the proximity issues that colour the relationships of the other dogs. It is no disrespect to each other, however close they come.

By the time they were three months old, the baby Huskies were confident and assertive balls of fluff that regarded anything as a potential plaything. As I was finishing the last chapters of 'Some Dogs', I had proudly boasted that our house suffered very little from dog destruction. This run of good fortune was about to end.

I can't remember the exact date when we first discovered that Inara found our leather sofa to be to her taste, but I do remember the horror I felt and the explosion of anger and colourful language that I gave vent to when I saw the damage she'd done. We had bought the sofa when we moved to Canada and it was one of three that matched, spread in a

U shape around the fireplace. It was a beautiful chestnut brown and we'd spent a considerable amount of money on it so as to get the best quality leather which, the salesperson had assured us, would last us for a lifetime. He hadn't told us that it also tasted really good. The attack on the sofa only affected one of its cushions, so I guess we got off lightly. We simply turned it upside down and pretended all was well. Until her next attack.

It seemed that Inara had developed a taste for things unusual and her taste was not limited to sofas. Next came socks. All of us suffered from finding half eaten socks that had been pulled out of drawers, laundry baskets, or off beds. Vaguely comical scenes would ensue when one of us caught her red pawed, sock in mouth, and would give chase. Usually it was much too late. She went too far when my favourite pair of socks got involved. It was a very good quality thick pair from the 'Life Is Good Company'. If you're familiar with this business, they sell wonderfully optimistic products, usually depicting a stick-man like character called Jake. Even better, Jake has a dog; and this pair of socks featured the dog. I loved them. So, apparently, did Inara. I was not amused.

Next came clothes; or to be more specific, my clothes. I had had experience in the past when Rittee, our beautiful Siamese cat, had decided to eat a brand new sweater. He didn't just chew it, he ate it, and I found it with an almost perfectly round eight inch hole added to the design. Since Rittee had moved on at the ripe old age of eighteen, some two years previously, I was sure that it wasn't him who had chewed the hood off a not inexpensive and prized Abercrombie and Fitch hoodie that I had bought in New York in better times. Clearly the culprit had good taste. The guilty party revealed themselves some time later when they brought it back up again; and of course, it was Inara.

T-shirts and other sweaters were to follow, but I thought she had to be crazy when she started in on underwear... If you are wondering why we didn't simply put everything away, ask yourself if you ever leave clothes out? There is always that moment where for convenience sake, something is forgotten. And these are just the moments when Inara would strike. It was as if she had a sixth sense, or had waited her whole week just for the instant when a casually discarded piece of clothing would become her prey. The funny thing is, it was always my clothing.

This less than endearing trait remains a feature of her personality today. And I should also add that we've now had attacks on six of the sofa cushions.

Over time you can come to accept, even though it still horrifies you, that these things are the price you pay for being surrounded by such (otherwise) delightful and loving creatures. An object is merely an object, whereas an animal provides for many other needs: love, comfort, companionship, entertainment. The list could go on and on. And although you can't sit on a dog, or wear a dog, these little tests of our commitment to our pack certainly helped us to prioritize our feelings about what was important in life; what matters and what doesn't. However, it wasn't too long before another form of behaviour began to cause us a completely different form of disquiet.

Without any apparent rhyme or reason, one day, out of the blue, the puppies decided en masse that they didn't like Briony, our 'second time around' avatar Poodle. We discovered all four of them chasing her wildly around the compound and snapping at her like a bunch of rabid dogs. If your first instinct is to think "poor little Poodle", don't. She may be small, but Briony can hold her own with pretty much anything. If pushed she can become incredibly ferocious and can put on one of the scariest faces of all of the dogs. Although she was the prey, she was managing to take them all on. However, we rushed to break it up because it was absolutely the antithesis of what we wanted. It was also utterly incomprehensible to us why something like this should have begun.

When you have a pack as large as ours, some conflict is inevitable. How much you get is a direct feature of how strong the pack leadership is. We are profoundly grateful that aggravation between pack members is limited to very minor spats, almost always over food, flashpoints because somebody wants somebody else's bone. The pack dynamics are in fact nothing like the knife-edge existence that logic dictates they should be.

Why aren't the pack dynamics 'knife-edge'?

It can reasonably be anticipated that when a large number of dogs get together, there will most likely be trouble. Those who have just two or three can tell you that the potential for conflict between them is great and the issue of position within the pack order is a major issue amongst canines. Mayhem and infighting are common features of multiple dog ownership.

So when people first hear that we have so many dogs, their first reaction is always one of shock. The next question we get asked is "How do they all get on?" When we tell them that they get on really well, there is sometimes a little bit of incredulity. However, it's the truth!

When Cesar Millan talks of the pack being 'healing', we can concur that this is very definitely the case within ours. We have experienced very obvious positive alterations in the behaviour of our rescues; conversely, we have been disturbed to discover that if a pack member leaves the pack for a length of time, they change quite markedly and become what can only be described as more 'doglike'. Although this transformation is reversible, it is nonetheless shocking to see.

It should be understood that the dynamics of our pack are somewhat different because of the sheer number of avatars within. Although they are full of potentially troublesome energies, many of their behaviours are subtly different from those of other dogs, particularly with regard to their relations with each other. We believe that there is a greater sense of knowing within them with regard to their purpose and the importance of the need for convivial interaction. As is recorded several times in these pages, their acceptance of troubled and damaged dogs is without question.

Frankly, I would never recommend anyone to have as many dogs as we do, if only because of the knife-edge dynamics that *could* result. No reader should underestimate the significance of the fact that all of the dogs that we take come to us because we are directed to take them. Rescue agencies ask us to assist with many that we cannot help with because we are advised not to. No pack member is brought in without guidance or instruction. It is only this assistance from the etheric that allows us to be confident that a new dog will 'fit'; although as will later be seen, not everyone is of the same belief!

It is a constant source of delight to us that all of our dogs get on so well and that they treat each other with such respect and tolerance. So this outbreak of aggression between pack members was not only threatening to their balance, but could easily end in tragedy if the puppies were seeing Briony as prey. It was unthinkable. Nonetheless, it was an isolated incident and so we chose to dismiss it as an aberration.

When there was a repeat three days later, our concern level rose. And when there was a third instance shortly after that, we could see a scary pattern developing. Sharon was mortified and almost in panic that this could be happening, incredulous that it was occurring between avatars. Of course, her first recourse was to Archangel Michael. Could he explain to us what was happening and why?

His brief and somewhat puzzling response left us reeling.

"Get a Maremma Sheepdog."

Close Encounters of the Maremma Kind

The first time I ever saw a Maremma Sheepdog in 'real life' was in the Abruzzo region of Italy, the place from which the breed originates. It was during one of my extended overseas trips, delivering multiple back-to-back management development programs in a small hotel, in a sleepy little spa town called Fiuggi. The town nestled amidst the beautiful mountains to the south of Rome, but to be perfectly honest, I hated the weeks on end that I spent there. Although the staff were wonderfully helpful, the hotel was not exactly brilliant and, as usual, it was somewhat depressing being away from home. Very intense, week long events, which began early each day and finished late, allowed only Saturdays free before a new batch of participants arrived on the Sunday. It became a matter of great significance how Saturday was spent, and my preference was to get out and about in the countryside. Sometimes I would drive for miles to visit places of historical interest like Montecassino; at others I would just hike amongst the rolling hills and mountains on the hotel's doorstep, enjoying the solitude after a week packed with people.

I quickly became aware that it was an inescapable feature of the landscape that whatever you did or wherever you went, you would encounter very large white dogs. They were quite beautiful, big, powerful and very like a Pyrenean Mountain Dog, (with narrower heads). In my early childhood I had watched a dubbed French children's TV programme called 'Belle et Sebastien'. It featured a rather touching story about a young boy living with his Grandfather in the mountains who befriends a much feared and misunderstood Great Pyrenees. I was about the same age as the boy portrayed in the series and ever since that time, I had romanticised Pyreneans.

However, the animals I encountered were not like the biddable and friendly creature Sebastien had played happily with in the Alpine meadows. These dogs were very threatening and implacable, snarling ferociously at anyone who came near them, and certainly not a dog to casually pet, talk to, or approach. Sometimes I would see them from a distance in fields where their bright coats stood out against the somewhat dull greys, browns and pale greens of the mountainsides.

When they spotted me, they instantly became alert and observed my passage with a gaze that felt discomforting, even from a great distance. If I went for a stroll through the town itself, in passing a house, I came to learn that there was a good chance that one of these terrifying beasts would suddenly appear out of nowhere, barking furiously and scaring the life out of me.

At first I was shocked by the very evident power and the ability to intimidate that exuded from such a pleasant and regal looking creature. Then as I encountered them more and more frequently, I began to wonder about why there were so many, and why such an obviously unsuitable pet was so popular.

A little research soon revealed that they were LGDs, or livestock guardian dogs. They were bred to live outdoors with the flocks of sheep and cattle that roamed the mountain pastures and ensure that no harm came to them. This they did with immense effectiveness. A single Maremma, it transpired, could protect a large flock or herd from wolves, with consummate ease. Its ferocity and raw aggression would be enough to scare off most predators; and if it came to it, it was also lethal in its ability to dispatch other creatures much larger than itself. Much later on I came to learn that two Maremmas, working together, could take on and see off a fully grown grizzly bear.

This obsession with protection extended to everything and everyone they regarded as their responsibility. It wasn't just an issue of animal predators either. Humans could also be regarded as a threat. Whilst they were apparently excellent with people whom they knew (even being affectionate, as well as loyal) they would guard against any intruder who was unknown to them. This certainly explained my experiences of the barking beasts that patrolled their owner's back yards. I was quite enthralled and would have loved to have watched them in action. Nevertheless, seeing the big white dogs defending a flock was something I envisaged I would have to leave to my imagination. Until, that is, an interesting little scenario occurred a few weeks later...

The courses that I ran for my client involved groups of 24 participants from all over Europe. They would work in groups of 6 and I employed a number of people to help facilitate the programs, each of us taking one group to work with throughout. One of my colleagues was an individual named Neil. I had known him many years before he came to work with me and he was a larger than life character in many respects. He was tall, bulky and bearlike, but gentle and sensitive, highly intelligent and very accommodating. His only flaw, at least as far as I was concerned, was that his energies were almost totally incompatible with mine and although I liked him a great deal and was actually very fond of him, I found being with him utterly draining.

How could Neil's energies have been draining?

If we allow ourselves to be aware of it, the experience of finding another individual draining is something that almost everybody experiences. Yet the idea of it happening with someone we like can be a disturbing one.

Everyone has differences in their energies. Our energies emanate as vibrations from our physical as well as our spiritual bodies and our vibrations are not necessarily compatible with one another. In some cases, the energetic 'collision' caused by one type of energy meeting with another will cause one to effectively feed off the other. The individual whose energies are being fed upon will most likely experience physical and emotional repercussions, both of which will be draining in their effect.

It is of little consequence whether or not personal like or dislike is involved. The draining effect may be regarded as a metaphysical one which is unavoidable. The occurrence of such circumstances is unlimited and may result from relationships between family members, friends, work colleagues or casual acquaintances. No group with whom you make contact is excluded.

What must be noted is that it is very often the case that people persist in relationships where their energies are not compatible. They are unable to get past what they perceive as the obligation of maintaining that relationship, despite its negative consequences (which, for the sake of convenience, they will often deny to themselves).

Michael has often reminded us that such feelings of debt or obligation are deceptions that we bring upon ourselves. We should, in fact, feel no burden from our attachments whatsoever. This is because we tread the ascension pathway on our own. We cannot ascend for others or with others, since their pathway is uniquely their own. If we bind ourselves to others, it is the equivalent of attaching anchors on our spiritual progression.

When we recognize our energetic incompatibility with others, it is actually an act of mastery to withdraw ourselves from the relationship, even when it is not accepted as such by the other party.

An imbalance of energies does not imply fault. It is just a natural fact.

However, if you seek to raise your vibration (which is an essential feature for achieving ascension), it is important to be aware that the likelihood of increasing incompatibility with those of a lower vibration is great.

When this story took place, I was not aware of the reasons behind my experiences of Neil. I liked him immensely and considered him a good friend, yet his draining affect upon me was undeniable. Eventually, and just because of his affect upon me, I had to 'let him go'. For years after I felt bad about it.

In hindsight, and with the revelations Michael has made about the 'deceptive' nature of relationships, I feel totally confident that my actions were for my highest good and the highest good of all.

As part of the program, the participants would always spend at least one day in the outdoors. Not only did it provide a welcome change from the conference room, it also provided a very memorable learning environment for whatever points I sought to convey in that time. At a personal level, I loved to get outside and breathe the fresh mountain air.

During this particular week, my group and I were walking along a high pathway on the side of a mountain, overlooking a valley full of open fields. In the distance we could see another of the groups making their way along the floor of the valley below us. They must have been at least half a mile distant and moving away from us but I could make out Neil's hulking form and bright blue waterproof jacket at the head, closely followed by the rest of his group. I was a little irritated because the facilitation technique that he was supposed to be using required him to trail along behind and not get involved. Yet here he was in the thick of the team, apparently leading them. I also noted with some chagrin that the area that they were walking in didn't even form part of the prescribed series of routes that formed their options! In fact, I wasn't even sure that they were on a public walking trail at all.

As I watched, the group stopped and seemed to register their error. They came together in a cluster, and then began to climb up a track leading out of the valley with fields on either side. I traced the pathway ahead of them to see where they would come out and when I got to the top of the valley, my gaze fell upon not one, but three Maremma sheepdogs scattered across the hillside, attending a large flock of sheep.

Immediately realising what would happen, I shouted a warning at the top of my voice. The distance and difference in height made my efforts futile. Our protestations simply rose up to the heavens and even when I solicited the support of my group, our combined efforts failed to carry the sound down into the valley. So we just stood and watched with growing disquiet as the group progressed up the hillside, totally oblivious to what was waiting for them.

By now, the dogs themselves were well aware that what they perceived to be danger was approaching. I have to confess that my concern turned to fascination as I watched their behaviour. First, the two outermost dogs ran to the dog closest to the intruders. They seemed to be holding a conference amongst themselves, and then they all ran to the edge of the hillside, coming plainly into sight of the group below. When their appearance prompted no response from the oncoming walkers, they spread themselves out approximately five metres apart and stood there looking down, with what I imagined must have been menace. When this elicited no response, they began to bark.

Neil and his group now became aware of their presence and their pace slowed slightly, but they were clearly unaware of *the nature* of what lay

49

ahead of them and they continued. This did not please the Maremmas. They began to run backwards and forwards along the ridge, creating an invisible line which evidently they did not wish anyone to cross, barking ever more furiously.

Still some 15 metres away, the group seemed to grow very hesitant. I could make out Neil, now several strides ahead, gesturing with his arm for them to follow.

The Maremmas began to jump up and down, their body language becoming very aggressive and the running backwards and forwards along the ridge now became small forays towards the group.

Neil, perhaps needing to portray himself as the fearless leader, or just plain clueless as to what was about to happen, pressed forward whilst we watched in silence, in awe of their stupidity.

When the group were about 10 metres away, the dogs closed their ranks and their barking reached a feverish pitch, the cacophony of sound travelling across the valley and beyond. They were very obviously making their final stand and this was their final warning. The group came to a halt and the humans regarded the dogs, whilst the united Maremma front edged menacingly closer.

I could almost see the instant at which Neil decided to call the dog's bluff. He took one more step. Then the Maremmas charged.

As one, the humans turned and fled. As one, the mass of white fur and fury pursued them, easily gaining ground on them with every passing second.

The humans were all flailing arms and screams. The fast ones sprinted out in front; Neil trailed up the rear, too scared to look behind him and probably moving faster than he had ever managed before in his entire life. He must have known that the dogs would be on him in seconds.

They never got to him. The Maremmas were quite content to chase the humans away without harming them. You could actually see them pulling their punch and slowing down their pursuit when they got too close. As we, the distant observers, began to realize that their intentions were not as blood thirsty as we had suspected, we began to enjoy the scene and it became quite hilarious to watch. The group was far too scared to slow down and their wild cries could faintly be heard as they rose up to us.

Meanwhile, the Maremmas were sitting side by side watching them with what I imagined to be satisfaction. At the floor of the valley, the group finally slowed to look back; and realising that the dogs were no longer at their heels, they stopped to get their breath back. Neil was bent over double, undoubtedly gasping for breath. Some lay down. The rest kept a watchful eye on the dogs, now several hundred metres on the hillside above them.

Only when the group finally collected themselves together and moved off out of sight did the Maremmas turn and race back to their flock. Within moments they had dispersed and returned to the positions in which I had originally observed them.

For my part, perhaps somewhat cruelly, it was a full five minutes before I was able to stop laughing. I rarely cry when laughing, but tears rolled down my cheeks. If I thought of what I had witnessed at any time during the rest of that day, I went into uncontrollable fits of laughter once more. It was ten years ago and I can still see the whole scene with absolute vividness. I still regard it as one of the funniest things I have ever seen.

That night when I met up with Neil and the rest of my colleagues back at the hotel, he did not relate the tale of his encounter with the dogs. When I suggested he seemed somewhat flushed he mumbled something about it being the effects of having spent the day in the mountain air. I asked my team if anything exciting had happened to anyone with their respective groups during the day. Still that story was not proffered. Finally, childishly unable to restrain myself any longer, I related what I had seen. The rest of the team found it very funny but Neil was quick to dismiss the incident as one so trivial, he had forgotten about it.

Curiously, from that time onwards, I observed a not-so-subtle transformation in myself. I had not only developed a great admiration for Maremma Sheepdogs, I also felt great affection for them.

Love At First Bite: Poppy's Tale (Part One)

As a result of all that is written in the previous chapter, the advice that we should get a Maremma Sheepdog was not entirely unwelcome. What was most intriguing was Michael's description of the affect that the dog would have upon the rest of the pack members.

He described the energies of the pack as they were evolving and the way in which they affected the energy line and conversely, its affect upon them. He explained that as energy entered through the Merkaba of which the line was a part, there would be corresponding effects on the dogs, particularly the younger and less aware avatars. The Maremma would be grounding for them and prevent the energies getting out of hand. Most important of all, it would protect Briony. Once she heard this, Sharon couldn't wait to get one through the door!

However, Michael made it quite clear to us that the dog would not be an avatar, so our enthusiasm was somewhat abated. In some respects it merely represented another mouth to feed. At this point, Michael revealed in a somewhat cryptic manner that the dog might be part of a 'knock on effect' and of more service to us in the future than we could imagine at present. Evidently there was more to the proposal than met the eye.

What is the 'knock-on effect'?

The intricacies of the relationship between events are astounding.

As we go through our lives we may experience them as a series of random and unrelated experiences, or we may notice the patterns within. The extent to which we have planned and prepared for what is to come in our lifetimes can almost defy belief, particularly since it is difficult for us to see beyond our own linear formulation of the way in which time passes.

It was revealed during one channelling session, that our preparation for incarnation takes, on average, around five hundred linear years; yet our actual time transitioning from one lifetime to another can take as little as six months. During this time, minute and seemingly inconsequential details of happenings to come are prepared for. When experienced during a lifetime, some are apparently trivial whilst others appear to be of monumental proportions in their affect upon our lives. What is seldom recognized is the way in which the trivial actually creates the monumental. Seemingly minor and unrelated events group together so as to create something of apparently far greater significance which, without them, would not otherwise have occurred. This is what Michael now described as the 'knock on effect'.

There are many very significant but apparently minor events that become part of the 'knock on effect'; however, if we were to look for them or get too hung up in our consideration of the implications of everything that happens to us, we'd eventually stop living our lives as we're meant to.

We began to conjecture as to precisely what was meant by this. It is extremely unusual that we are given any information about our future because of the likelihood of us distorting our freedom of choice to make a particular outcome a reality. Obviously there was a greater purpose in sharing this information with us now, but the only conclusion we could reach was this one:

When we first knew that we were coming to Canada, we had discussed keeping alpacas. Our affection for them dated back to a time when we had taken the children out for a Sunday morning alpaca trek some years previously. A local farmer had enterprisingly bought a small herd and offered four hour treks around the local countryside, for a not inconsiderable sum. Since money was no object at that point, and it sounded like fun, we decided to go along. It was a wonderful morning and between the four of us, we had two alpacas to lead. They were quirky and unusual, surprisingly good walking mates and just plain good to be with. So we developed aspirations to get some. To this end, my forty fourth birthday present from my parents was an alpaca husbandry course, and thereafter, I spent a great deal of time researching the needs of these potential pets.

We believed that in coming to Canada, we would be able to buy considerably more land than we had owned in the UK, and this proved to be true. However, when we eventually bought our property, we ended up owning thick forest, with a house nestled in the middle, on terrain not really suitable for alpacas. And then of course, one or two more dogs came along who took up a not inconsiderable amount of our resources. However, the desire to have alpacas still remained. Perhaps a Maremma would be useful in providing protection for them if we got to the point of owning some in the future?

We already knew from my research prior to our emigration that Maremma Sheepdogs seemed to be almost as common in Alberta as they were in Italy. Their skills as LGDs were much sought after by local farmers; it was from our Province that the stories of the dogs seeing off grizzly bears emanated. We had even come across several Maremmas living in houses off the same highway as ourselves. We were certainly in the right place to begin a search.

Then somewhat to my horror, I realized that for the first time in many years, I was searching for a dog without getting any angelic assistance whatsoever. For the briefest of moments, I began to question whether or not I would make the right decision, but I reminded myself of a piece of guidance given to Sharon some years earlier regarding the importance of using our own freedom of choice.

Michael on freedom of choice

When I first started to channel it was, for Sharon, like a guidebook for life had been opened up. With the nightly channellings that formed part of my learning, she would have access to vast amounts of wisdom from a diverse range of beings and personalities in the etheric, and so, if only to make their visitations worthwhile, she would ask them questions about anything and everything. I used to tease her that she would ask Archangel Michael what we should have for dinner that night, and although this was not really true, she was developing a reliance upon the guidance from beyond.

On the trip that we made to Canada prior to our emigration, we took a walk together, in temperatures of minus twenty eight degrees Celsius, along the side of Lake Louise, and then back across its frozen surface. As we walked, with such close proximity to the Etheric Retreat at the Plain of Six Glaciers, Michael could be heard loud and clear. He chose to relay feedback to Sharon regarding her growing dependency, and it went something like this:

From the angelic perspective at least, our freedom of choice is the most important and valuable facet of our experience as humans. It is an unassailable right that is not shared by beings who are in the Etheric.

Yet once we possess this right, so many of us seek to give it away!

We do this by seeking answers, guidance and direction outside of ourselves, believing that someone else's version of what is right, good or best for us is better than our own interpretation.

If we repeatedly require reference sources outside of ourselves, be they angelic or otherwise, we eventually arrive at a point where we do not exercise the greatest gift that we have been given. In other words, using our freedom of choice is a matter of habit which we can lose.

In this way, we also abdicate responsibility for the decisions that affect us. We tend to do it because it seems to make life easier for us. It allows us to be victims. It allows us to not have responsibility for all those things that affect us, when really we are fully responsible and need to acknowledge this. Quite simply, if we are not choosing for ourselves, we are not learning for ourselves and our progression along the ascension pathway is significantly slowed.

Most certainly, we can ask for assistance and there are a host of beings in the Etheric only too willing to offer their support. On the other hand, it is probably best to save our requests for those occasions when we feel hopelessly lost.

And anyway, in giving guidance, an angel will never tell you directly what to do!

With that message remembered, I began to search in earnest and discovered local farmers in Alberta charging a few hundred dollars (and

56

less) for their dog's offspring. We had even come across those who gave them away.

Somewhat perversely, in consideration of the way our financial situation had been going, I felt that these dogs would not be right for us and continued to search, eventually finding what I considered to be a highly suitable breeder in Minnesota, who coincidentally had just had a litter of eleven puppies. The parents were awesome looking dogs, large and sturdy and with more than a passing resemblance to Great Pyrenees; much finer examples of the breed than the Maremmas I had seen in Italy.

Images of Belle floated before my eyes! Somewhat ironically, in a probable fit of nostalgia, I had bought the DVD of the ancient TV series 'Belle et Sebastien' some time before the Maremma question ever arose. I now watched it again with Tristan and I was amazed at how a black and white children's television programme made in 1965 could still hold great appeal for both teenagers (Tristan was by now fourteen) and adults. I enjoyed it infinitely more than I had in my childhood and saw facets of the story and the emotions portrayed that had been beyond me forty years previously.

However, the romance of the dog aside, we now came to the issue of arranging for the purchase and I contacted the kennels by email to make enquiries. It transpired that there was just one puppy left, a female (which was just what we wanted). All seemed to be working out fine until we came to money. The breeder in Minnesota was charging a comparatively huge amount for her puppies. In addition, we would have to pay a sizeable sum to have the dog shipped to us.

To say that our financial situation had become dire would be an understatement. If we couldn't pay for something with cash, we couldn't pay for it; so the issue of getting the money to the breeder, irrespective of the amount, was in itself an issue. It was with some trepidation that I broke the bad news to Sharon and after a brief discussion, we both agreed that we couldn't get the dog after all.

With some regret I emailed the breeder to let her know that we wouldn't be taking the puppy, although perhaps in future we'd come back to her. She sent a very nice reply saying "not to worry" as she'd had another enquiry just after our contact and that person would be delighted to take the remaining dog.

During the course of the day that followed, we must have come across half a dozen references to Maremmas. Since, in the average month, we might never see so much as a single reference, we took this to be meaningful. However, I wasn't prepared to push the issue or even point out what was happening.

Of course Sharon, by now, was every bit as attuned to such goings on as I was and eventually she confessed that her higher self was telling her that we should get the dog, whatever. I concurred.

That didn't exactly deal with the expense problem. Irrespective of this, we both concluded that since getting the puppy appeared to be the right thing to do, it would be provided for, and that belief was enough for us.

<u>How would it be provided for?</u>

Only a few years prior to these events, our financial circumstances had been somewhat different. We had enjoyed heady days of major income and carefree spending. These were now replaced by a total absence of work and penny pinching 'in extremis'. By this time we were living a life of borderline destitution.

Knowing this, you might then be surprised that we were foolish enough to embark upon the expense acquisition of yet another dog that wasn't even an avatar.

It basically comes down to an issue of trust and a lesson that we have come to learn time and time again.

If something is 'right' and meant to happen in your life, then it will be provided for, irrespective of your circumstances or whatever else happens to be going on in your life.

This doesn't mean that a life should be lived devoid of any attempt to secure that which is desired by the person living it. Far from it. This refers to the fact that when a lifetime is being lived 'according to plan', i.e. in accordance with the learning that was intended and in compliance with the contractual obligations that have been made, the etheric can be relied upon to make happen that which is meant to happen. And this includes the provision of material needs.

This learning was to assume great meaning for us in times to come and will be returned to later.

Blind faith did not deal with the likelihood that the remaining puppy had now been allocated to another purchaser. When I got back to the breeder, she confirmed that this was indeed the case. We were chasing a lost cause. Perhaps it wasn't 'meant to be' after all.

We were both a little disillusioned at the way in which we had misinterpreted the signs, and so it was something of a relief when the next day, the breeder got in touch again to ask me if, instead of the remaining puppy, we would like to take the 'pick of the litter'. She had been keeping this one particular female to breed from as she was such a fine specimen. Now she had suddenly felt that she should let us have her, if we were still interested? It was a no brainer!

She sent us a charming video of a mass of fuzzy balls of white cotton, all falling over one another in a barn. It was as if I was watching snow, such was the brilliance of their coats. They looked incredibly like Harp Seal puppies, with gorgeous pelts, deep pool-like eyes and shiny black button noses. How could one even tell them apart? Jokingly, I wrote to ask: "Is ours the white one? The instant reply was "Nope, yours is the white one with the black nose".

Sure enough, the universe provided and at the last moment, as on so many occasions before, just the right sum of money was delivered into our hands. So it was that a few weeks later, Sharon and I made our now familiar trip to the cargo depot at the airport to collect our new puppy. Although she had been coming a relatively short distance, the convoluted journey required multiple changes. By the time we collected her, our puppy had been in transit for a horrendous thirteen hours. It would have been quicker for her to come from the UK! It was after ten that night before we were allowed to liberate her from the cargo handlers.

We had already told the breeder that she was to be named Poppy, and we were later to discover a hand written note on top of her crate, explaining that she would get lonely in transit and could the handlers please talk to her as it was her first time away from her family. The note was written with such care and tenderness that I found it deeply moving. So it was all the more distressing that when I went to collect Poppy, I could hear the handlers talking to her in the warehouse that adjoined the offices. Or to be more accurate, cursing and shouting at an obviously terrified animal who was crying pitifully in fear.

We got her out of there as fast as we could, trying to wish the freight handlers only the learning that was surely coming their way.

<u>What was the learning coming their way?</u>

I imagine that there will be very few people who read this book who haven't already understood the precious and very important nature of our relationship with those creatures in the animal kingdom.

The way in which we choose to relate to them, respect them, value them and treat them, is a direct reflection upon ourselves and the learning we have attained within our many lifetimes.

Although these individuals were not being nearly as horrendous in their treatment of Poppy as some may be with what they think of as lesser creatures, even their manner in dealing with a helpless and frightened creature betrayed their utter ignorance of the synergies of our lives and those of animals.

I am sure that her cries were irritating to them, but their intolerance and lack of kindness revealed choices incorrectly made. I am equally sure that if it had been a child crying, their response would have been different. Even if they had not cared, societal norms would have forced them to at least feign some semblance of a compassionate response.

If they believed that an animal didn't warrant it, just because it was an animal, they sure had a lot of learning to do.

Poppy was clearly parched, starving and scared, so we quickly drove to the same grassy spot where previous arrivals at the airport had been allowed out of their prisons to renew their faith in the existence of grass and fresh air. We then discovered not only the breeder's note, but also a lovingly prepared pack of food and bottles of water, with instructions that politely requested the handlers to ensure that she had access to both. Of course, she had had neither.

We lifted the crate on to the grass and attached the lead to Poppy's collar before opening the mesh door. Sharon knelt on one side with me on the other, as we prepared to welcome and comfort our new arrival. There, inside the crate was a simply stunning little bundle of fur with agonisingly sad eyes, just waiting to be loved and cuddled. I eagerly opened the door.

In a flash, Poppy leapt out through the opening and sank her teeth deep into my thigh, neatly puncturing my jeans and causing an instant red flood of blood to stain the material. Then she made a break for it, leaping over me and heading off over the field to the beckoning freedom beyond. She got about six feet before her motion was brought to a very abrupt halt. Thank God her leash was on. What a beginning!

Just as Sharon had forgiven Saffy in her unthinking outbursts, the bite was nothing to me. It hurt like hell, but it was impossible to recriminate with the animal. She was clearly very frightened and probably furious with her treatment. Perhaps she even equated me with the unkindness's shown towards her by the cargo handlers. After giving her much needed water (she refused food), we returned this fire-brand to her crate and headed for home as fast as the speed limit permitted. Clearly she would be better off in our home compound.

Yet much to our surprise, when we arrived within its safe confines, Poppy would not leave the crate. For twenty minutes we tried to coax her out, inducing her with treats (that she would not take) and encouragement (that she ignored). Neither of us wanted to risk putting our hand inside to attach the leash again, and we didn't think that being dragged into your new home would exactly be a pleasant experience for her.

By now it was approaching midnight. Poppy needed to be bedded down. There were nineteen other dogs to meet before that could happen, and here we were, playing this silly game. So eventually, in desperation, I tipped the crate up thinking that at least gravity would facilitate an exit. Poppy wedged herself in the back of the crate. I increased the angle and she splayed herself out in the back of (or now, the upper reaches) of her travel box. Exasperated, I raised the crate until it was vertical. Still she clung on. By now it was a matter of pride that I felt I had to dislodge her. So then I lifted the plastic box a couple of feet above the ground and shook. Nothing happened; except that it caused Sharon to fall about laughing at the comedy of the scene. No matter how hard I shook, this dog was not going to shift. Finally, exhausted by the strain of holding up the large crate with a heavy dog inside, I put it back down again.

For the second time that night, we were passed by a white streak. Instead of going out of the wide open garage door that was right in front of her, Poppy dashed around the side of our SUV, and secreted herself beneath the engine.

At this time of night, I wasn't about to go crawling underneath the car so instead, we decided to let the rest of the dogs come and meet her, in the hope that this might make her feel at home. The other dogs were whining and scratching at the door from the house to the garage. They clearly knew there was another dog on the property and they wanted to come and see if it was a friend or a foe. So we opened the door from the house to the garage and they poured forth like the closing waters of the Red Sea. As one, they raced towards the car in excitement. What followed was as comical as it was shocking.

Suddenly, all of the dogs stopped dead in their tracks. In a single instant, they had all simultaneously realized that at the back of the garage lurked not a nice friendly dog that might join their number, but something ferocious and terrible. From underneath the SUV came the rasping, snarling, guttural utterances of a creature from hell. As one, the pack fell into silence. Some whimpered. All backed away. One by one they sloped off into the night, silently anxious to get away from the horrors within. A few of the brave or foolhardy lurked around the area of the garage door, occasionally daring to set a paw inside, only to retreat with haste. None would approach whatever monstrosity lay within.

What on earth had we brought into our home now?

The Amazing Psychic Dog: Poppy's Tale (Part II)

It was so late that Sharon decided to go to bed. I was left to get the dogs in and they, for the most part, retired to their usual sleeping places. There was more than a little edginess about them. They were plainly disturbed by the frightening thing that was in their midst.

I shut the outer garage door and Poppy was left alone inside. Imagine my surprise then, when a few minutes later, I opened the connecting door between the house and the garage, and in walked Poppy as if it were the most natural thing in the world! Her gait was confident and her body language totally relaxed. She sat down and looked up at me, her tongue lolling out of the side of her mouth and a pleasant smiley look on her face. I cautiously bent down and she licked my hand enthusiastically, greatly appreciative of the attention she was receiving. What on earth was going on? Anxious to test the transformation in her personality, I opened the door that lead on to the kitchen and there sat five of the dogs, in muted anticipation, clearly in some trepidation of might happen next.

They need not have worried.

Poppy strolled into the house, allowing the others to sniff her, as friendly as could be, and appearing to enjoy her new surroundings. She was tolerant of all the attention that she received, and made no complaints at their curious sniffing. She licked one or two of them and made herself quite at home. So I offered her food, which she eagerly accepted, whilst the others looked on in stunned silence, not even trying to steal from her bowl, as they might normally do with each other.

By now, several more had realized that 'it' was now amongst them, and other cautious heads began to peek around corners. The sheer lack of noise was deafening. One by one, they all assembled to greet the newcomer, showing an inordinate amount of respect to a creature that was, to many at least, a fraction of their size. And then, without any bidding, Poppy went and lay down on the nearest bed and was soon fast asleep.

The rest of the pack shuffled around, now bemused more than frightened and unsure of what to do next. So I instructed them to go to bed, and that's exactly what they did. When my head finally touched the pillow, it was 2:15am.

If I expected something to be different the next day, or if I had anticipated the normal period of slightly strained adjustment that follows a new pack member's arrival, it didn't happen. The next day dawned just like any other. There was no period of transition whatsoever, just instant assimilation. Poppy was a part of the furniture who joined in as a member of the pack in all things, and has never, to this day, repeated any of the behaviours that we witnessed that first night. It's bizarre.

So it shouldn't be surprising to also note that by the end of the morning, she was treated with about as much deference as anybody else. She was chased, rolled over, nipped and pushed around as much as any other new entrant. For her part, she took it all in her stride and gave as good as she got, playing with as much energy as those who sought to play with her. Mostly, this was the younger Huskies. Because she was already a large puppy when she arrived, her size and weight were almost on a par with theirs. As we watched, we wondered what would happen as she got bigger and stronger. She could easily grow to Indy's giant size.

Over the coming days she worked out her place in the pack order with no disruption whatsoever. As usual with new arrivals, some dogs treated her with aloof disdain; others wanted to be her best friend. To our astonishment, Indy was not only more tolerant of her than any other incoming pack member thus far, he also seemed to like her. A lot! Perhaps he saw in her a future "big dog bride" and was almost lavish in his attentions.

Kachina was the most interesting to observe. She never let her come close and watched the fluffy white ball from a discreet distance. Only then did it occur to us that the original purpose of the Maremma breed had been to kill wolves. What had we done?

It was slightly surprising to us that after a few weeks, Kachina began to take more than a keen interest in Poppy. In part, our expectation of the antipathy that would exist between the two species caused us to be taken aback. We had also anticipated that Indy's obvious fondness for Poppy would provoke jealousy on Kachina's part. Instead, it produced an almost opposite response. The wolf and the livestock guardian dog became the very best of friends. It was almost like watching the old Disney movie 'The Fox and the Hound' played out between much larger animals.

To this day, no two of our charges play together more often, more roughly, or more good naturedly than these two. They are fairly evenly matched (Kachina is slightly taller, but Poppy is slightly heavier) and will rush headlong at each other, meeting with such force that the impact sends them both flying. They rear up like heraldic beasts doing battle and try to push one another backwards. Both are very agile and masters of the full body check and other clever wrestling moves that could have been borrowed from the WWF circuit. Their mock confrontations can last for twenty minutes before they are too tired to go on; yet despite the gusto with which they attack one another, they have never fallen out. If the instinct to protect the herd from wolves is as in-bred as the Maremma reputation suggests, it has not over-ridden the discernment of the individual dog. Poppy understands that Kachina is no threat.

Other behavioural traits within a livestock guardian dog are much more deep rooted. A dog like a Maremma needs something to protect and there are many stories of families taking one into their suburban homes and then discovering that they bark at anything that moves, wander away from home if left outside, and frighten away all-comers to their houses. Needless to say, the dogs are quickly branded as something they are not, and wind up in shelters, often with no chance of being rehomed. It is quite a different story in rural areas where stock need protection from coyotes and even more voracious predators. In these communities they are highly valued and seldom in need of rescue. They do not get bored and therefore do not become liabilities. Nonetheless they still need something to protect. Since we live in a rural area but have no stock, we harboured nagging doubts about how Poppy would react to our environment. Needless to say, we shouldn't have had any concerns.

From the first day it was as if she believed that every single other dog was her responsibility. She would walk the perimeter of the fence line, peering through the wire and watching for the slightest little movement. She would patrol the whole area and then, content that nothing bad was lurking outside, would find a position that afforded her the best view of the area where the most dogs were playing. There she would sit and observe, occasionally breaking off to join in with the games, but always returning to her vigilant watch. If the majority of the pack was indoors, she would come in too. Every few hours, she would need to go outside to visit a variety of strategic positions which, we realized, allowed her to note all activity both outside and inside the fence line. We were very impressed with her constant alertness. Even when she appeared to be asleep, the slightest sound or movement would cause her to be instantly upright and ready to defend her charges.

It therefore came as a great surprise to us when we began to notice that the patrols decreased in number and that her determination to be where the majority of the pack was totally fell by the wayside after only a few weeks. Instead, she would be quite content to lie around the house, as chilled as any of the other dogs. Had her natural tendencies been subverted by their lackadaisical attitude?

If this worried us, it needn't have. It soon became apparent that Poppy seemed to use some other source of reference to determine whether or not there was any need for her to go into livestock guardian mode. It was fascinating (if a little annoying, initially) to watch. Poppy would be (apparently) fast asleep and snoring and suddenly wake up barking her head off. She would instantly become a study of alertness and ready for action. She sounded an alarm that would alert the whole household, be she in basement or bedroom and once she began, there was no stopping her.

Most frequently, the result of these barking fits would be a full on charge to the recess of the bay window to maximize her view of the compound at the front of the house. She would wait for us to catch up with her, still barking frantically; or if someone was already there, she would immediately demand access to the outdoors. Once outside she would race to a very specific point on the fence line to see off some creature whose presence we were unaware of; or occasionally, throw her considerable weight between other pack members whose game playing was getting a little too rambunctious.

Gradually, we began to recognize that she had some form of inbuilt 'badness' detector. If anything was amiss, anywhere, she would instinctively know about it and consider it her duty to sort it out, and although her definition of 'amiss' might have varied from ours, we gradually began to appreciate the useful, if somewhat noisy, service she was providing.

However, our gratitude didn't last long. After a few weeks she developed an additional pattern of beginning her barking routine *without* following it up with the obligatory trip outside. This only seemed to occur in the evenings when we were in the basement. Most usually, we would be watching a movie with most of the pack sprawled all around us, when (often at a crucial moment, or so it seemed) her klaxon like bark would go off. She would race for the stairs and be desperate to get to the mid-level, but then instead of laying siege to the front door, she would stop in the kitchen, suddenly noiseless. This was puzzling and annoying and I would berate her for interrupting the movie, shooing her back downstairs and demanding her silence. Then after a while, we began to notice that the instances of her adopting this behaviour coincided with subsequent discoveries of wrong-doing in the kitchen: stolen food, raided waste bins, illicit cupboard searches or worse, the decision by a dog to use the carpet as a lavatory. And then it finally dawned on us that she was letting us know when the other pack members were up to no good. Not only did she see it as her role to protect the pack from what lurked beyond the fence line (or from each other when occasion arose), she also wanted to ensure that there was no criminal activity in the house! There were two aspects of the bizarre in this: firstly, she seemed to know at an instinctive level what constituted inappropriate behaviour; and secondly, she knew what was going on without even needing to see it! Our irritation turned to awe that we now seemed to be living with a psychic dog.

If her psychic powers serve her well, her eyesight doesn't always. When we have visitors to the house, she is initially very wary of them. She will give them a good 'barking at' that can last for many minutes, despite reassurances from us that they are meant to be there. Then she will stay in their proximity so as to ensure that they are not up to bad things. Unfortunately, if they then make the mistake of going to the washroom, their return will be greeted by the same process all over again. She seldom seems to recognize that the person who just returned to the room is the same one that she had sat next to quite happily for the previous two hours.

In fact, visual stimuli seem to mean very little to Poppy. Anything that defies her expectations of how things 'should be' will provoke the barked response. On one occasion, I mistakenly believed that I had heard the sounds of conflict between the dogs outside. I had just got out of the bath and raced downstairs to prevent whatever I imagined was taking place. As I did so, I dropped my towel and burst through the front door, stark naked. Although I was invisible to all human eyes, due to the privacy of our house, Poppy was positioned just outside the door. My bare appearance was obviously too much for her to bear and she began to let me know in no uncertain terms. She either didn't recognize me without my clothes on, or thought that I need a good telling off for having the audacity to appear before her in this way. I was barked at until you'd have thought she'd go blue in the face. Only when I retreated indoors was her fury assuaged. I collapsed in fits of laughter.

So Poppy has developed a role as guardian, keeper of the peace, policewoman and arbiter of moral standards. I always think of her as being a little like the robot Gort in the 1951 movie 'The Day The Earth Stood Still'. He polices all, is harmless unless provoked, and is programmed to save people from themselves. And so, apparently, is Poppy. (NB. If you have only seen the 2008 remake of the movie with the somewhat more sinister version of Gort, trust me, the original one is a little less intimidating.)

For those of you who can still remember our reason for getting Poppy in the first place and are anxious to know if her presence has affected Briony's lot... Not since the minute she crossed our threshold has a single Husky ever touched the poodle. She has lived a totally hassle free existence. At the slightest hint of trouble between any dogs, Poppy is there like a one dog United Nations Peacekeeping force. But then you knew that would be the case didn't you? It is exactly as Michael had said.

Three wheels on my wagon

Amidst all of these dog related stories, you might well get the impression that there wasn't much else going on in our lives. And funnily enough, if you drew this conclusion, you would be quite right.

For months we'd been struggling with very limited income and there seemed to be no prospect of work on the horizon. I'd long known that from the Etheric's perspective, only now was I doing what I was 'supposed' to do, and whilst I had begrudgingly accepted this fact, I had not really expected that this meant that I would receive no other income.

As I alluded to in 'Some Dogs', my work as a consultant had certainly begun to dry up and it was as if I had become invisible. Even as I tried to generate alternative sources of income, a sense of futility started to overtake me. Initially, I began by contacting the types of business around Calgary that you might expect to employ someone with my experience. This includes pretty much any company concerned with the quality of leadership within their business. I was confident in my resumé since my experience is almost unique in both its depth and breadth. There aren't too many people who can include in their repertoire that they have had very extensive global exposure, written a bestselling business book, run a successful international business, set up (and sold) a software company, been an advisor to a national government, created a development program (legendary in its time) attended by hundreds of all-comers, coached top business leaders, media personalities and even a politician(!) on leadership skills, spoken at international conferences and appeared as a subject matter expert on the media. Apparently, this all now counted for nothing. I couldn't so much as get an interview for a job or a sniff of interest from a potential client. It seemed as if my past counted for nothing.

In a year, I managed to get only one job interview. Ironically, it resulted from interest expressed by a business that had come across me on the internet, rather than one I had approached. The interview went well and those interviewing me were very enthusiastic about what I could bring to the business. But when their report of our conversation was relayed to the Vice President of Human Resources, she apparently concluded that I was 'too big for the role', a message that was conveyed to me with great embarrassment by the interviewers.

After months of trying, someone suggested that I 'dumb down' my resumé. Unfortunately, even when I did so, there was not so much as a nibble of interest. Finally, despairing, I decided to apply for a job in Chapters Bookstore. I was happy to do this and even quite looked forward to the prospect of working in a place where I was surrounded by books. I took even more out of my resumé. They didn't even bother to reply to my application.

So our income was now based solely upon delivering personal channelling sessions, monthly public channellings, household energy clearings, guiding people on hikes to Archangel Michael's Etheric Retreat, and running the Balance Class. Whilst this actually provided a not inconsiderable amount of regular work, it is best seen in context. During the 2009 tax year, I earned less money than I could have earned in two and a half *hours* of conference speaking, in my 'former' life.

This may stretch credibility in the minds of some readers, but with absolute honesty, I can say that this really was not a problem for either Sharon or I, from an emotional perspective. In fact, we were happier than we had ever been in our lives together, and that continues to be the case today. Certainly, it created a host of practical problems such as do we buy food or gas today; or can we reasonably let the car go any more than fifty thousand kilometers past its last service interval? And it is also true that I developed an intense dislike for opening mail in case it brought more bad news; and a similar dread of the telephone ringing. Yet the experience opened us up to an amazing understanding of what is of value in our lives.

The big problem was that our household costs, dogs aside, were based on the income level achieved in my consulting days, and not the channelling ones. Consequently, we had a mounting debt problem and just servicing this now became a major problem.

If you are of a certain age, you may remember a song, a favourite with children, which described the plight of a wagon train pursued by Cherokee Indians. In today's climate it might be thought of as very much less than politically correct. In the 1960's, it was amusing if only because during the course of the song, the singer describes how, one by one, in his attempt to evade his pursuers, the wheels fall off his wagon. Nonetheless his wagon, improbably, "keeps rolling along". In the last verse, there are no wheels on the wagon and he's been captured. Amazingly, the music is written by the great Burt Bacharach, and the song was originally recorded by legendary song and dance man, Dick Van Dyke before it became a massive hit for the New Christy Minstrels.

Music trivia aside, viewed from an adult perspective, the really interesting feature of the narrative is that despite all of the troubles the lyrics describe, the singer constantly asserts "but I'm singing a happy song".

As 2009 progressed, I found the song going through my head on an almost daily basis. There were most definitely less than three wheels on our wagon, yet miraculously from our own perspective, we were still rolling along and still managing (most of the time) to be 'singing a happy song'.

This time also really began to reveal to us the true nature of friendship and who our friends really were. We were humbled, and still continue to be humbled, almost on a daily basis, by the support we receive from so many. Although the true extent of the desperate nature of our plight was not something we readily revealed, there were many who instinctively or spontaneously came forward with stunning acts of generosity.

I have lost count of the number of times that we did not have enough food in the house to feed us all, and no money to buy any with that day. If it came to a choice, as it regularly did, between feed us or feed the dogs, the dogs never went hungry. And the funny thing is, neither did we. No one could possibly have known what was happening, yet at the eleventh hour, we would *always* get a phone call from someone asking us if we would like to come round for dinner. With alarming prescience, our friend Wayne would show up with food he had bought and ask if we would like to share it with him because he'd bought too much. Or Shannon would come up with vegetables that one of Scott's relatives had grown in their yards and ask if we'd like some as there were so many. Our friends even kept us supplied with luxuries which, in the darkest times, helped to keep us 'singing a happy song'. When you get to the bottom, it's amazing what lifts you up and for us, the good coffee and wine friends gifted us always did the trick!

The recurring incidence of the fortuitous intervention of our friends was way beyond coincidence, and our luck in help coming out of the blue wasn't just related to food.

Needless to say, with old dogs in particular, there are vet bills to be paid. Although our vet kindly allowed us a certain amount of leeway in when we paid, we tried very hard to keep up to date, and were only overcome when there were surgery issues to be dealt with. On one occasion I remember being presented with a bill for forty five dollars that, whilst relatively minor compared with others we had received, was still more than the five dollars I had in my pocket. As I took the five dollars out and put it on the counter, it unfolded to reveal a crystal pendant (of a type I'll explain later). A passing client had her eye caught by it and asked if I would sell it and if so, for how much? I told her in absolute honesty that I sold the crystals for thirty nine, ninety nine. She immediately handed over forty dollars and refused the change. I added it to the five dollars already on the counter, my bill paid in full.

As if to draw an even closer parallel with the song, one day we discovered our SUV had a slow puncture in its front left tire. At first it would take several days to deflate to the point where the pressure sensor would pick it up, but as the weeks passed, the puncture got worse and worse. Departures from the house were impossible without ten minutes of tire inflation. Then we would go out and not be able to return, save for carrying our compressor with us and reflating the tire before setting off again. On long journeys, we would have to stop every half hour or so to feed the tire more air. Finally, it got to the stage where after a night in the garage, I would find the car tilting wildly and down at the front end. It looked just like there were only three wheels on our wagon!

If you're wondering why we simply didn't get it repaired, the tire was already bald, totally unroadworthy and desperately in need of replacing; as were all three others. We simply couldn't afford it. After a few months of this ridiculous and highly inconvenient situation, it happened that we were visiting our friend Susan. When we came to leave, she walked us back to our car (parked some distance from her house) with Wexford and Jock and was perplexed to see me having to plug in the compressor and do the usual reflation. Her response quickly turned to dismay when she looked at the tires and saw their appalling and unsafe condition. So concerned was Susan for our safety that the following weekend we had a brand new set of tires put on the car. Susan had insisted on loaning us the fifteen hundred dollars it cost, researched exactly what we needed and had even arranged the fitting.

What it is to have friends!

As Michael had said, we would be provided for, which was just as well. Things were going to get a lot worse and all too soon the last verse of the song would be going round in my head.

Incidentally, The New Christy Minstrels who sang 'Three Wheels On My Wagon' were precisely the type of group gently and affectionately parodied as 'The New Main Street Singers' in Christopher Guest's excellent mockumentary, 'A Mighty Wind'.

If you can't work out what this has to do with dogs and this story...

Christopher Guest also made the superb mockumentary 'Best In Show'. This is an absolute 'must see' movie for dog lovers, especially those who know anything about the world of showing dogs. Only the dogs come out of it well!

Now those of you who've read 'Some Dogs' may remember Melody, the dog that a lady called Joanne had owned. She wanted me to find out if she was reincarnating. In telling her story I mentioned that Melody was not only an awesome dog, but a movie star. That's because she was in

'Best In Show'. Watch the film and study the final line up. Melody is the gorgeous Husky not being shown by one of the movie's actors. That's because it's actually Joanne herself showing her. Even more fascinating, Christopher Guest was so taken with Melody that he wanted to rewrite the ending so that it was Melody who won.

How's that for a segue?

A Matter of Life or Death

When I meet or hear from people who have read 'Some Dogs', I am unceasingly delighted to hear how the book has affected them. I am also surprised. When I was writing it, I wasn't really conscious of the potential impact that it might have on readers, and although it obviously didn't get to everyone who read it, it was evidently doing what Michael had said it would. One day, for a reason I now forget, I started reading it myself. Bizarrely, when Sharon came to get me to go out for a channelling, she found me utterly enthralled by it and waxing lyrical, amazed at what had been written. It was a very odd experience. I didn't have time to read it all but it's impact on me caused me to reflect upon one of the most affecting books I have read to date: Raimond Gaita's 'The Philosopher's Dog'.

Even though it is a work of 'popular philosophy' i.e. one that attempts to make broad philosophical tenets accessible and easily understood, I found it a difficult work to get through. In common with most philosophy texts, there was no definitive conclusion. Such is not their purpose. Frankly, I'm not even sure if I correctly interpreted what was being said. However, there was one element that had stuck with me and, to a certain extent, tortured me ever since.

The author reflected upon the ease with which humans are prepared to assume God-like control over the lives of their dogs. We will comfortably choose to override natural processes of life and death and have our pets 'put to sleep'. We call it euthanasia and it is defined in the dictionary as 'painless killing to relieve suffering'.

Yet euthanasia laws prevent this with humans. It is accepted that we are a 'higher life form'. This implies a higher degree of sentience. If this is so, then we experience pain and distress to a higher degree. So shouldn't the motivation to prevent suffering be correspondingly higher? Instead, it seemingly becomes less acceptable. This is because we consider that it is totally unacceptable to terminate something that we consider to be so 'alive'.

In our society, as I write this book, euthanasia is only legal in a handful of countries and three States in the USA. The principal reason for this is the need to ensure that such a system is not abused. After all, unscrupulous individuals could use it as a method to rid themselves of troublesome or inconvenient relatives. Euthanasia is also defined differently in the law, where it is termed 'assisted suicide'. In other words, it is dependent upon that individual's choice. Therefore, the consent of the individual is paramount in ensuring that the termination of life is allowed to happen. Even then, a great many medical 'proofs' of the justification for such an action must be provided. Above all else, great pain must accompany the desire of the individual, but not in so much as it clouds their judgement and ability to make a 'rational' decision.

Many lives end in what may be deemed 'poor quality'. Almost as a given, the elderly can expect to experience the ravages of old age. Impaired sight and hearing, joint issues and immobility, loss of memory and degrees of dementia, susceptibility to all manner of illnesses, and potentially embarrassing personal issues such as an inability to bathe one's self and incontinence; all these things potentially await us as we grow old. Individually, they are daunting. Combined, they create a portrait of impending agony. Yet they still generally lack the essential criteria for euthanasia. None of the above criteria would make it permissible. Therefore, instead of taking this irretrievable, life ending action, we seek to alleviate the suffering of the old in whatever way we may; usually at whatever cost.

Ironically, I read Gaita's book at a time when Kaiti was our only dog, although we also owned our two Siamese cats, Rittee and Sasha. I was left confused and unable to reconcile the issues it raised in my own mind; the intervention of knowledge from an Archangel didn't help much either. It only served to muddy the waters.

<u>What was the knowledge from the etheric?</u>

Put straightforwardly, it was that the termination of an animal's life by their owner could affect their progression upon their ascension pathway if the decision to do so was not part of a prior agreement that this was the way in which their life would end.

78

Some eight years later, we chose to have Rittee 'put to sleep'. He was eighteen and he began to cough blood. His kidneys were failing. It seemed the kind thing to do and I had neither qualms nor regrets about the decision.

Yet I am constantly aware of owners who make decisions based on 'convenient' kindness. I have long ago lost count of the number of dogs that I have heard of that have been put to sleep because they have impaired sight or hearing, joint issues or immobility, loss of memory or degrees of dementia, susceptibility to all manner of illnesses, and potentially embarrassing personal issues such as an inability to bathe themselves and incontinence. Sound familiar? Isn't this an abuse of our power over them?

I have also come across some hideous situations where the animal was put to sleep simply for the convenience of the owner. The worst case involved a couple who decided it would be fun to have a dog. They wanted a cute one so they chose a Chow Chow, with apparently very little understanding of the breed's temperament or indeed, much knowledge of dog care at all. They both worked, so the dog stayed in their house all day. It began to chew furniture in its boredom and loneliness. To solve this, they then left it in their yard all day. It barked constantly in its boredom and loneliness. So then they kept it in their garage all day. There was nothing to chew and nobody reported being disturbed by the barking, so there were no symptoms of boredom or loneliness, right? Nonetheless, they did come home to a dog that was highly distressed and frantic. And after a very short while, the dog became aggressive when they tried to put it in the garage. So they had it 'put to sleep'. This was not euthanasia. This was killing. They didn't even try to rehome it and a vet did it for them.

Although I have many others like it, that particular story troubles me very much, even to this day, for all sorts of reasons.

You could be forgiven for thinking that in countries where euthanasia is legal, there must be a rush amongst those in acute pain to check out and avoid the burdens old age imposes upon them. Yet in actual fact, a miniscule percentage of the population actually elect to end their lives in this way. They value their lives so greatly that they would rather endure the torments of physical decay than miss one more day that is available to them; one more meeting with loved ones; one more chance to look at the sky and be glad to be alive.

We know this because they can tell us. Animals can't.

Just because this is so, it doesn't mean that they don't cherish every single living moment; every kind word; every loving touch of their owner's hand; every poorly sensed scent; every last look at the sky that makes them glad to be alive.

Readers of 'Some Dogs' may recall the story of Susan Palliser and her quest to get her dog, Buddy, back. Her other dog, Wexford, whose illness had precipitated our meeting, suffered from failing eyesight, kidney problems and an intolerance for proteins. Yet Michael assured us that Wexford could go on for at least another two years, and sure enough, it is now over two years since the occasion of our first meeting. As I write this, and despite his increasing old age (he is now eighteen) Wexford is still managing to enjoy every day of his life. However, every few weeks, Susan finds herself in the midst of one of his numerous health crises and has to spend a fortune at the vet to try and hold back the encroachment of decrepitude. Many others would have given up on him a long time ago. Few would wish to spend the thousands of dollars it costs per year to help sustain his life. Yet if you were to experience his joy in his life, in spite of his very much less than perfect health, you would understand in totality why she seeks to alleviate his suffering in whatever way she may, at whatever cost. With cast iron confidence, I guarantee that she will only stop doing this if he begins to suffer.

Of course, not all people can afford to do this.

It was once put to me by a friend that our making of choices on behalf of our pets is simply the equivalent of that which occurs in the natural world. Nature 'decides' for a wild animal that if it is too old or too weak to survive, it will simply die of cold, starvation or death at the hand of predators, or even its kind. He believes that this argument tops all of the ones I've put forward above. Veterinarians may agree. Why prolong the suffering of old age?

However, a dog is not a wild animal. It is highly domesticated and it has few natural predators in a man-made world apart from motor vehicles. Few homes will be so exposed that an animal occupant would die of cold within them. Only the most callous of owners would stand by while a pet starved to death. And the dogs live in this domesticated state alongside us because *we* have chosen that it is so.

Why have we chosen that it is so?

I have stated and reiterated on numerous occasions now that our association with animals, particularly those that are domesticated, serves a far higher purpose than them being an entertaining distraction for us. It's worth saying again in a slightly different way:

In many respects, for so many of us, a pet represents our only connection with the wider animal kingdom which, in turn, may be thought of as a representation of the natural world (as opposed to the man-made one we have created).

From our perspective, these creatures are less sophisticated and therefore simpler than we are. They seem to be 'lesser beings', and we may all too easily come to think of them in this way. Yet the reality is that although they are less complicated in their needs, demands and expectations, they are far more content than we are, far more at ease with their lot and, I believe, far more aware of the need for balance on their ascension pathway.

I do not intend to paint a portrait of animals being sainted. Far from it. We know that their world can be brutal when need requires it. However, their relationship with the natural world is seldom damaging (as ours is), and they are not prone to behaviours and actions that represent anything more than an understanding of a need for non-destructive co-existence with one another.

Most of us will never have the opportunities to live amongst truly wild creatures that may be afforded to naturalists. However, we *can* co-exist with domesticated creatures. In these relationships, which are far more precious than even our love for them would suggest, we are provided with immense opportunity for learning.

We agree to our co-existence with them before we incarnate. Their purpose and the nature of our relationship with them is contractual and powerful. Yet so often we break our contracts and do not seek to expand our understanding of the basic 'why?' we have them in the first place.

As I am frequently reminded by the etheric, a dog is every bit as alive and every bit as sentient as a human being. Despite the fact that we, as owners, have loved them throughout their lives, we perhaps decide that we are being kind in having them 'put to sleep' rather than treat our pets in the same way that we would a human, by seeking to alleviate their suffering in whatever way we may; usually at whatever cost. Perhaps it is too easy to rationalize or excuse what we are about to do by relying upon that dictionary definition of euthanasia which is 'painless killing to relieve suffering'.

In reading this chapter you might feel a little uncomfortable. Please accept that in writing all of this, I don't seek to judge anyone. For my part, I've never managed to reconcile for myself the arguments that Gaita began for me. I accept that euthanasia may end a great deal of suffering; but make no mistake, ending an animal's life is NOT assisted suicide. Suicide is a choice. Ending an animal's life is our decision not theirs.

The idea that we may be affecting them in their progression upon their Ascension Pathway is difficult for me to say the least. Over the coming months, my feelings about the whole issue were about to be tested to the full.

I would be found severely wanting.

Before she came to us, Kenani Breeze had to be permanently chained up.
Would you have spotted what she is?

As Kachina, she soon found herself attracted to Indy
whom she clearly regards as her mate.

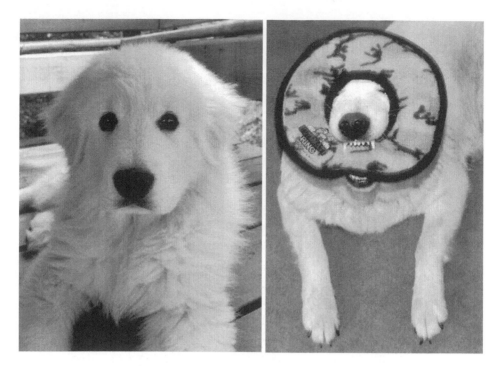

Although the seal pup lookalike on the left possessed the lethal teeth shown on the right, after that first occasion, she has never used them – on us!

Growing up big and cute. An Italian dog from the US,
Poppy is nonetheless a true Canadian patriot

Zoe was the smallest of the Husky puppies and had the most difficult birth.
Now she's the prettiest and always reminds us of a little fox.
That's very appropriate considering the company she keeps.

As soon as we saw that tongue, we should have known that Inara's principal way of
demonstrating affection would be to lick everyone in sight.
She's even featured on a YouTube video, apparently trying to lick Tristan to death.
Here I get a brief respite before she recommences facial assault.

It's hard to imagine that Idaho was once a small puppy. He's the biggest Husky we have by some way. Here he's elected to chill-out in a crate, oblivious to the fact that such things are used to whisk dogs off to the vet clinic...

Aura has always been on the mad side, so it's quite unusual to catch her in tranquil repose. Nestling amongst the roots of a tree is an interesting variation on the holes that the Huskies dig in the earth to lie in and keep cool in summer.

Dougal (above) out for a dash in the snow, while Emily (below) prefers the more sedate approach to life. Or it could be that she's trying to lull us into a false sense of security before her next escape attempt...

Briony enjoying her 'Poodle privileges', which basically means that
she's a lap dog that is allowed to sleep on our bed (sore point!).

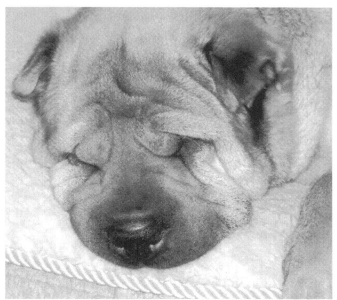

Kaiti doing what comes most naturally to a fourteen year old Shar Pei.
It's only now at mealtimes that she becomes (very) active.

Timba and Lara, the proud(?) parents.
Yes, he is wearing glasses but he only needs them for reading.

Cinnda keeps a watchful eye on the world.

Here Indy is snuggled up with Timba; so perhaps in retaliation,
Kachina teaches her 'mate' a lesson by choosing to get cosy with Briony.

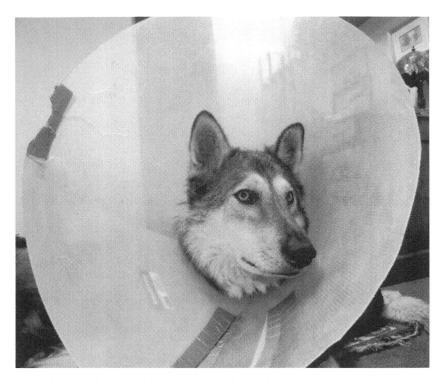

Feeling like 'The Wolf in the Iron Mask', Kachina is temporarily trapped inside the collar of terror before her frenzied behaviour forces us to remove it. Her eyes say it all.

Sharon amidst one or two dogs.

Me with Indy

A Time For Goodbyes

When Saffy had come to us, we had very little expectation that she would live for long. Her skeletal form and lack of energy certainly did not bode well. Yet within weeks we were delighted that she grew both in strength and stature. Moreover, she displayed an amazing character for such a sickly creature.

Saffy wasn't exactly what you'd call a 'nice' dog, but she was certainly enchanting, funny and a major personality. Her range of facial expressions was quite unusual for a dog and they varied from her most usual 'frightened rabbit' look (which was a feature of her physical form rather than any emotion she experienced), through to a very intense attempt at trying to be a big ferocious dog, which she certainly wasn't. The latter came at meal times, not hers, but ours. She would force her way to the table through the melèe of dogs and put her head in Sharon's lap. If any of the other dogs came too close, she would assume a hideous expression with teeth bared and make a strange 'arrgh' sound that was neither a growl nor a grunt. For the most part, none of the other dogs took her seriously, as in her highly advanced years, she posed no physical threat. Even as a fully fit, mature adult, she would have been very small for a husky and in her emaciated state, even the smallest of the puppies could have batted her frail frame aside. Yet all seemed to respect her and allowed her the self-deception that she was still a powerful and important member of the pack. Perhaps they knew that the end was coming.

Saffy's deterioration began a matter of days after I had finished writing about her miraculous recovery in the previous book. Perhaps I should have known better than to tempt fate.

It started with minor dysentery that developed over the next few weeks and was uncontrollable by anything the vet could prescribe. During the day, it was not a big issue for us. Saffy had the presence of mind to scratch at the door when she needed to go out. Night time was a different story altogether. Saffy could not 'do' stairs due to her advancing feebleness, and we had always let her sleep in the carpeted lounge on the main floor of the house. Now, in the mornings, we began to find dark brown spots as big as a one cent piece in various locations across the carpet. Each morning there seemed to be one or two more than the previous night and I quickly got into a routine that involved greeting the day with our carpet washer. Then one morning, the carpet could best be described as having taken on a polka-dot appearance. Clearly the dysentery had been very bad that night and the cleaning operation that followed took six hours.

We moved Saffy into the 'dog room', usually occupied by the puppies, which had a tiled floor. She was severely weakened by the events of this night; her ability to withstand the outdoors or even stand up was now very limited. The 'dog room' quickly became a bathroom and we entered into a cycle of bed and floor washing that was relentless. Sharon shouldered much of the burden of this with a cheerful disregard for the unpleasantness and a determination to allow Saffy to be alive for as long as she wanted.

However, the whole experience presented us with something of a dilemma. We desperately wanted to give Saffy every chance possible to live out whatever life she could have with us. At the same time, medicines were having no effect, and neither was Sharon's energy healing producing a sustained result.

Why wasn't the energy healing working?

Sharon's healing work on animals is normally stunningly successful. She has some great testimonials for the things she has been able to accomplish, so it was a source of frustration for both of us that nothing would 'stick'.

Upon questioning, Michael reminded us of a fundamental of energy healing, it has to be *desired* by the recipient to be successful.

As we had previously discovered, a great many of the issues that relate to an animal's health, and particularly those that involve issues of life and death, are decided upon by their higher self.

It was almost as if her higher self had recognized that her third dimensional body was failing rapidly and it did not wish to prolong her presence whilst in this state.

Thus, anything that Sharon did had only a very short term impact. Regardless of how she could affect the physical form, the etheric version of Saffy seemed to have decided that enough was enough.

Sometimes what 'seems' is not what 'is'.

We certainly did not want her to suffer. It was as if Saffy had gone into a holding pattern that would see her one day reasonably lively, alert and characterful as ever; the next, apparently at death's door, with us expecting her demise at any moment. On these days, Sharon would spend a great deal of time with her. In part, it was because she didn't want to lose her; and perhaps because she wanted Saffy to know, in what could be her final moments, that she was loved and wanted in a way that she had never been before she came to us. Just Sharon's presence seemed to produce a recovery of sorts, and throughout, Saffy showed no sign that she was in pain.

Matters finally came to a head when, after about three weeks of 'dog room' living, Saffy's deposits contained blood. The vet had warned us that this would be a sign that her system had gone into complete collapse, and so we made the inevitable phone call.

I now found myself experiencing a curious range of emotions. It was clear that we would not be returning from the vet's with Saffy, but the idea that we were about to make that life or death choice for her was something I struggled with greatly.

Raymond Gaita's inconclusive ponderings collided with my etheric given knowledge and I began to question whether or not we actually had the right to end Saffy's life in this way. We had no knowledge that this was what she would want and our actions could affect her own learning, spiritual development and the experiences she had chosen to have.

Of course, the argument about ending suffering is an immensely compelling one and that was exactly what we encountered in the vet's office. It made it easy for us to decide that this was in her best interests. And it would be wonderful to be able to report that in those last moments, she simply slipped gently into a blissful and relieving sleep.

That isn't what happened at all.

Saffy fought her death in a way that we would never have believed possible. Although this diminutive dog was as frail as you may possibly imagine and unable to stand, she still managed to resist the vet's attempts to give her the tranquillizer that is the precursor to the fatal dose of medication. She was uncooperative and feisty, and the fact that she had nothing that was recognisable as a vein didn't help. After ten minutes of attempts that were highly stressful for all concerned, Saffy finally relaxed enough for the next stage. Unfortunately, that didn't go well either.

The vet was unable to find the right place to inject the liquid death for long minutes on end. Constant reinsertions of the needle were required and although Saffy was in a totally soporific state and blissfully unaware of what was transpiring, it didn't stop us fretting. Finally, the injection went in and we waited for her final breath. It didn't come. The injection had been given in the wrong place and so the whole process began again. Time dragged by and the passing minutes seemed to go on forever. By the time she had finally let go, a full fifty minutes had passed. It was agony for both us and the vet, who had acted with utmost professionalism and sensitivity throughout. We were grateful beyond measure for the knowledge that Saffy, by comparison, felt nothing.

In the dark hours that followed, you might imagine that we would have asked Michael for clarity. Had we acted in accordance with her highest good? All throughout the process, I had been seemingly unable to communicate with the etheric. My heightening levels of stress and grief had caused me to shut out all of those voices that could have supported us. I didn't even try. So now we were left with the grim analysis. Had we done the right thing for her?

We didn't ask. It wasn't that we didn't want to know, we were just totally numbed by the events that had taken place and it never actually occurred to us to ask. It would be fair to say that our confidence in the 'rightness' of the decision we made stopped us from seeking a greater analysis of what had transpired. In fact it wasn't until I began writing this chapter today, nearly eighteen months later, that Sharon asked me the question: "Did Saffy actually want to go?"

When I referred the question to Michael, his response was brief and totally without rancour. "No. She wanted to stay. She wanted to transition naturally." He explained that the value of every moment of life was greater to her than the suffering she experienced. It was her higher self that had intervened to try and prevent what was happening on her behalf. It had clung on to her life force with all the power of intervention that it could possibly muster, substituting, in those moments, her physical energetic presence for its etheric one. It had wanted her to transition naturally.

If anyone could have heard its pleas, surely it would have been me? Its efforts were all to no avail and the pleas fell upon deaf ears. Neither of us, in those slowly passing, tortured minutes, had been able to see any reason behind what was transpiring. I had neither tried to, nor been able to listen to the intervention it sought to make. Perhaps it was simply not convenient.

Hearing the truth now is difficult and painful, despite the fact that Michael counsels that I should feel no guilt.

Why should I feel no guilt?

An animal's life is filled with an unimaginable degree of imponderables and uncertainties. This is totally by design.

The defining feature of human existence is our freedom of choice, our free will and the right to exercise it. If this seems to contradict the notion that our lives are, for the most part, planned and pre-determined, almost to the nth degree, consider the following: The relationships, events, circumstances and happenings that we plan for ourselves before incarnating are simply opportunities within which we may utilise our free will so as to bring about outcomes.

In all this, the most important element is perhaps our discernment, our ability to use that which we have already learnt so as to make choices that are for our highest good and the highest good of all. This is the experience that we are supposed to gain and it defines the parameters of our existence.

For an animal, the same does not hold true. For a domestic (or domesticated) animal, their range of ability to exercise their free will is limited by the nature of their relationship with us humans.

Therefore, if the choice we made was made for our highest good, it effectively overrides theirs.

Quite apart from all of the above, guilt is a wholly negative and futile emotion that lowers the individual's vibration and should be banished from our emotional tool box.

A friend asked if Saffy would be coming back and if so, would we find out the location of where she would reincarnate. We already knew that she was a relatively young soul and that most certainly, she'd be coming round again. We were also told that it would not be appropriate for us to try to find her.

<u>Why wouldn't it be appropriate to try get to Saffy back?</u>

It was all too easy for us to assume that coming back to be with us again would be the absolute best thing for Saffy. After all, we already had that experience with Sage returning to us as Timba. And if she'd tried so hard to stay, wasn't that in itself evidence that she would want to return?

However, Michael explained with some tactful reasoning that Saffy had already had five months with us. The environment we provided for the dogs to live in was becoming increasingly rarefied due to the ever increasing numbers of Avatars. Whilst it worked really well for them, it no longer represented a 'normal' or even a 'typical' environment in which to learn the lessons necessary for progression along the Ascension Pathway. At Saffy's level of progression on her journey, she could learn more lessons elsewhere.

It wasn't that we couldn't get her back. It just wasn't for her highest good.

As for trying to stay, that had more to do with her love for her life, in whatever way she was experiencing it, than it had to do with us.

The sense of misery and numbness that can surround the death of any pet enveloped us as we began the brief journey home that day. Perhaps the worst part was having to tell Jenny and Tristan what had happened. Both had been expecting to see her again and had not had their chance to say goodbye. At home we sat glumly trying to console one another, totally unaware that her passing was soon to be followed by another.

There's One More Angel In Heaven

I was once running a team development workshop for the Chief Executive of a business and his four Senior Vice Presidents. At one point in the discussions, one SVP made a comment that if his aged dog died, he would need to take a day or two off work. At first there was a stunned silence, which quickly turned to incredulous looks and laughter as his colleagues lambasted him for his stupidity. It was only a dog. As he tried to defend his position, one against four, he was heckled with scornful abuse by the others. Finally the CEO decided that he would end this foolishness with a definitive statement: "If you take time off for a dead dog, you won't have a job to come back to." In an instant everything became very serious. Then I realised that the guy was nearly in tears and trying desperately to hide it.

It is a personal rule of mine during team development interventions, that as the facilitator, I never direct outcomes, demonstrate bias or take sides; but by now I was appalled. Rules be damned. Shamelessly, I used my position as a 'neutral' observer to verbally eviscerate the four and put forward my own agenda. I unleashed a tirade of abuse upon them, laying into them for their extreme insensitivity, lack of tolerance for the views of others, feeble ability to empathise and woefully inadequate communication skills. I was able to make (quite justifiable) references back to the whole of the business and made it look like I was talking about the general malaise in their leadership skills. At all times I talked about the love of dogs as if it was a convenient parallel, which of course, it was not. The ferocity of my assault upon them surprised even me, and by the time I had finished they were cowed into silence, with a great deal of staring at their hands going on. It was absolutely not what I should have done, but boy, did it feel good! Then to my amused amazement, the CEO thanked me for my very helpful and insightful feedback, and apologies were murmured to their colleague before we took a convenient break to ease the tension.

About three year later, the dog loving SVP was on another event with me. He told me that in the intervening years, his dog *had* died. When he had gone to tell his boss, it had been insisted upon that he take the rest of the week off. In truth, he needed it.

Grief affects different individuals in unique and contrasting ways. As the weeks passed, we had begun to get used to Saffy's absence from our lives. Sorrow over the loss of a pet can stay with you every bit as that experienced over the loss of a relative or friend, or even more so. From the perspective of those who don't experience grief from the loss of a pet in this way, this can be a thing of mystery, ridicule or even intellectual discomfort, as the previous story illustrates. There is that part of us that says that an animal is inferior and that as a consequence, strong feelings of grief following their departure is unreasonable. From the etheric's perspective, there is a somewhat different explanation.

What is the etheric's explanation?

Grief in itself is not a good thing. The pain that it causes us lowers our vibration.

If we were to be able to appreciate the true nature of life and death, we should celebrate the lives of those who have departed. We should also be confident that we have not seen the last of them since those animals that share their lives with us are undoubtedly part of our soul group and we will encounter them again in the etheric, in future lifetimes and possibly even in this lifetime.

All this said, grief can provide us with an opportunity for us to gain mastery over ourselves and come to terms with the learning that is written above; but why should we believe that this learning must be attached to humans?

We can have deeper and less troubled attachments to animals than we have to humans and created for ourselves far more learning opportunities with them than we may with human partners, offspring relatives, friends or associates.

Therefore, although this may be shocking to hear, your animals may be more important to you than some people. From the etheric's perspective, this is just how it should be, because that's the way you planned it!

Saffy was the first dog we had lost since Sage, almost eighteen months previously. At that time as now, we were lucky to have so many other dogs around. They proved a good salve to help us cope with loss. They simply didn't allow us to feel morose and they certainly were nothing less than their normal cheerful selves. It wasn't the case that they could immunise us from pain but they helped us get over it with more than reasonable speed. This, combined with helpful and supportive input from the etheric regarding the transition process generally, plus knowledge of what would become of Saffy meant that we restored our emotional equilibriums with some ease.

What did we know about what would become of Saffy?

The planning for a being's next lifetime and the course that it will take becomes apparent very quickly after they enter the etheric following their passing. I had been shocked that on occasion, within hours of their transition, I would be told where dogs (and people) would return. I was aghast that the planning could have been so instantaneous and it didn't seem to give much indication of a well thought out process!

Needless to say, it was my interpretation that was flawed; not that which was designed by the etheric! Patiently Michael explained the following.

Our perception of time causes us to measure it in a linear fashion as if going in a straight line from one point to another. We measure it with the construct of our creation, that we think of as time, and allow it to become a regulatory or controlling mechanism.

The true nature of time, as alluded to in 'Some Dogs' is very different. Etheric time bears little resemblance to ours, and may be perceived as operating on an approximate thousand to one basis. Thus, if someone passed four hours ago, it would be as if they had been in the etheric for nearly six months.

And since time loops and folds back upon itself, it is certainly the case that very extensive amounts of planning might already have gone into a reincarnation within a very short space of time after a being has passed.

We knew with absolute certainty that Saffy had chosen a next life where she would not have to experience the discomfort of liver disease, nor the manner of interactions that had caused her to be dismissed by her adoptive family because of her age and infirmity.

In short, during her next lifetime she wanted serious pampering!

Nonetheless, her passing was still unsettling, if only because of the breach in our hereto (apparently) invulnerable pack life. Having so many elderly dogs almost implied that we could expect transitions on a regular basis, but like all pet owners, we preferred to think of them as going on forever. In those weeks, I reviewed each pack member and studied their health. I concluded that I need have no anticipation of anybody going soon.

So the first time Sharon found Joe having a fit, we thought, or rather hoped, that he was simply twitching in his sleep. It was a shocking sight as, since joining us, Joe had begun to thrive. If this were a portent of his passing, that prospect was unbearable.

The journey back to Alberta from America with Joe and Saffy now seemed like a life time ago. We had always half expected Saffy to go; but Joe, in both manner and physique, if not actual years, was a much younger and stronger dog. He adapted to pack life wonderfully, and although he and Indy never got on, he fit in fine with everyone else.

After a couple of weeks of suspicion, he formed a very close bond with me and he would follow me everywhere. When I sat typing at the computer, he would lean against me and nuzzle his nose under my arm so that I was forced to hug him. His immensely thick and beautiful red coat, almost shocking to see in its brightness, made him appear to be a very big dog and he dominated a space with his presence almost as much as Indy could. Having him in the house was like having a big woolly teddy bear around. He was always ready to be cuddled and established himself as a firm favourite with visitors.

So the notion that this adorable creature might now be falling prey to epilepsy or some other condition was so alarming that I tried to ignore it. After all, he was an Avatar and surely such things could not happen? Although I had not seen the incident, I assured Sharon that it was probably nothing, and sure enough nothing more happened.

For a week.

Joe had his next fit lying beside me at the dinner table. His eyes rolled and his tongue lolled out of his mouth. It didn't last more than a few seconds and his confusion afterwards was very short lived. He was back to himself within minutes, desperate for affection and food! I tried to push away concerns again and succeeded.

Until the next day.

In mid-afternoon Joe had another fit. It was clearly much longer and more intense than the previous ones. Sharon performed healing upon him, but within minutes a second started. And then a third.

The fourth began as we were trying to get him into the car and the fifth on the way to the vet's clinic.

Immediately upon our arrival he was put onto an intravenous drip to administer a sedative to relax him. Worryingly, it wasn't strong enough to prevent another and the vet, having initially been quite 'up' about his condition, began to look concerned. We outlined his history of neglect and starvation and her face became grimmer with each new revelation. This was, she believed, much more than simply epilepsy (which could have been treated with preventative medication). She felt that it was something far more ominous and the beginning of something a lot more unpleasant for him. She believed that his main organs were beginning to shut down.

As Sharon and I stood there in disbelief, big tears began to roll down both of our cheeks. It was twenty nine days since we had lost Saffy. We had rescued them both at the same time. Surely it wasn't possible to lose both of them like this, so close together? For my part, pain in the butt though he could be at mealtimes (when his dogginess certainly overcame his angelic core), I had come to adore Joe; and he seemed to reciprocate the feeling. He had become my dog. He was big and funny and comforting, loving and silly and huggable. And most of all, he was Joe. Major character. Doting pet. Avatar. We couldn't lose him. I couldn't lose him.

Nonetheless, there was the vet, telling us that it was not in his best interests to go on. And there were all of the 'Philosopher's Dog' arguments nagging at me again. The vet left us alone for a few minutes in the operating room he'd been brought to so that we could decide what to do. Joe lay on a steel operating table, the IV in his leg, his body the most relaxed it had been for the past two hours, his back turned to us.

It was all I could do to make eye contact with Sharon, let alone speak. I was quite resolute that this would not be the end, yet I couldn't get the words out. So I turned to look back at Joe, his massive hairy form filling the table. At that moment he pushed his head right back, straining his neck to see us behind him. He made very deliberate eye contact. I cannot remember ever being fixed with such a kind and gentle, but sad and knowing gaze. That gaze was filled with love and understanding. It is a look that I found heartbreaking and will never forget.

Then a voice in my head said, quite clearly: "Let me go".

"We've got to let him go" I whispered and Sharon nodded. We ushered the vet back in and while she administered the fatal medication, we stroked his beautiful coat until he was truly asleep and gone from us. Then the vet left the room and Sharon and I took it in turns to bury our faces in his fur, offer our apologies, gratitude and love for him. And then we left.

We had only just pulled out of the car park before Sharon revealed that she had quite clearly heard Joe ask her to "Let him go" at the very moment he'd made eye contact. Neither of us was in the least bit shocked when I said I'd heard too. It was a comfort to both of us, but only for a moment. We carried on in agonized silence, the grief raw and palpable, worse and more painful than it had been with Saffy. He had seemed to be so strong and his departure so unnecessary.

As we drove on I mused upon the sound of the voice we had both heard and its peaceful nature.

We were no more than a mile away when it started to speak again.

By Special Request: Sienna's tale

In the midst of the earthly angst, it was almost possible to forget that Joe was an Avatar. His transition to the etheric was therefore quite unlike it is for humans and the immediacy of his communication should have come as no surprise.

What happens when a soul transitions to the etheric?

Most people have heard stories about those who have had near death experiences. The description of the tunnel of light and being met by all those who they have known is now commonly accepted and is very close to the truth of what occurs.

The tunnel of light is a link between the third dimension and the etheric. It appears as a physical manifestation in this way, because for a transitioning soul, it is easiest to cope with in this form. The blue light actually begins as purple, but quickly becomes an increasingly paler shade, rapidly fading to blue before it eventually becomes white. The colour shift represents the changeover between the third dimensional vibration and that of the etheric. The tunnel may appear long, stretching off into the distance, although the process of transition is actually quick and easy.

Within the tunnel may be found anyone and everyone the individual wishes to encounter. Whilst we may reasonably anticipate that we will encounter those who have passed, you may meet with literally anyone with whom you have a connection, even if they are still alive and physically present in the third dimension. This is because their higher selves are in the etheric and they may therefore also be met. However, because at this point, the soul is still trying to 'get to grips' with what has happened, the 'living' are rarely encountered. Effectively, the whole transition process is governed by what we would expect.

The sensation of love that is reported is also a vibration. It is so powerful that it produces a palpable quality and it is difficult to describe it as anything else but love. However, it should also be understood as a profound sense of peace and rightness. The soul has (albeit temporarily) returned to being part of the whole that the etheric most often describes as 'the great oneness' and sheds all issues of the physical, emotional, intellectual stressors that may cause it disturbance in the third dimension. Although the perception of emotions is somewhat different in the etheric, our stressors are replaced by surety of total acceptance, which is most often experienced as love.

The experience of reconnection may last for as long as we need it to. We may 'party' or do whatever we wish with those whom we encounter, for a time of our choosing. This will be an aspect of our need in the moment and eventually, we come to a realisation that everything is of our own making. Our connection to those around us is both a tangible and an illusion at the same time because we are never actually separate from anyone, since we are all aspects of the same thing. When we understand this once more, we are ready to move on and the preparation for our next life begins.

For a returning avatar, the experience is somewhat different. Upon transitioning they find themselves in the very instant they left experiencing the moment as if they have merely blinked. The integration of their experiences as third dimensional beings has already taken place and they are immediately ready to continue with their purpose and angelic tasks.

However, what Joe then said to us was surprising as his very first request was that we "now consider getting Sienna".

This will mean very little to the reader, and even less if you haven't read the first book. So here's a recap and an explanation:

We had collected Joe from a lady in Montana called Helena, in response to a suggestion from Archangel Michael. When we had arrived at her rescue facility, she had been kind enough to give us a tour. What I omitted to mention was that amongst her sixty plus dogs, with guidance, I was able to identify three more Avatars. I was concerned that they were in a shelter in the first place, but Michael had explained that it was a good place for them to be, so loving and caring was this wonderful lady. He also pointed out on two occasions that the avatar was not meant to be with us anyway. I did not ask the reasons since, if I'm honest, I was rather grateful. At that stage I thought we had more than enough dogs. After all, there were twelve!

However, almost at the start of the tour we were introduced to a dog named Sienna who was lying somewhat dolefully up against the wire of her enclosure. She looked a little like Joe, with a thick red coat. She was terribly affectionate when I stooped to pet her. She seemed reluctant for me to go and her energies were very intense. Michael rather casually commented that she was an Avatar, but said nothing more on the subject.

Sadly, I tore myself away from her and caught up with the others. I enquired about her origins and it turned out that she had been the pet of some people who had become missionaries and decided that dog ownership conflicted with their purposes, despite the fact that they were to operate domestically within the US. These were by no means cruel, thoughtless or uncaring owners. Quite the opposite. They had loved their dog but been surer of their calling than the need to be dog owners. They had been greatly conflicted in their choice and almost immediately I understood what her purpose with them had been. Sadly, like Joe, she had not been successful in its achievement.

What was Sienna's purpose?

Sienna's family were mid-term souls caught up in one of the most major dogmas that affects humans: Religion.

Mid-term soul experiences are typified by an on-going need (that spans many lifetimes) to overcome some form of dogmatic belief that stays with the individual. Most typical amongst these is religion. It holds a great power to sway the mind since it allows the individual to place the responsibility for their lives in the hands of another i.e. that which they conceive of as God. Religion is seductive in how comforting it appears to be, yet it is an illusion in its representation of our purpose.

The choice that came to Sienna's family was an odd one. From their perspective it appeared as 'choose the dog you love or choose the God you love'. I won't dwell on the similarity of the letters.

With their perception of God and what 'He' meant to them, they were unable to see the God in the dog.

Yet the vibration of the etheric from Sienna was palpable. She is a fully conscious avatar and her effect upon the family would have been strong. It *could* have been strong enough for them to see the situation differently and break away from their dogma. But when they came to the crossroads that their choice presented for them, they chose the God route and their piety ensured for them a further mid-term lifetime to come.

Alas, Sienna had failed in her purpose.

Now she had been in rescue for two years and nobody wanted her. The people's children regularly enquired about her and were deeply saddened that she had no home to call her own; although undoubtedly Helena showered her with love. I wished that we could have given her a home, but as we were due to collect Saffy as well, we could not take another dog under any circumstances.

We were greatly troubled by her plight thereafter. The knowledge that such a gentle Avatar was languishing in the enclosure came to me over and over, as it does with all of the other Avatars that I know of and am unable to assist. So over the coming months, I occasionally enquired of Helena how she was doing. "No takers" was the stock response.

When Joe suggested that we get Sienna, our answer was instant and affirmative. Of course we would.

In the short minutes that it took us to get home, Joe explained that, with our permission, he would now remain within our home in the capacity of what he described as a 'house angel'. He wished to watch over the dogs he had formed an association with. That was no problem for us, in fact it made the parting a little less sorrowful. There was something very comforting about him still being around. And even now, over a year later, I really value and enjoy being able to speak with him and consult on pretty much any matter with total ease. His presence is constant and reassuring in a way that is difficult to describe. Sometimes I wonder if we will eventually end up with dozens of former Avatars living with us.

However, his continuing presence, albeit in a very altered state, would subsequently prove to be something of an issue for Tristan! More of that later...

On our return, the second action I took was to email Helena. It was a sad outpouring of grief at Joe's loss (I felt that I couldn't tell her about his instantaneous return); an expression of deep regret that we hadn't been able to protect the loving soul we had been entrusted with from the ravages of illness; followed by a plea that she consider us for another one of her charges.

Her response was instantaneous. It was kind, supportive and most oddly, filled with joy. She wept with sadness for Joe and with happiness for Sienna. She would be delighted if we took her. And so it was.

I must pause at this point and go off on a slight tangent. I mentioned in the last book that as I wrote their chapters, all of the Avatars (except those physically unable to do so) had come into the room and lain at my feet as I wrote their chapters. Well true to form, Sienna just pushed her head under the arm of my chair and started to lick my hand as I was typing. The affection is very typical. Interrupting me when I'm typing is a complete first. Normally she'll be respectful and just nudge my elbow to let me know she's there and then wait. This is a fully fledged 'I know this is about me' intervention. Now she's settled at my feet. On with her story!

The prospect of making the long journey to Montana and the consequent expense was a daunting one for us. As fate would have it, it turned out that Helena was a good friend of Karen's, who spent a fortnight each year at Helena's assisting her and enabling her to get much needed rest. Karen did this in addition to running her own very active rescue and she lived about half way between us and Helena. I previously said that 'the second action I took' on getting home was email Helena, because the first thing I had done was email Karen. I asked her if she thought Helena would consider giving us Sienna and if it would be OK to ask. She had given me an instantaneous "Yes!"

When I emailed her to tell her of Helena's response, with the immense kindness and generosity of spirit that is her trademark, she offered to meet Helena at a location convenient to her and then bring Sienna all the way to our house. It was too good an offer to refuse. I also saw further opportunity in it.

By now I had amassed quite a back catalogue of 'orders' from people who wanted me to find what I always call 'second hand avatars', i.e. those that have found their way into rescues. Knowing that both Helena and Karen had them pass through their doors with some frequency, I proceeded to look at their current 'stock' and try to match them against my orders!

Why did these two have a particularly high throughput of avatars?

To my mind, it is something of a tragedy when an avatar finds its way into a rescue. The reasons why it happens are explained in detail in the first book and it is a risk that they have an awareness of before they incarnate in dense third dimensional form. It is also a risk that is assumed with quite a high level of probability that failure and a sorry ending will be the outcome. Apparently, it's worth it.

However, wherever possible, those Angels that are actively supporting them in their purpose attempt to ensure that if rehoming does become a reality, the rescues where they find themselves are at least ones where there are loving and caring humans to look after them (although due to the intervention of free will, it's not always possible to bring about).

Both Helena and Karen emanate light. Their love of the animals goes beyond what one might typically expect. As you might imagine, we have now had a great many dealings with rescues and rescuers. By my reckoning, to even be participants in rescue work, these people must, by

104

definition, be fairly wonderful; or at least have some semblance of an understanding of the importance of the animal kingdom. But in comparison with the majority, Helena and Karen are positively light filled.

For an avatar that is unwanted, it experiences the equivalent of being set adrift in stormy seas. They are never abandoned by their fellow Angels and those who watch over them in the etheric attempt to guide them to safe harbours. It comes as no surprise to me that they choose people like Helena and Karen for this purpose. By comparison, they are proverbial lighthouses in the sometimes forbidding mists and density of the ether.

To be perfectly honest, I get many more requests to help find Avatars than I am actually able to help with. There are two reasons for this. Firstly, it is very difficult to find one since only one in three thousand dogs are avatars; so it can be a little bit like finding a needle in a haystack. I have to be guided to find them otherwise it can be a futile pursuit involving looking at the (most often) heartbreaking stories of literally thousands of poor abandoned creatures. Secondly, not everyone is meant to have one. Because of their rarefied energies, they are invariably trouble in some way, shape or form and can potentially cause more disruption to the households that they go to than they can do good.

How do avatars cause disruption?

The principal cause of avatar disruption stems from their energy. Upon first encounter, most avatars will certainly appear as perfectly normal dogs. However, prolonged exposure to them will engender quite a different experience.

The vibration they possess, very much like the energy line upon which our house is situated, will accentuate aspects of being in all those who are around them. This may just as easily result in negative behaviours as positive ones. They can be very unbalancing for humans. Ironically, this is in part the reason why they may easily fail in their appointed tasks. Again, the risk is worth it.

Then there is the fact that their own energies can be difficult to contain in bodies the size of even large dogs (avatars seldom chose to incarnate in small dog bodies because of this); as a consequence, this can make them unusually boisterous, difficult to control or just plain irascible.

Despite my explanation of this fact in the first book, I regularly receive emails from owners telling me that they have an avatar. They know it is one because it's so sainted. I disagree at my peril!

So I will only find a 'second hand' avatar if Michael says it's for the highest good of the individual(s) involved. And even then, it can take many months of searching before the right one appears.

Readers of 'Some Dogs' may remember our protracted hunt for an Avatar for our friends Angie and Diego? Well at this point in time, the search was still on-going and despite having found several potential dogs for them, there was always something about the circumstances that prevented them from adopting successfully. To their credit, they were endlessly patient and quite philosophical about these failures. Angie would always be the first to accept that it was not 'meant to be'.

Now, Helena made me aware of a Husky she had with the awesome name of Madame Ruby La Rue who needed a new home. She would be perfect for a family, and as soon as I saw the (not very good) photo of her, I realized that she was undoubtedly an avatar. Despite the fact that she by no means matched the family's specification for their ideal dog (white, male, blue eyes, young) as she was red, female, blue eyed and middle aged, Michael was absolutely insistent that this was the dog for them.

I presented Ruby's case to them without revealing the insistence of their friendly neighbourhood Archangel. I didn't want them to feel obliged to take the dog as this was surely a recipe for disaster if things did not work out. I was only able to show them the not very good photograph of her and there was, somewhat unusually, zero information about her background and how she had come to be in rescue. I reiterated the difficulties of taking an avatar and issued my usual dire warnings about the extent to which the dog would inevitably disrupt and inexorably alter their way of life.

Nevertheless, upon seeing her, they all fell in love instantly and agreed to take her in a matter of seconds. Clearly Michael knew exactly what he was talking about. So having facilitated an application to Helena (which was subsequently accepted) I arranged with Karen that Ruby would also be brought along with Sienna.

Also at this time I had been looking for an Avatar for our friend Colleen. She had no preconceptions about what type of dog she would welcome into her life; she simply wanted to offer a refuge to an Avatar. In discussion with Karen regarding a dog for Angie and Diego, it had come to light that she had a white female Husky called Nakita who Michael had identified as an Avatar. She came from a very troubled background. Although she was very gentle, her experiences of humans had been deeply unpleasant. She now lived in constant fear and could best be described as 'damaged'. She would not make a suitable dog for a family with young children (as she was particularly frightened of them), so that had already ruled her out for Angie and Diego. So I now wondered if Colleen would consider taking her. Again, Michael was quite adamant that this would be the right dog for Colleen.

To my great relief and pleasure, she agreed; so we arranged that Karen would bring all three dogs with her a few weeks hence.

Thus it was that after a journey that sounded as if it was something straight from hell, Karen arrived at our house with all three dogs where we, along with Colleen, Angie and her girls Valeria and Natalia (Diego was overseas), all waited eagerly.

The contrasts in the dogs were amazing. Sienna stepped out of the vehicle as if it were the most natural thing in the world and as if she had always been expecting this eventuality to transpire in her life. (As it turned out, she had, but more about this later.) She jumped out of the RV with absolute confidence, greeted us warmly, trotted briefly around outside, then made her way indoors. She was totally unphased by the rest of the pack and they in turn responded to her confidence with instant acceptance of her presence. She obviously knew that she was home and there was no way she was going anywhere else!

Madame Ruby was an altogether 'different kettle of fish'. Unlike Sienna, who was a relatively known quantity thanks to our previous meeting, we had not set eyes upon this dog and therefore relied totally on Helena's description of the avatar. We knew that she had been reported as loving, gentle, laid back, generally gorgeous but slightly overweight. What we encountered was a stunningly beautiful, growling, snarling, fearsome, obese canine with major attitude. Had there been some mistake?

Of course, we trusted Helena totally and knew that never in a million years would she misrepresent any dog in her care, because of the potential repercussions of doing so. We also knew very well of the high stress such transitions can bring for a dog. But that didn't stop me feeling great concern for Angie and the girls who were now faced with having to take home this potentially vicious creature. As they tried to coax her into the back of their SUV, it really looked like she might bite them at any moment. Her apparent aggression was not reserved for the other animals around her. Eventually I had to lift her into the back for them and they drove off, perhaps slightly shell-shocked and in some trepidation over what was to come.

By even more stark contrast, Nakita was too frightened to even leave the RV. She curled herself into a tight ball and exuded misery and upset. It was as if she was trying to make herself invisible. It was obvious that she was a very attractive, fine specimen of a Husky dog (which, as it transpired, had a great deal to do with her troubled life this far) but she displayed zero levels of confidence and absolute lack of interest in all that went on around her. My heart went out to Colleen. I knew that she had been so excited about Nakita's impending arrival. She knew she was getting damaged goods, but to be confronted by a totally unresponsive and reserved animal. Was this really what she wanted?

Despite all of my experiences, I am still prone to doubt the wisdom of the etheric and the guidance given by Michael when it conflicts with what I see before my eyes. I forget that from their perspective, Angels can see so much more than we are ever able to. In making his recommendations, Michael already knew exactly what the outcomes would be.

A Dark Past: Nakita's Tale

Colleen's journey with Nakita began as an uphill battle on the side of a slope that had an incline rising sharply away from her with massive odds stacked against her and boulders rolling towards her. When Michael revealed her full background, this fact became as obvious as her past was disturbing.

Nakita had been rescued from a puppy mill operation. Her good looks, excellent breed conformation and fine fur had caused her to be singled out at birth to become a breeding machine. From the earliest age, she had been mated with other Huskies. She apparently had strong genes, resulting in a knack for producing pure white, blue eyed offspring. These were in great demand amongst those who were more fashion conscious of their dog's looks, or had a stereo-typed belief about what a Husky 'should' look like. Therefore, they also attracted a premium price from buyers. Nakita was a very good revenue earner. The price she paid for this was high.

To be a malleable resource for the owner, she was needed to be highly submissive and non-confrontational. She lived in a kennel (although the term should be used loosely, since it was little more than a very poor wooden shed) at the back of the owner's land, a long way from their house so that the occupants would not be disturbed by any noise she might make. There was a twelve by six foot run attached to it. There she remained for four years without being allowed out. She was visited only at feeding time and when mates were brought to her. She had no company, no-one to play with, no-one to take her for walks. Her puppies would be taken from her at eight weeks and she was expected to breed again as soon as she came back into season. Eventually she had enough and turned on the unwanted mate that was forced upon her. He received the full force of her pent up anguish with this agonising existence, and he was badly injured in the process. 'The worm had turned'.

After this episode, the mill-owner (I will not dignify him by calling him a breeder) realized that she was now damaged goods and could not be used for further breeding. So rather than attempt to rehome her, where her less than usual personality would be recognized and likely render her unadoptable, she was left to starve.

Without any apparent reason, and having known of this operation for many years, a neighbour suddenly decided to alert animal welfare and the mill was raided. I have no doubt that he was led to do this by those in the etheric who watched over one of their own.

Although she had been liberated, by now Nakita was at death's door. The vet recommended that her miserable existence be terminated and so she was put on to the perpetually full roster of those awaiting their unhappy departure from this life at the end of a needle.

In another unlikely twist of fate, Helena just happened to visit the pound to which Nakita had been taken. She saw beyond the terrified eyes and ravaged body and her heart went out to the emaciated dog. She begged to be allowed to take her and the dog pound was only too grateful to be able to save themselves a few dollars from their over-stretched budget by not having to administer the fatal dose of liquid death.

After months of rehabilitation with Helena, Nakita had been nursed back to fine physical health, but could still only be described as a shell of a Husky. Her spirit was broken. She would lie listlessly, shunning all contact with the other dogs and only responding to the love Helena showed her for the briefest of moments. The breed is an immensely resilient one that is capable of enduring tremendous hardships of a physical nature. But here was a dog that had suffered psychologically. Ultimately Helena recognized that any progress that she might make from this point onwards required a different environment, away from dog runs and in the midst of a home where she could be lavished with attention around the clock. Only then might she begin to forgive what had been done to her.

When we discussed her, Helena pulled no punches in revealing what a difficult proposition Nakita presented. She would not consider anyone who offered a less than ideal home for this battered soul. Colleen was an easy sell. Amidst a lifetime of helping others, she had actually run a nursing home for the psychologically damaged. If anyone could understand the dog, it would be Colleen. In return, when describing the dog to Colleen, her issues were like water off a duck's back and she was not deterred one iota. All she saw was a soul that needed to be reached out to and an etheric being that had been there for a purpose.

So our friend had now taken an emotionally scarred being into her world. Her extreme shyness and apparent fear of everything around her continued, even despite the gentle and loving treatment she received from her new mistress. She would choose to spend long hours in a room apart from Colleen, alone with the demons that haunted her, never daring to venture out and experience the new home that surrounded her. It was weeks before she would leave one room and go to another of her own volition. Even the walks that provide such excitement for most dogs were something of a difficult chore. Nakita would show some initial enthusiasm, but once she had left the confines of the house she would experience panic attacks and try to drag Colleen homeward as soon as possible. If they encountered other people, this would set the dog off even worse. It was almost as if the contrast with the confined quarters that she had spent so many years within had left her with a form of agoraphobia.

It has to be said that in all of this, Colleen's behaviour bordered on the saintly. At times it seemed that for every two steps forward, Nakita would take twelve backwards. Yet Colleen accepted her new dog for what she was and where she was, encouraging her with unending patience and tolerance. From an outsider's perspective it may have looked like the dog was an unrewarding one to own. But all Colleen saw was a being that needed patience and help. Not once did her resolve waiver. Not once did she have any regret about the choice she had made.

Because she is a close friend, we received weekly updates from Colleen on Nakita's progress. Basically there were very few that revealed any headway being made. It was many weeks before we got an excited phone call to let us know that Nakita had finally decided to experiment with visiting a different room in the house. An even more excited one sometime thereafter let us know that the dog had actually greeted Colleen upon her return from shopping. It was a tiny step, but above all else, it represented a major triumph for Nakita and Colleen was thrilled for her.

Anyone who adopts a rescue dog at some point reflects upon what their new charge has lived through and hopes that they are now totally happy. So it came as no surprise when Colleen requested some information about Nakita's past; and more specifically, what her purpose had been as an avatar. Had she fulfilled it? Beyond the circumstances of the scenario that had required the rescue, we knew little of her day-to-day life and treatment. Michael, on the other hand, knew quite a lot. But Colleen soon wished she hadn't asked.

As a major part of the mill owner's initiative to instil Nakita with the qualities that would make his life easy, from the earliest moments of her puppy life, she was shown no kindness. What physical contact she was offered was brutish. Within days she had learned that to approach a human could result in a stinging reproach. Quickly, she understood that she need not fear abuse if she just did nothing when in the proximity of humans. Whereas most pets learn and respond to a name, Nakita was simply not spoken to. The exception to this rule was that if she looked in the direction of a human, she would receive a harsh rebuke. Relief might have come when the owner decided to put his young son in charge of taking the dog its food; after all, children love puppies, don't they?

Michael did not describe the boy in any way, but he did describe his actions. He used the word "monstrous". The child took perverse pleasure in grabbing the puppy by the scruff of the neck and twisting the fur until she was at the point of choking. Her paws and leg joints became targets for unnatural manipulations. He would force her neck over the side of his arm, almost to the point of snapping the vertebrae and if she resisted, the treatment was accompanied by blows to the head and body. On more than one occasion she was physically thrown across the cage. Finally, after months of systematic torture, the father was alerted by the pitiful yelping noises made by the dog and caught the boy in the act. He was severely punished, not because of the hurt he was inflicting on the poor defenseless creature, but because there was a risk that he might damage the future breeding machine.

114

Ironically, the beating the boy received probably saved Nakita's life, but it did not end the abuse. Thereafter, the child became more adept at inflicting his tortures upon the animal in a way that hurt, but would not actually break anything. When she cried out, her muzzle was slapped. Hard. Gradually, she learned not to cry out and take her punishment. On one occasion whilst she was receiving the harshest of treatment and the most severe of physical abuse, she dared to look plaintively into the boy's eyes in the hope of sparking compassion at some level or another. Instead she was met with cold reproach and showered with a tirade of abuse and violence. It was a fateful moment for both of them. She had fulfilled her purpose and he, beyond his wildest imagination, had reached a crossroads in his life.

What was Nakita's purpose?

As we go through our lives and follow our uniquely individual learning paths, we *all* do good and bad. This is the way it is meant to be, for how can we understand one without the other? Through our experience and learning we are meant to apply our discernment in recognising that which is for our highest good, and make life choices accordingly. Some learning is easy. Some is difficult.

Occasionally we get caught up in beliefs that become cyclical for us. We miss learning opportunities that then loop and revisit us on multiple occasions within any one lifetime; and if we still don't get it, between different lifetimes as well. Usually when this occurs, the magnitude of the lesson expands exponentially so that we cannot miss it (although we may still choose not to apply our learning). These are the lessons described as 'dogmas' in the previous chapter.

This boy was caught up in just such a dogma. To explain briefly and simply: over the course of many lifetimes he had struggled with the (not uncommon) belief in the supremacy of his state of being over others. Whilst I was not allowed to see his previous lifetimes, Michael explained that they had usually involved acts of cruelty and particular contempt for the natural world and creatures therein. He explained that such an experience of life was absolutely valid, and that although I might find it abhorrent, many have this pathway to follow. He also counselled that all overcome it, eventually.

However, this particular individual had gone through so many iterations of this state of being that he needed a more than usual amount of assistance in order to break free of the constant loop he had gotten into. And since the impact required to do this was very high, he would now go through a lifetime of relatively extreme experience.

As a way of assisting him in breaking free and coming to terms with the challenge of himself, he elected to meet with a 'signpost' at an early stage of his life. This would provide him with a chance to experience an awakening and overcome the learning need. The signpost would come in the form of a pet, a creature that would evoke all of his issues. In theory, any creature would 'do' to serve this purpose, and many 'normal' dogs do undertake similar roles with their owners, albeit for those with less severe learning needs; or even for the sake of their own experience.

However, of key importance in this situation was what would emanate from the dog at the very moment when the lesson was to be presented to the learner. It must reflect a higher state of being that prompted recognition in the observer. The boy needed, in that moment, to be touched by an understanding of what he consistently failed to grasp: that in hurting something else, he hurt himself. In an instant, he needed a vital reminder of his own etheric origin and to extend his consciousness outside of his limited third dimensional reality.

All of this could not be conveyed by a 'normal' dog, since the essence of their being is as an incarnate form. So an angel was required and Nakita, acting out of pure love and in full knowledge of what would transpire, volunteered.

The opportunity to gain learning extends across a lifetime. The opportunity to apply that learning is decided upon in moments. So brief are these moments that we may not even be conscious of our opportunity to exercise our discernment. Yet the choices made in the instant of the moment may reverberate in their impact across our whole lifetime.

An avatar may live a lifetime with a purpose that lasts throughout, or merely for a moment that may occur at any point in that lifetime. For Nakita, the desperate plea for pity conveyed by her pained eyes *was* that moment. Her beseeching look delivered the awakening message, clearly and directly from the etheric. In that almost imperceptible instant, the boy was reacquainted with lifetimes of learning and presented with a blinding glimpse of the meaning of the moment. Then he was given a simple choice: Stop what you are doing, for your own sake.

Or continue.

From an adult perspective, and in the light of the consequences which you as an observer may be fully able to comprehend, the choice, in its implication, may appear to be of great magnitude. Was it therefore beyond the mind of a child? When I asked Michael about this he explained that an infant may be ignorant of the ways of the world they will come to grow up in; but in so many other ways, a child's discernment may be far more sophisticated than an adult. Consider that as yet, they have not learned to encumber their thought processes with concerns of political correctness, vested interest or self-deception. More importantly, the learning and knowledge that has been gleaned in previous lifetimes (and contained in their soul DNA) is actually much more accessible. Choices are more easily made because their points of reference in making them are far purer in their nature. Therefore, a child acts more with their hearts than their heads. This choice was well within the boy's powers of understanding.

Yet still he chose to ignore the guidance that spoke within him and the violence recommenced.

I asked Michael if it would be possible for the child to undergo some kind of epiphany later in his life? The answer was a "yes" delivered with very little conviction. When I queried this, he commented that direct intervention had been given from the etheric *only* because of his pre-existing difficulty with acting upon a piece of learning he already possessed. And only in the most extreme cases of need would this be permitted. Once the intervention had been made, never again in this lifetime would he be the recipient of such mighty assistance from the etheric. Instead, he consigned himself to a further series of repetitions and a ramping up of the extremity with which the learning point would be presented to him. Unfortunately, it would be without a corresponding increase of ease with which the learning would be made obvious to him.

Michael went on to explain that lifetimes in which we fail to apply discernment, when we have already understood the learning points that allow us to make effective choices, may more deeply engrain inappropriate choices and actions. This also provides an explanation of why so many lifetimes are lived within the mid-term soul range.

I was left in two minds by the explanation. On the one hand, I was deeply saddened that the result of Nakita's suffering amounted to nothing. But I realized that my concern was for her. If I revisited the horrendous unkindness of the boy, I struggled to find any empathy with him.

Michael, on the other hand, was much more philosophical. I was awed by his ability to regard the situation without judgement of the boy. He reminded me that those in the etheric simply see the souls of the individuals in their true higher self form. Even though the actions affected one of his own kind, the actions themselves were deemed inconsequential. He was supremely accepting of what had come to pass. He was also absolutely confident that the child would eventually 'get it', however long it took. And I was once more reminded that time in the etheric has very little meaning.

Ultimately, from a totally third dimensional perspective, I fear for the adult the boy may now become; for all our sakes. Pleasure in abusing animals, when observed in children, seems to be taken as a portent of much darker things to come.

This child was only ten years old.

It was at this moment in her life that Nakita first came into season. This natural biological process committed her to a further form of brutalisation, but saved her from another. Now that the dog was able to be productive, the father would take care of her, exclusively, to protect his investment. The key to her cage remained in his pocket and from that point onward, the boy was only allowed to sneer through the fencing wire, his abuse now verbal.

And so it is that even now, if she encounters children, Nakita experiences the wildest panic of all. Her apparent terror will not abate until some considerable time after the offending youngster has been left far behind. To add to the problem, Nakita has luxuriant white fur and a cuddly polar bear like quality about her. She is large and powerful with blue eyes, very attractive and she looks very approachable. All in all, she's a recipe for a child magnet. Therefore, it is a source of some sadness for Colleen that she constantly has to keep a look out for children or move the dog away from eager little hands when they inevitably seek to connect with her. There is no risk to the kids as Nakita is quite harmless. It is the canine that would be traumatized. At least we now know why.

They say that time is a great healer, but nobody ever specifies how much time is required, or in what proportions to the time that has caused the hurt in the first place. So it made sense to us to assume that if it was going to happen at all, Nakita's road to recovery was a (unspecified) matter of time. Over the months that followed, we would see her at regular intervals and we were delighted when she overcame her fear of being with our pack. Gradually she accepted that the harm that had been inflicted upon her was not from her own kind, although I can only imagine that she must have viewed her enforced and oft repeated matings as a form of rape. I was relieved that she perceived no threat from our dogs.

About a year after the dog's arrival, Colleen decided that she and Nakita would join us on one of our hikes to the Plain Of Six Glaciers, the site of Archangel Michael's retreat at Lake Louise. Since this has the effect of awakening in avatars at least a modicum of knowledge of what they truly are, we were very pleased that this would be happening. To facilitate the process, I run energy through them whilst in the midst of channelling, and it can produce some spectacular effects. On this hike, the channelling for the group as a whole had been quite extensive and I had not realized that Colleen had an appointment in the evening and needed to return to her car much sooner than everyone else. As she was bidding farewell to all, Sharon reminded me that I needed to 'infuse' Nakita; so in a somewhat rushed fashion, I bent over her and began the process. Since I do this with my eyes closed, I will leave it to Sharon's account of what happened next. *"When it began, Nakita stood very still. Then all of a sudden we all got a sense that something powerful was entering into her third dimensional body. She stiffened slightly and looked about her, trying to see where the energy was coming from, but she didn't resist. She actually seemed to be enjoying it. Then all at once her eyes and the expression on her face changed. It was as if she was overwhelmed with a sense of peace and calm. If she'd have been human, you'd have heard a long and satisfied sigh of relief."*

For my part, I sensed the flow of etheric energy into her as if it was a ball of electricity that passed from my hands to her body. I could feel it coursing around her frame and her fur seemed to stand up. This would correspond with her stiffening. With my eyes closed, I suddenly saw a blast of brilliant white light as if what had gone within her had now permeated every individual hair of her coat and burst out of her. Her whole body then relaxed, and this is Sharon's 'sighing' point. When I opened my eyes, she turned her head slightly and made momentary eye contact. "OK, I get that."

Colleen herself was absorbed with the need to get home. It was her daughter's thirtieth birthday and she could not be late for the large celebration that was planned for that evening. So it took her a while before she started to notice the full force of the effects upon her dog. Over the course of the coming weeks, Nakita took on a new and much higher level of confidence. She walked out with Colleen in comfort, clearly finding enjoyment in sharing time with her owner and not worrying about those things that went on around her. And when she visited our house, she was perfectly happy to come indoors and rest comfortably, even amidst the madness that our pack can create. Even better from my perspective, when I approached her, she let me fuss with her and smother her with affection. And she licked me! What an honour.

However, Nakita was not yet out of the woods and our understanding of her and the lessons associated with her state of being were still unfolding.

Things That Go Bump In The Night

Learning can be a tall order and so a drip feed approach is perhaps best. Perhaps that's why we only got to hear Nakita's story in bits and pieces. The floods of information which can be delivered by the etheric can all too easily become overwhelming.

Much of what Sharon and I have come to know defies commonly perceived wisdom and challenges belief systems about almost any subject you may name. Some of it is almost too incredible to be accepted without some degree of personal struggle. Even in writing these books, I have been aware of deliberately 'pulled punches', where the etheric wishes the reader to have information revealed in a manner which is appropriate to both their level of comprehension and preparedness to accept. If you imagine it's any different for the channel, I can assure you it's not.

By now, the idea that I could trace reincarnating dogs, allow beings from other dimensions to communicate with me and even explain in some detail the presence of alien beings amongst us, was by now second nature.

Explain the alien beings amongst us!

It would be a naïve misconception of our place in the known universe to imagine that we are the only ones here.

When we look into the night sky and see it full of other planetary bodies we assume them to be lifeless. We have pursued our understanding of them through photographs and scientific analysis that is based on what we understand at this point in time, and what we believe to be possible.

We are massively unaware of all that is.

We imagine other planetary bodies to be dead because we are simply not able to see with our eyes the vibration of that which exists there. In fact, the astral forms all around us are teeming with life.

Life forms which we cannot begin to imagine occupy them and are all pursuing their ascension pathway. They have different purposes and vastly different experiences from ours.

Sometimes our lives overlap, but not in the ways we would conventionally conceive of. Science fiction can contain both truths and deceptions.

What I haven't yet discussed, but will already be apparent to those who have visited our www.angelsincanada.com website, is the fact that our daily lives now include dealing with residual energy vibrations, or what are more commonly described as ghosts.

I can't remember the first time Michael asked that we assist with such an issue but when he did so, it seemed like a perfectly normal extension of what we were already doing. Curiously enough, for years across our married life, Sharon had experienced recurring dreams about dealing with evil and demonic possession. Whilst I now dismiss these concepts as something of a distortion, there is a certain irony in the path our lives have now taken.

Why do I dismiss evil as a distortion?

It didn't take very long at all for somebody to ask in a public channelling about the nature of evil and 'the Devil'. The answer, as usual, was very matter of fact.

We need what we would describe as 'evil' in order to experience 'good'. We perceive these two as the opposites of one another and without polarity we cannot undergo a range of experience. Therefore, 'evil' as a concept is a valid thing.

The Devil as a being is a little more fanciful. There is indeed an archangel called Lucifer, but it is by no means a 'fallen' angel. Far from it. It is as good a being as we would perceive archangels Michael, Gabriel or Raphael to be. It simply has a responsibility that encompasses the spectrums of experience that include good and evil and is therefore associated with evil. This does not make it evil!

The being that we think of as 'the Devil', the embodiment of evil, has no form or presence. It is a construction of the church, originally a device to instil fear into people so as to more easily control them.

Initially I regarded Sharon's fixation with these matters to be a by-product of her devout Catholic upbringing, but once we had begun this work, the dreams abruptly stopped. Obviously her higher self had been trying to make an aspect of her purpose clear to her.

For my part, I had no such dreams and certainly no aspirations in this area! As a child and even into early adulthood I had been greatly fearful of anything remotely scary. I avoided movies with any horrific content and I found stories of the supernatural or occult disturbing. So to now find myself being asked to conduct what were, for want of a better description, exorcisms, was an interesting progression. Nonetheless, this is what has now come to pass.

We began with what we termed 'energy clearing', changing the vibration that existed within a certain space to a more acceptable one. It is worth understanding that any vibration that is created may take lifetimes to dissipate, depending upon the space in which it is confined and its nature. By integrating with another vibration (or attaching itself) it may move and change the space it occupies. The more powerful it is to begin with, the longer it may be sustained.

A simple domestic argument creates a vibration that may be perceived as 'an atmosphere'. A murder creates one that is entirely different and likely to be far more powerful in its sustainability. The vibration resonates between the walls of a building where it is trapped, and does not leave simply because doors and windows are opened.

The most common way of dealing with these energies is to use sacred white sage in a process called smudging. This has been accorded great ritualistic significance in the way it is normally carried out. In fact, smudging uses the vibration created by the smell of the sage to 'dampen' the pre-existing vibration. It does not however, get rid of it other than in cases where it is not too powerful to begin with. A lot of the success of a clearing of this nature has to do with the vibration of the person carrying out the smudging. Thus Shamans (perhaps the most well-known exponents of the method), can achieve considerably more success in its use than the average individual who buys a bunch of sage from their local new age store. This is not to say that smudging is of no value; simply that its effect may not be sustainable.

The first time we did an energy clearing, I hadn't a clue what we were doing. I was content to let Michael instruct us as to what should take place and I didn't even understand what we had done until half a dozen clearings later when I thought to actually ask. The method we use is a three stage process using sound as well as scent to firstly dampen, then remove, then replace existing vibrations with much more positive and beneficial ones. I also had to be a willing participant in allowing etheric energies to be run through me. Michael explained that only in this way would a vibration be totally removed. It's a shame it wasn't as easy as just smudging; that would have been a lot quicker. The average house takes at least one and a half hours to clear.

It wasn't long before this simple energy clearing led us to encounter the causes of some of the vibrations, which more often than not seemed to involve the energies of a departed being (or ghost). At this point, I guess it's worth explaining what a ghost is, as it has been elucidated to me by the etheric. This description has caused me to fall out with a lot of people who seem to want them to be something else. Judge for yourself.

What is a ghost?

A ghost is simply the residual energetic vibration of an individual that has been left behind in a certain place. It's not the actual person. It is an emanation of their energy that is trapped by its own inability to completely remove itself through the blue light tunnel that was made available to it upon its passing.

The reasons for this always relate to the free will of the individual and the selection of choices that go against that which is for their highest good. In an earth bound soul, this freedom is so sacrosanct that we may even contradict our higher selves (even though it knows a lot better than we do what is best for us!). Thus we may, in our dying moments, choose not to go, for whatever reason.

126

Unfortunately, our bodies are scheduled for departure, regardless. This leaves the vibration of the being in a state something akin to being shipwrecked on a desert island with little cognisance of their state of being, and no way of getting off the island until they themselves realize that they can float away!

Thus stranded, they can remain almost in perpetuity, their own energy sustaining the vibration that maintains their presence. It is not totally limitless and may be thought of as having the equivalence of a radio-active half-life, dissipating over (potentially) thousands of years. The longevity of its presence is a feature of the conviction to remain earthbound at the moment of passing. The stronger the desire, the longer it remains. However, the energy may be fed by the vibration of others:

When earthbound beings become aware of the presence of a ghost, their thoughts about this 'entity', which emanate from them (irrespective of their intentions) add to its energy and may by themselves sustain its presence. In certain cases, they may substantially add to it and even fundamentally alter its nature.

Since the ghost is largely unaware of its state of being i.e. it doesn't really know that it's dead, it tends to get frustrated and may seek contact with the living. When it is able to do so, the upsurge of energy it experiences reinforces its sense of self and therefore, it seeks more connection. We tend to call this a haunting.

Some living beings emanate far more energy than others. Children in particular, being closer to their point of entry into incarnation from the etheric, are much more vibrationally powerful. Therefore, many residual vibrations of this nature are attracted to them. This does not mean that they are harmful; simply that they feel more alive when around children.

Energy may be witnessed. Thus ghosts can be seen, if only for the most fleeting of moments. (Since children experience far greater ease in seeing them, this also helps to perpetuate their presence.) We are surprised if we see them and we have an alarming tendency to fear what we do not understand. A ghost is therefore generally regarded as a thing of fear, when in many respects it is quite a natural (if rather unfortunate) phenomenon.

A haunting begins when a vibration has been able to make itself known or has been perceived. The fact that it now exists in a state of awareness not only increases its energy, but also furthers other's awareness of it in the living world by word of mouth communication. In essence, the more people who know about something, the more the vibration gains in energy.

However, if people think about it negatively, the more negative energy is transferred to it. And so it may become something that it was not originally. This is also known as a 'construct', something that is the product of collective consciousness that has actually given it life.

Distortions of its energies may come by the expectations that the living have of its purpose; in other words, we endow it with something other than that which it would naturally possess, most commonly, evil intent. We tend to do this because our collective consciousness, fed by the media, relishes the salacious and finds that fear sells. We have learned to fear ghosts and assume that they are bad. Movies that intentionally play upon fears, like The Exorcist, create an expectation that becomes its own self-fulfilling prophecy.

Many hauntings that would otherwise be quite innocent and harmless assume proportions that are based upon our fear, not upon the original intentions of the being that has not properly transitioned. That is not to say that the intentions of the departed being were automatically good; simply that we may, by our own devices, alter what is there.

A residual vibration cannot in itself be harmful. It can certainly affect our own vibration and cause a cascade of emotional and consequent physical response, but this in turn is a matter of our own choosing. If we are in mastery of our own thoughts, it can have little effect.

The more fear based responses that 'feed' a haunting, the greater its ability to impact the vibrations of others becomes, giving it the semblance of something that may be capable of intentionally performing harmful acts.

In truth, a residual vibration or ghost, is to be pitied not feared. It needs help in getting to where it should be as its progress upon its ascension pathway has been waylaid by an unfortunate mistake in the exercise of its freedom of choice.

In dealing with ghosts or hauntings, we quickly found that these shipwrecked beings were actually very willing to move on. We were very easily able to sense their presence and Michael was usually more than prepared to fill us in on what had caused them to make the unfortunate choice to remain in the third dimension. Many of the stories were sad. Very few involved bad intentions and although we have had some unpleasant experiences, these have only involved the sensing of the vibration and the recognition of its negativity.

After communicating with the etheric about the ghost, I am often able to see the blue tunnel open up and beings of the etheric leading the entity away. Normally there is a sense of relief at their departure and once a being has gone, it cannot return.

The ghosts were not exclusively human and on more than one occasion, we found ourselves dealing with the vibrational residue of animals, specifically (of course) dogs. I found this odd because of the more powerful role that a dog's higher self plays in its life and death. Perhaps needless to say, I also found their reasons for remaining deeply saddening since they invariably involved selfless commitment to their former owners.

I found myself wondering why these ghosts would not respond if beings of the etheric asked them to move on. Why did it need the intervention of people playing 'Ghostbusters?'

Why is human intervention required?

Those who find themselves in this position still regard themselves as of the third dimension. In death as in life, they are simply unable to see beings of the etheric because this is what they choose.
When they are presented by the living communicating with them, they are able to accept their situation far more readily.

If you're beginning to wonder what all this has to do with dogs and avatars, your patience is about to be rewarded!

On one occasion we were asked to do an emergency house clearing. The occupants of the house were experiencing some majorly distressing energies that had been most disruptive for their dog. It had begun rather suddenly, but the situation had deteriorated within hours to the point where the dog had to be taken into veterinary ER. No ailment could be detected, yet the dog was very obviously in a state of high anxiety and physical distress. Their vet could offer no cause or solution and the owners feared greatly for their pet's life.

Hearing that we dealt with such things, the owners asked that we come out immediately. We agreed, but as we came to leave, had great difficulty with Lara who made it very clear that it was her intention to come with us.

Lara can be an awkward dog at the best of times. She is very strong willed, obstinate and determined. When she sets her mind to something, she always seems to get her own way and gets an unfair degree of support from the etheric in achieving her ends. (Readers may recall our futile attempts to get her spayed when she wanted to have puppies.) On this occasion, repeated attempts to get in the car without her presence failed miserably and eventually we gave up and decided to take her with us. Even more unusually, she insisted on being in the main body of the car on the back seat.

As we drove towards the troubled property, we were about five kilometres away when suddenly Lara stood up and stared intently ahead, her furry head poking between the front seats and her gaze unwavering upon the road ahead. Although she had sometimes travelled on the back seat, she had never displayed behaviour of this nature before. We could neither understand it, nor make out any reason for it. There was nothing ahead upon which her gaze was fixed. She just stared, unblinkingly. Finally, just before we pulled into the driveway, she sat down again, curled up on the seat and was instantly asleep.

We entered the premises with the bad stuff inside and prepared for the worst. Since we had both developed a great sensitivity for misplaced vibrations, we were greatly surprised to discover that all seemed to be quite fine. I asked to meet the troubled dog, but before she could be led to me, she arrived of her own accord, none the worse for wear from the experiences she had been having, and wagging her tail happily. I conducted a detailed recce of the house and found nothing out of place. I reported back to the owners that the clearing we had come to do seemed unnecessary and would be a waste of both their time and money. Somewhat embarrassed, they explained that their dog seemed to have made a full recovery only minutes before we had arrived, as if something miraculous had transpired. They paid for our gas, thanked us for our time and we went back to the car, more than a little bemused.

"So what was all that about then?" were my first words to Sharon, but before she could answer, Michael was already in there. "Lara removed the energies before your arrival. Their force necessitated her avatar intervention. It is her purpose in being with you."

Finally, the penny dropped. We had initially got Lara knowing that she was an avatar but without questioning why she was coming to us. It happened almost as an afterthought when we sought to get the reincarnating Sage back. We had never even thought to consider whether or not there was purpose for us in her presence and had glibly accepted that it was just to have babies. Now she had proved her worth. It wasn't to be the last time.

It doesn't happen that often, but on several subsequent occasions when the occupiers of houses have warned us of grievous things that lie within, Lara insists on coming with us, and we don't ignore her resolve to do so. Interestingly enough, Timba, who always likes to come out in the car whenever we leave the property, never shows signs of interest when Lara is being insistent.

As ever, we find ourselves in awe of the range of purposes for which the dogs have entered our lives, and it is nice to know that Lara has an objective of such magnitude. It makes perfect sense to us that the emanation of her powerful avatar vibration can be so affecting of another. Of course what we don't understand is precisely what energies she assists with clearing.

However, we do understand the mistake Max Von Sydow made in 'The Exorcist'. He didn't take his Husky with him!

Where the wild things are

In coming to Canada, we had moved to a relatively 'wild' place, surrounded by open forest in which a great variety of creatures were free to roam. We had already known about the dangers of coyotes before we moved, but we soon discovered that a wide assortment of creatures would regularly pass our doorstep and that it was quite easy to bump into intimidating creatures whilst out walking.

I considered it prudent to have an awareness of what we could expect to encounter, but also to be able to recognize potential danger from the tell-tale signs that could be seen all around us. Thus, I bought a book with the catchy title 'Animal Tracks and Scats of Alberta'. After a few days study, I considered myself reasonably competent in spotting a whole host of creatures from the footprints left in the copious amounts of snow all around us; although older, slightly melted or dog damaged tracks could be deceiving.

Much more reliable was a good poop deposit and I developed a growing fascination with the sheer variety of droppings that were available for viewing. These were also of great interest to the dogs, particularly as some of them seemed to taste very good. Often, I would have to haul dogs away before all evidence of an animal's presence was consumed.

Such awareness, whilst advisable, can also be quite disturbing. Hiking with the dogs took on a new dimension when one day I was out with Kaiti and Indy. They are a good pairing for a walk because Kaiti is too old to pull on her leash; and Indy can be totally trusted off leash. Since it was a day when snow lay quite deeply on the ground, I didn't want to risk being pulled over. We hiked on a forest road in the gorgeous wilderness of Kananaskis where a plow had already removed most of the snow. Indy trotted a few feet ahead of us while Kaiti, as usual, was going a great deal slower, apparently trying to enjoy the scent of every living creature that had ever been that way. Even by her standards, she was remarkably slow that day and her fascination with the invisible lingering smells of previous visitors bordered on the obsessive. Whilst waiting for her to move on from the latest distraction, I idly gazed around and noticed how clear Indy's large footprints were in the snow. I recalled with amusement a time on a hike when we had encountered a pair of young walkers who had come up behind us. They were relieved to discover that they were not, after all, following a bear. His tracks had appeared huge to them. I had thought them a little unrealistic at the time since his paw prints weren't *that* big, but today as I looked at them freshly made in the snow, they did indeed seem remarkably huge. And I was somewhat embarrassed to note how long his claws must have become. I made a mental note that we must get them cut.

We walked fifty metres more following his prints and I was impressed with the length of his stride today. He was clearly stepping out. Then Kaiti came to a complete stop again and I turned to find her with her nose deep in one of Indy's tracks. "Oh for God's sake Kaiti, what's so special about his tracks? He's right behind you!" I chided her, and gestured to Indy who was himself sniffing tracks twenty feet away. I gave the leash a jerk and set off again, returning both my thoughts and attention to the impressive tracks Indy had made in the snow.

It took about a full minute before the penny dropped.

If Indy was twenty feet behind us, how could I see his tracks stretching ahead of us? I froze and for the first time took a proper look at the paw prints. I glanced back and was shocked to note that Indy was rooted to the spot fifty feet behind us. In the silence that prevailed once the noise of our trudging through the snow had stopped, his whimpering could be clearly heard. I could almost feel the colour draining from my face as the grim realisation finally dawned on me. We were following a cougar. And what was more, it probably wasn't that far ahead of us.

Rapidly I began to walk backwards, scanning the receding whitened roadway for tell-tale flashes of colour that might betray the whereabouts of this deadly predator. The words our neighbour Scott had spoken months before rang in my head. "If a cougar's going to attack you, you won't see it; you'll already be dead." Although I was scared for myself, I was terrified for the dogs. How could I have been so stupid as to lead them into this danger? Even with his great size, Indy would be no match for a mountain lion. And as for Kaiti... With every footstep, I expected the cougar to have outflanked us and spring from the concealing trees that bordered our walking route. After a few hundred metres, I turned and ran as fast as Kaiti could manage.

I didn't relax again until we reached the spot where we had left the car, the dogs were safely stowed behind the tailgate of our SUV, and I was in the driver's seat with the door locked behind me. I sat with my chest heaving, gasping for air and beginning to shake. At times like this, it is very difficult to connect with the etheric, but nonetheless, Michael came through loud and clear, seemingly quite bemused, if not a little amused, by what had transpired.

"Why are you concerned?" he asked. "Are you not aware that you are protected at all times? Have you forgotten that you have two powerful avatars with you? Do you really think that harm may come to you in this way? This is not what is intended for you."

What does 'not intended for you' mean?

A great many aspects of our lives are planned out to a very fine level of detail even before we incarnate.

One of these is the manner of our demise.

I would not say that it's a good thing to know what this is in advance, but on this occasion it was nice to know that I wasn't due to be eaten by a cougar!

Instantly, a sense of calm came upon me and I felt much better. I remembered that I should have anticipated that I would be watched over at all times anyway, but the insight into the knowledge that this was not what was meant to happen to me was also quite comforting. In effect, it was a minor glimpse of the future and as I drove home, I reflected upon the implications of such knowledge. Was I immune from any harm that might come from the world of nature? Would this mean that I would never again experience any concern for my safety when out hiking?

As it turned out, no!

About eighteen months later, Sharon and I were out on one of our crystal planting hikes. The hike had taken us 'across the border' and into British Columbia where we were on a remote and (obviously) seldom used trail that took us far away from any point where we might encounter fellow hikers. It was a pleasant and sunny day in the fall, but snow was already on the ground. I was at the front walking Timba. Sharon and a friend trailed behind somewhat with Lara. Indy was running the gauntlet between the two groups.

It was actually the second planting/second hike of the day since we were trying to complete the western points of two separate grids we were creating. The first hike had been to a lake in a delightful location that I had, as usual, arrived at before the others. I was thrilled to see an otter playing in the lake and the joy that this sighting brought me stayed with me for hours afterwards.

Now, about three hours into the second hike, I got another type of sighting, and this one was not nearly so welcome. Although Timba made many tracks of his own and destroyed others on the pathway, I began to notice large but poorly formed tracks in the snow ahead of us. Closer inspection of them was spoiled by the dog's excited toing and froing, but my suspicions were immediately aroused and I felt the hairs on the back of my neck begin to stand up.

After going about one kilometre further, the pathway went into a deep rut and Timba quite happily jumped down into it. However, whatever had been making the tracks had obviously no intention of being in this low area and had shifted its progress to the higher ground on the right of the pathway. For the first time I could clearly see the tracks and my heart almost stopped. Not only were there the footprints of a large adult cougar, but by its side a perfect replica of them in smaller form. The cougar was a mother with its cub. And we were following it.

It had begun to snow gently so I could tell that the tracks, unfilled as they were, had been made quite recently. There was no sign whatsoever of anything immediately menacing up ahead of us, but we could only see for a few hundred metres ahead before the pathway became obscured by aspen trees and bushes. I immediately stopped to warn the others of the potential danger and for a few moments, we were all paralysed with indecision about what we should do next. To make matters worse, Lara had now arrived with Sharon and began to take great interest in the scents. Huskies are definitely not scent hounds (had any of the BGVs been with us, they would have started their unique and disagreeable hound baying at the first whiff of any animal) and for the most part, they rush on, seemingly oblivious to whatever has been in their path. However, when she was young, Lara was walked with the hounds and this seemed to instil in her some of their curiosity for the smells of the outdoors. Now, she started to move rapidly back and forth between the tracks and look ahead with apparent apprehension. Indy too, seemed reluctant to go forward.

It took Archangel Michael to persuade us that we would be safe. When we had first begun the crystal planting hikes, we experienced some disquiet regarding that other great perennial threat to hikers in the Rockies: bears. Initially I had carried bear mace and been very concerned about the threat they posed; but we had been told in a channelling that we should not be concerned. I had never really considered cougars a threat, but now the old fears returned. A brief piece of communication reassured us that our planting was of importance and that we would be protected.

Just how much can the etheric protect us from?

It's a fairly popular belief that there are angels looking out for us all of the time. That's a very appealing proposition because it makes us feel safe. But it's only true to a certain extent.

Everybody has a pre-determined expiry date and a method of departure that is also agreed upon in advance. If our time is up, it's up and there's nothing anything in the etheric can do to prevent us from 'shuffling off this mortal coil'.

However, if we find ourselves in peril and endangered through no fault of our own, angels will do whatever they can to avert us leaving before our time.

The one thing they absolutely cannot protect us from is ourselves. Our freedom of choice allows us to check out early through intentional acts (suicide) or foolish acts of omission. Sometimes, things happen that aren't meant to because we are rash and foolish in the valuing of our lives. And this can also be a major learning point for us.

Suicide is a VERY bad idea. I recently heard someone espousing the belief that suicides go straight to the front of the reincarnation queue and are instantly reborn. Not so.

If you take your own life and it's not intended (and it's extremely rare to be a valid learning opportunity), the time taken for you to recycle in third dimensional linear terms is around two thousand years. Normally, it would be six months. The relative time spent in the etheric for normal recycling is about five hundred years.

Now do the math. Suicides can spend five hundred thousand years waiting to return.

The reason?

Incarnate life is considered a massive privilege. To cast it aside is a very, very bad idea.

Another couple of kilometres later we had arrived at the appointed planting location, and the cougar tracks had ceased to be visible, the animals probably having wandered off somewhere to the south. We had just settled down to a reasonably relaxed break when suddenly all three dogs went into a state of high alert. Their ears pricked up and their noses twitched manically, all pointing to the south east of our location. And then we heard it.

Somewhere in the distance was the distinctive low grumbling growl sound of a cougar. I recognized it instantly from wildlife documentaries I had watched since my first cougar track encounter, when I had sought to educate myself more about these awesome yet intimidating creatures. It came several times whilst we all listened, hardly daring to breathe, and desperately trying to work out whether or not the sound was coming closer. It was a real struggle not to let fear get the better of us and it became an object lesson in the importance of mastering this particular emotion.

What's so important about fear?

Fear is one of the most destructive emotions that we can experience. It alters our focus, damages our level of balance and can all too easily cause us physical repercussions, especially if it is maintained over an extended period of time.

In my days of training people to be leaders, I have taught motivation from the perspective of understanding it from a psychological point of view, and also techniques for creating it within others. One of the most unsettling aspects of this learning comes from the understanding that fear is the most powerful motivator there is, at least in the short term. It is also a sad fact that a very substantial portion of any workforce will respond better to fear than any other motivational technique, since this is the way they have developed as individuals.

This piece of information calls to mind one of my favourite phrases: 'A life lived in fear is a life half lived'.

From the etheric's perspective, a life lived in fear is a wasted one.

When we'd finally got a grip, we dug the hole and went through the planting ritual in record time. We didn't even stop to do the usual channelling that follows such an occasion. Even Sharon, who isn't exactly the fastest of hikers, walked away from the area with a speed an Olympic athlete would have been proud of whilst I made up the rear. It wasn't until we were an hour and a half, and several kilometres away, that we stopped to listen to the messages of the day from the etheric.

On the way home Sharon and I were able to laugh and joke about the adventure; but there was a certain edginess in both of our voices that betrayed the concerns we each felt, not just for ourselves but for the dogs.

Little did we know that the experience of one of our pack members with cougars was only just about to begin.

Big Cats and Dogs

Kachina's rush into and out of the house routine continued for many weeks. Patience was vital to win her trust, and we needed to fully accept that we had a wild animal living in our midst who did not think or act like a domestic dog. This meant tolerating her many peculiarities, mood swings and differences. Eventually, the perseverance paid off and Kachina would come into the house (usually following Indy) every night.

Still, it was a matter of relatively little concern to either of us when, one night, she refused to respond to the ajar door. I went to bed without any worries at all. And sure enough, next morning, she made her mad dash indoors to receive her food as if everything was fine and right with the world.

So it was somewhat to my surprise when Sharon called me a few moments later to ask "where the trail of blood in the hallway was coming from?" Nobody seemed to be in any pain, so thinking it must be from a broken claw or relatively minor issue, I unhurriedly went to make an inspection of the blood; and as there wasn't that much of it anyway, I dismissed it as nothing to worry about.

That didn't stop me from coming running when some time later Sharon very loudly exclaimed "Oh my God". I found her pointing, horror-struck, at Kachina, who was quite happily eating her food without a care in the world. Yet extending vertically down her left side, just behind her front leg, was a six inch long, two inch wide, gaping and bloody gash through which her ribcage could clearly be seen!

Our first thought was not prompted by panic, since she was so obviously quite at ease with whatever she was going through. Instead, we asked "How?" Our minds raced to find a logical explanation. There was no evidence of any fight having taken place between pack members and only Indy was big enough to have done anything like that to her anyway. And he simply wouldn't do that. Neither could we think of anything upon which she might have caught herself to inflict such an awful piece of damage.

Finally, practicality overtook shock and we made an urgent appointment for Kachina to visit the vet.

Fifteen minutes later we stood in the foyer of the clinic whilst the receptionist pronounced that she most likely caught herself on the branch of a tree. I took this to be faintly ridiculous, but she assured me that it was possible. Or even more likely, that we had a nail sticking out somewhere. In return, I assured her that I was intimately acquainted with the enclosed area of our property and that no such thing was possible. Our fence line used no nails whatsoever, and there were certainly none projecting from any of the buildings. Besides, even if she had caught herself on a nail, how could it come to pass that the gash was vertical not horizontal?

The argument was interrupted by the vet who made a quick examination and confirmed a slash from a very sharp and very large claw. Surprise was expressed that Kachina could possibly have survived such an attack; but also at her demeanour, apparent lack of pain and low blood loss. Nonetheless a general anaesthetic was hastily administered so that she could be sewn up.

We went away while the procedure took place and reflected on how utterly calm Kachina had been throughout. She was not fazed by the car ride, the clinic, the vet or the examination. Amazing!

We drove home and in spite of myself, I immediately scoured our compound for tell-tale signs of blood from protruding branches. Instead I found a part of the fence line where there was an unusual dipping at the top, right next to a tree which was on the inside of the perimeter. And there, high up, were fresh marks that could only have been left by the claws of a cougar as it jumped up to scale the seven foot high fence.

Upon our return a few hours later, a slightly groggy wolf awaited us. The gash had gone through many subcutaneous levels and she had required three separate 'layers' of stitching before her skin could finally be sewn up to cover the wound. Now she had a huge shaved patch of fur around an unsightly and very tender looking scar.

Nevertheless, she seemed at ease and was quite happy to make the short journey home with us. Needless to say, she had to be kept 'quiet', which basically meant that she now needed to be indoors and we anticipated that this might present some problems for her. So we were pleasantly surprised when she settled down on a dog bed and was perfectly content to remain inside.

As with all animals that have received stitches, there is an issue of understanding their benefit and a natural inclination to want to remove them. For a 'normal' animal, you might perhaps attach a post-surgical plastic pet collar to their usual collar. But we were only too aware that Kachina is not the sort of animal that would respond well to such an appendage.

So instead, upon the vet's recommendation, we put a T shirt of mine on her. Her front legs went through the arm holes and her head through the neck. We tied a knot in the hem so as to bring the shirt tighter to her body and not have it flapping around. She looked quite fetching in it and didn't seem at all bothered by wearing human clothes. It was a 'Roots' shirt of which I was quite fond, that featured a Great Grey Owl (a bird I am in awe of every time we see one). Perhaps she appreciated the nature theme.

Or perhaps not.

That night I led her upstairs and she slept on a bed by my side as if it was the most natural thing in the world for her. She settled down very peacefully. The next morning I awoke to find my T shirt shredded and lying all around her. Even worse, there was the same gaping hole that we had seen the previous morning, all the way through to the ribs.

A dash to the vet, a further surgery, and some four hours later, we picked up a slightly groggy wolf who had required another three separate 'layers' of stitching before her skin could finally be sewn up to cover the wound. And the same problem of how we would stop her pulling out the stitches without a post-surgical collar. Reluctant to lose another T shirt, I decided to give the collar a try after all. Bad move.

To say that Kachina did not like the collar would be a ridiculous understatement. She hated it. It terrified her. When I gently lowered it over her head, she greeted its descending form with the horror that Alexandre Dumas' 'Man in the Iron Mask' must have felt when his whole head was enclosed. It sent her into a blind panic and she thrashed around, crashing into walls and furniture, sending water bowls flying and creating havoc in seconds. Worse still, we feared the injury she would surely bring upon herself. Clearly it was time for me to sacrifice another T shirt.

This time I chose more carefully and picked one I wasn't quite so fond of. But I still wasn't willing to let another shirt be torn to pieces; so cleverly, I loosely wrapped the shirt in the strongest substance known to mankind: Duct tape.

The next morning, the Duct tape bore the evidence of an attack by a fearsome creature with big teeth. But it had triumphantly survived.

Until the next morning.

This time the floor was covered in nasty sticky pieces of grey matter, plus another ruined T shirt and the same gaping hole that we had seen twice before, all the way through to the ribs.

A dash to the vet, a further surgery, and some four hours later, we picked up a slightly groggy wolf who had required yet another three separate 'layers' of stitching before her skin could finally be sewn up to cover the wound.

Needless to say, two days, some Duct tape and a third T shirt later, we found ourselves in the vet clinic being told that it was now impossible to sew up the wound since the skin and flesh tissue around the area of the wound was effectively in tatters. There was simply nothing left for the sutures to go through. Our only option now was to try a 'honey bandage'.

This was something we had never heard of. It involved coating a piece of gauze with organic Manuka honey and applying it directly to the wound, bandaging it in place, leaving it for twenty four hours, removing it, bathing the wound in running water for ten minutes, then starting all over again. This we would have to do for, perhaps, two weeks. We were slightly sceptical about the success of the process. To us, this seemed very unscientific. But the vet freely admitted that we were now in desperate straits and that this was pretty much the only thing we could do. We sought out the honey, bought supplies of gauze and bandages and headed home to try it out.

The worst part for Kachina was undoubtedly having the wound washed. To achieve this it was necessary to put her in the bath, attach a shower head to the faucet, then get in with her and hold the shower head close enough to her to gently wash the wound out. Getting a wolf into a bath is not necessarily an easy thing, but to her credit, she was relatively co-operative and never became even slightly unpleasant about this indignity. It was vital to hold her collar before beginning the process as she would always try to jump out of the bath. And the ten minutes of bathing rarely went by without her feeling at some point that enough was enough. Afterwards, the application of the gauze was met with interest and excitement. She seemed to like the honey a great deal and if I hadn't been quick enough, she would undoubtedly have liked to have eaten it, and probably the gauze too. A wide, self-adhesive elasticated bandage secured the gauze in place and Kachina was free to go. Amazingly, she objected to the bandage not one iota, and I did not need to call upon the Duct tape.

Over the coming days, she got used to the whole process and to keep her happy, I would let her lick small amounts of the honey from my fingers. The truly remarkable thing was what happened to the wound. After the very first application, whilst bathing the fleshy hole, I could no longer see Kachina's ribs. Instead, I was greeted by the sight of very healthy looking tissue deep inside the gash. Around the edges, there also seemed to have been an immediate repairing and the livid looking ragged flesh seemed to have knitted back together. On the second day, things were even better and by the third, the hole in her side had reduced to half its original size. On the forth, it had all but closed and on the fifth, there simply was no hole.

We reported the success of the treatment to the vet and even she was surprised with the speed at which this healing had come about. Sharon and I were delighted and stunned at the same time. To us at least, this was truly a miracle of nature.

As I write this, it is over a year since all of these events took place, but we are still amidst the positive repercussions from this whole incident. Despite how nightmarish it was at the time, it fundamentally altered Kachina's state of being. During her enforced period of being housebound, she effectively became what we termed a 'housewolf'. Her comfort level with being indoors and dealing with us went up immeasurably. She had to accept the close physical proximity that the circumstances created and, apparently, even grew to like it. Although once outdoors she immediately becomes a creature of the wild again, actively avoiding any physical contact and preferring to keep her distance, she now comes and goes from the house in as relaxed a manner as any of the dogs. Crucially, apart from one single occasion, she now spends every night indoors.

The second odd outcome of these events was the recognition for us of the power of nature's healing gifts. Since that time we have used honey bandages on ourselves, on several occasions. The affect is always powerful and as successful as it was on Kachina.

There is also a curious footnote to this story that relates to Kachina sleeping indoors.

Several months later I was housesitting for friends. Every night I would leave our house at around 9.30pm and drive the eighteen kilometres to their house. As I left the house, Kachina was still outside, but as usual made no attempt to leave the compound when I opened the gate.

As I drove down the road, about six kilometres from our house, the headlights picked up the silhouette of a dog in the distance, just starting to cross the road. As I drew closer I saw that it was quite a large breed and I began to wonder if I could stop and check its I.D. tags. (People in our neighbourhood regularly look out for stray dogs since they are in danger of falling prey to coyotes.) The closer I got, the more impressed I was by its size. The tail in particular was remarkably long. I began to speculate about the breed as I drew right up to the dog. Then it turned its head lazily towards the car, curled back its mouth and showed me it's very large teeth. My blood ran cold and a shiver went up my spine. I found myself staring straight into the eyes of a large cougar.

It continued to cross at a leisurely pace and I watched for another thirty seconds before it disappeared into the blackness of the undergrowth at the roadside.

That night Kachina, despite Sharon's best efforts, refused to come in. All night long she kept up a watch at the fence line. Only in the morning did she allow the vigil to come to an end.

One thing may strike you as strange in this story. Even a very small cougar will weigh upwards of 65 pounds. Their claws are lethal and their jaws can exert a phenomenal amount of crushing pressure, to say nothing of their tearing power. They can easily run at speeds in excess of 55 kilometres per hour and scale tremendous heights. They have no natural predators in Canada apart from hunters armed with high powered rifles (although hunting them is prohibited by law). They are pretty much a match for anything apart from a bear, and once their purpose is set, not many creatures have a chance against them.

So how did Kachina not only survive, but also see off the cougar?

It was a question we asked ourselves and had to ask of Michael. It is another of those drip feed pieces of learning that I'm told not to reveal yet. It relates further to Kachina's true nature. I'll tell you how in the next book.

The Tell-Tail

As I remarked in 'Some Dogs', the impact upon our children of living with so many dogs was more in making them blasé about the connection than revelling in the experience. As with so many things, you only know what you have when it is gone. So it came as no surprise to us that when our daughter Jenny went to UBC in the fall of 2009, the greatest hardship she faced was not so much homesickness, as dogsickness. All at once she became aware of not only the simple pleasure of their companionship, but also the tremendous benefit of being the recipient of their energies. A house without the dogs suddenly seemed all wrong, and throughout her first year she struggled with their absence. Her return at Christmas became a celebration of reconnection with them as much as anything, although oddly, the joy of this didn't persuade her to help out with them!

Of course, separation can also be created by the passing of one of the dogs and although the presence of so many others does a lot to assuage the pain, that doesn't mean there isn't any. Oddly enough, Tristan was greatly affected by Joe's departure, but in quite a positive way.

Tristan is 'special needs' and has struggled academically at school. However, this has always been more than made up for by his innate ability in art. Specifically, he loves to draw cartoons and although he had always preferred to draw superheroes, a la comic book representations of them, he had been struggling for some time to create his own, unique character. To date this had come in the form of a rather unappealing creature he called 'Rockmoose'. It bore a striking resemblance to Sonic the Hedgehog from 1980's video games, and this alone prejudiced me against it. I'd had a very hard time trying to convince him that from the audience's perspective, it wasn't necessarily the most alluring of subjects to follow, but he was resolute in his desire to create scenarios around it. Finally, I managed to persuade him to ask his schoolmates what they thought of Rockmoose, which he bravely did. The result left him in no doubt that he was indeed pursuing the wrong character. But now he was without a hero again.

The day Joe died Tristan decided to draw a caricature of him. It depicted a younger dog, as he might have been, emphasising his portly appearance and his love of food. It was a bitter sweet picture for us to see, but clever, touching and funny. It was also very well drawn. That day Joe was reborn not only as an angel in our house, but also as a cartoon character.

Over the coming weeks, Tristan developed a number of cartoon strips, as professional as any cartoon you might find in a newspaper, and demonstrating considerably more warmth and wit than some we had seen in local rags. He showed them to his teacher and they were quick to commission a regular 'strip' for the school magazine. Since the cartoons were produced on a computer graphics package, he was also able to upload them on to the internet, and a 'Joe Husky' Facebook page was born with a small, but loyal and enthusiastic following. Compliments flowed in, and an appetite to see more.

Sadly, over the months, his fascination with drawing the character gave way to his greater fixation with drawing superheroes and now, Tristan seldom draws Joe; but the Facebook page remains as an unusual testimony to this particular avatar's life, and I like to think that it helped us all deal with Joe's loss from our physical world.

However, if he was gone from the physical, he was certainly still very much present in the etheric. And if the knowledge that Joe was in our midst pleased Tristan at first, it didn't do so for long.

My ability to communicate with Joe is easy and instantaneous. It is as if he is sitting on my shoulder, and it's very comforting. True to his designation, he remains within the confines of the house and so when we leave, I can no longer hear him. For the most part, he is content to give advice about aspects of the dog's behaviour. For instance, there have been occasions on which he has warned us that Timba was going to make a break for the great wide yonder whilst we were out. We very quickly learned that he was *never* wrong and that we ignored him at our peril. He also gives health advice and explains both physical and emotional issues that are affecting the dogs. His experience as a dog makes him the ideal advisor in these matters.

With regard to broader issues, he always defers to Archangel Michael and will seldom proffer an opinion that falls outside the scope of what he perceives to be his proper sphere of influence. However, this does extend to the humans in the house as well, as we first discovered when we came home after a public channelling about three weeks after he passed.

There is an unbreakable rule in our house that Tristan is not allowed to watch DVDs from my very extensive movie collection without my express permission. This is firstly because he has his own, and secondly because he has a track record of damaging the supposedly indestructible discs. Admittedly, this occurred when he was considerably younger than he is now; but as a film buff, my collection is precious to me and I take the protection of the films very seriously. Thus, the 'no watching without supervision' rule stands. So you might understand why I was mortified when, upon our arrival home, Joe, in the middle of an update about the welfare of the dogs in our absence, somewhat casually announced that Tristan had been watching my movies.

Tristan was duly summoned and I began with the opening salvo "Joe tells me that while we've been away, you've been watching my DVDs." I presented it as a fait accompli, not a question, and Tristan's face was a picture. The shock that I had discovered his naughty secret was palpable. Instantly he confessed and in the hope of avoiding my wrath, made unequivocal commitments that there would be no repeat of this incident. Then he went away muttering to himself about how unfair it was that Joe had 'ratted him out'. It wasn't to be the last time.

A few weeks later, a hole a little bit smaller than a nickel mysteriously appeared in one of our kitchen tablecloths. Sharon, Tristan and I sat and puzzled over its origins for some time since it wasn't in a place where the dogs could have bitten the cloth; neither did it seem to have been caused by a kitchen implement piercing the material. Just after Tristan went away and we had decided to let the mystery rest, Joe volunteered that the hole had been caused by Tristan. Apparently, he had spilled some sauce or other on the cloth, making what he decided would be an indelible stain. Curiously, he had decided that the best way to deal with the spot was to simply cut it out! Only then did he realize that the hole was worse than the stain, and with a dawning of realisation that we might perhaps not be that pleased (especially as it was one of Sharon's favourite tablecloths) decided to say nothing to us about it, hoping that we might not notice.

Once again, Tristan was summoned to hear the evidence provided by Joe's intervention. This time, he visibly paled as we relayed the information, and instantly owned up to what he had done. To his great credit and without any prompting, a few months later Tristan surprised us both by using his own money to replace the cloth.

Joe's policy of volunteering any information that he thinks we need to know continues to this day. He has relayed tales of quarrels between the children; the real cause of inexplicable damage to other household items; incidents between the dogs and sundry other random incidents. The list goes on and on. Most recently, having bought a two steak pack for Tristan's dinner that he would cook whilst we were out, Joe explained that through a little carelessness, the dogs had eaten the steaks. He did this well in advance of Tristan telling us himself. (Although he did not try to conceal it, it had somehow escaped his memory to tell us this.)

Now, if I am suspicious of what has been happening at any point, I simply ask Joe for confirmation. The children very quickly learned that he sees *everything*. Consequently, if ever anything is in doubt, I will be exhorted to "Ask Joe" since he will provide a defence for them that will allay any scepticism I may have. Funnily enough, if my misgivings are true, they never request that I "Ask Joe." Needless to say, now that Jenny has left home, it is Tristan who suffers most as a result of his unwanted intervention. What he doesn't necessarily understand is that they are made out of love and with his highest good in mind.

Why are the interventions for Tristan's highest good?

Our ability to understand and (perhaps more importantly) accept what is for our highest good is often coloured by our uniquely personal perspective upon the world. It can be difficult to view our lives and the learning that comes to us from an objective standpoint.

In all things, the decisions we make that inform the actions that we take should be based upon the sum of our learning to date. The consequences and outcomes of these decisions and actions affect ourselves as much as they do anyone else.

As I write this, Joe assures me that by no means does he tell me everything that transpires in our absence. It would neither be appropriate, nor necessary. Only where learning points may be extracted is there benefit in his 'tale telling'. In actual fact, it is very much for Tristan's benefit, since it helps him to understand and define parameters of behaviour within the safe setting of the house that will ultimately form the parameters of his actions in the outer world. Getting to grips with right and wrong when you are 'special needs' is not always easy.

The funny thing is that it never strikes any of us as remotely strange that we routinely take guidance from a dog that we used to own that is now somewhere unseen and has returned to being an angel. Neither does it seem to discomfort those who visit us when we refer to Joe for reference. In fact, it's all too easy to get to the point where it's more surprising when people don't accept intervention from the etheric than when they do.

Of course, not everyone does.

Annie Come Home – Annie's tale

Not too long after Sienna came to live with us, Michael requested that I visit a rescue site totally unknown to me, that of the Collie Rescue Network. I was asked to seek out a Rough Collie called Annie. Although perhaps as a child, I had sort of liked Lassie, the breed was not one I'd ever felt drawn to. In fact it would be true to say that my only encounter with a Rough Collie pre 2009 had been when Sharon and I had visited Universal Studios in Los Angeles. We attended an animal training show and as 'Front Of Line' pass holders, had been invited to meet one the dogs that starred in the 2005 remake of the movie Lassie. The dog was so highly trained that it was sadly sterile in its behaviour. It would not interact with us and merely responded mechanically to its trainer's instructions. In the photograph we have taken with the poor creature, I always feel that the soullessness is apparent in its eyes. It is fixated on complying with the demands of its trainer and there is precious little evidence of the 'real' dog within.

I was a little taken aback when Michael made his request, but looked up the animal nonetheless. Annie's history was tragic. She had spent almost five years living as a stray in a rural area of Alberta where people in the area occasionally left food out for her. Sometimes a shed door would be left open when the weather got really bad or she might be allowed to sleep under a porch. She would wander around and find the food left out and if there was none, she would seek out garbage or, more likely, just not eat.

At one point, Annie was hit by a car and left in a field to die alone, in pain and probably very scared, with no medical or human intervention. But Annie was an avatar and thus she eventually recovered, returning to her life as nobody's pet.

Ultimately a newcomer to the area saw Annie, brought her into her house and called the Rescue Network. Once there she received kind treatment and apparently, her joy at things like heated rooms, air-conditioning in the summer and beds just for dogs was heartbreaking to see.

After some time she was adopted and was very well treated. Sadly, her family moved away and were unable to take her, so she was returned to the rescue.

At this point Michael had me look her up. I was certainly moved by the story; but after multiple rescues and already having so many dogs, one has to steel oneself against even the most heart wrenching tales, basically because you can't take them all. I also noted with some interest that Michael had simply told me to look up her details. He hadn't even suggested that we might like to offer her a home.

However, a few days later I was talking with an individual who claimed to be actively involved with the Collie Rescue Network. I mentioned Annie to see if this person knew anything about her plight. During the course of the conversation that ensued, the individual made it clear that the requirements for Rough Collie adoption were very stringent and although they actually weren't any different from those for other breeds we had adopted, it was suggested that we would not even get a look in if we tried to adopt Annie.

I was somewhat taken aback, but I left with a clear conscience that any efforts on our part would have been fruitless anyway. I felt further exonerated when a few weeks later I checked on Annie's progress and saw that she had been adopted and her listing had been removed from the Rescue website.

About two months passed before Michael requested that I 'visit with Annie'. Puzzled, I looked up the CRN site and sure enough, there was Annie again. It turned out that she had been successfully adopted, but returned almost immediately. This time Michael asked us to consider submitting an adoption application. Still nonplussed by the idea, I did as I was asked, simply because I was confident from the previous conversation that there was no chance of us being accepted.

I was not in the least surprised when a week later we received a pleasant letter from the CRN which read as follows:

Hi Mark,

I just wanted to send a quick note to say we received your application for Annie. I think Annie would be happier in less of a pack environment. She was fostered originally in a foster home where she was one of seven and she was never truly happy there. In her current foster home she is one of two and is just blossoming. She seems to thrive with a lot more one on one attention and therefore we'll be placing her into a home where she is either the only dog or perhaps has only one other canine companion. Her life on her own before coming to rescue seems to have left a big emotional need in Annie for constant human companionship and a home where she was the centre of attention is what she will need in the long run.

That said, I think you're doing a wonderful thing for the dogs you do adopt and that fit well into a multi-dog environment!

I accepted their comments and advice totally. It seemed perfectly reasonable to me and I saw that these kindly people absolutely had the dog's best interests at heart. I felt very pleased for Annie that she had such loving individuals looking out for her. It also made some sense since, although dogs are by nature pack animals, their nurturing experiences can mean that they develop preferences that are otherwise untypical. So if Annie now preferred to be with limited canine companionship, I could totally 'get it'.

At this point, the story could have come to an end, at least as far as we were concerned. However, that night I was dog sitting at our friend Murray's house. This could be a tale in itself since it involved looking after a Standard Poodle, two Miniature Poodles, four Miniature Poodle Puppies and a Whippet. When I arrived, Murray had left a note for me which detailed all of the instructions for their care and welfare, ending with the curious footnote "And watch out for your toes". I thought nothing of it until I released the puppies from their cage. Immediately they began biting my feet with very sharp little teeth and I spent the evening walking as if I was wearing flippers so as to try to minimize the pain they dealt out.

When I eventually retired for the night, I looked forward to a restful sleep since the puppies apparently slept quite well. But by the next morning I had experienced one of the most disturbed nights of my life.

Every hour, on the hour, I was woken up by Michael. Each time he reminded me of Annie's plight and requested that I seek to adopt her as a matter of urgency. The onslaught was relentless and by morning I had the clearest fix within my head – ever – of what we were meant to do with this avatar. We *must* bring Annie home to our house.

Although I usually accept everything that I am told, on this occasion I questioned what I was being told with some vigour, since I actually agreed with the rescue people. As always, Michael's explanation was to the point. Here it is, only very slightly paraphrased.

"This being's purpose as an avatar has been somewhat unusual. Her presence affected a large number of people; whereas avatars usually come for the benefit of one person or a family. Her difficult life and her gentle acceptance of the hardships and suffering she faced was apparent to all who encountered her, and in the community in which she lived, many were aware of her plight. In observation, she provided an opportunity for them to experience their compassionate side, to reflect upon the dignity with which she bore her lot, and open up their hearts, and even homes, to her. Some received this message, at least in part. Others did not."

I reflected momentarily upon the many dogs that experience hideous lifetimes, such as those struggling to survive in the favelas of Brazil. Weren't they doing the same thing as Annie? Did they also provide opportunities for human learning? Michael gave me a brief reminder about soul level experiences and continued.

"The role this avatar has played should be viewed in the context of the setting in which the events of her life occurred and with her own physical form. It was a rural community, neither wealthy nor poor.

Feeding a dog presented no conflict for the residents with providing for their own families. The opportunity for choice in the compassion they demonstrated was an issue of the application of the learning already achieved by each and every individual. Her task is complete.

We now wish to have this avatar join your home so that her experiences of a third dimensional lifetime are not coloured simply by relentless experience of displacement. Those concerns expressed by her current guardians are based on a failure to comprehend her true nature and are of no consequence."

That was pretty clear. However, it didn't deal with the troubling question of how we were to achieve getting her in the face of the equally clear "No" we had already received. Surely I couldn't write and tell these kind and experienced people "Sorry, you're wrong. An Archangel says so, and you must give her to me!"

Well, in actual fact, that's pretty much what I did. Here's the exact letter I wrote.

Hi XXX,

Many thanks for your email. We totally understand your thinking, so please let me apologise in advance that this may be one of the most bizarre emails that you've ever received!

At this point I think I need to tell you a little more about us and what we do. As you have probably gathered, we offer a 'forever home' to a lot of dogs. Many we adopt are considered too old to be taken in and we end up with a regular round of heartache as we lose our beloved adoptees, although we are honoured to have given them homes in their last years/months. Some are terminal cases as we take them; others are just geriatrics! Most have been abused, some quite badly. We also have younger dogs. In fact our current age range is 8 months to 14 years.

All of our dogs are 'house dogs' with the ability to come and go as they please and run freely within a securely fenced two-acre compound. They all sleep indoors and with the exception of those with special needs, they are all fed on the B.A.R.F. diet. It is a surprisingly balanced pack. We currently have 4 males and 15 females. Our vet's bills are large but we have a very understanding vet.

This is pretty normal so far. However, what is not apparent is the reason for having the dogs, and here the story takes a turn for the unusual. I hope what I am about to explain does not offend your belief systems in any way.

Some years ago I discovered, quite by accident, that I was what is called a 'channel'. Some would describe it as a gift; others as an affliction. Whereas a medium is apparently able to communicate with dead people, channels literally act as mouth-pieces for angelic beings. This, so it transpired, was my lot. I had been a very successful international businessman, running a people development company and authoring a bestselling business book on leadership development. To cut a long story short, after my discovery that I was a channel, it soon became apparent that my own destiny was not totally within my own control. Amongst the more unusual aspects of communication from the angelic realms was the revelation that some dogs literally are angels living lifetimes as what is called an avatar. This is perhaps best explained by following this reference:

http://www.somedogsareangels.com/some_dogs_are_angels_041.htm .

This is the chapter from a newly published book that tells our unusual story.

We then began to be guided to find avatars that had been cast aside. I would be told the names of rescues and the dog that was being looked after, and sure enough, the dog would always be where I'd been told. We rescued a couple. We relocated from the UK to Canada bringing our (then) pack of six with us (at a cost of $16,000) and set up home on our current acreage. Then the guidance began in earnest. Having been here for 3.5 years, our pack has grown to its current level of 19 with dogs coming from as far away as Taiwan. Some we have helped find excellent homes for, some we are instructed to keep. Twelve avatars are living *with us for the rest of their lives, at the moment. Some have already passed.*

I was first alerted to Annie a little while ago and told that she was an avatar. I spoke to a person who you may know of for her rescues here in Calgary. She assured me that CRN would never let us take her, I accepted this and shortly after that her listing was removed. But as you may have gathered, somewhat to my surprise, I was alerted to her presence once again. This in itself is somewhat surprising, so I thought that I should at least try to see if we would be considered.

Your response came as no surprise and we totally accepted your quite valid reasoning. So last night, after reading your message, I wrote a reply that basically said "We quite understand. Thank you for considering us". For some reason it didn't send.

Then during the night, I was repeatedly disturbed by instructions that I must try again. It was explained to me by an Archangel, very directly, that Annie is supposed to come to us, that she would actually thrive in our pack environment, and that I must tell you all that has been revealed above.

As I write this, I can almost hear you speculating that you are in touch with a complete nutcase! I can only assure you that almost the complete opposite is true. So following these directions, I must ask if you would be prepared to reconsider.

As you might appreciate, with such a range of ages and breeds (a Shar Pei, an English Pointer, a PBGV, 3 GBGVs, a Leonberger, a Poodle, an Alaskan Malamute, 8 Siberian Huskies, a Maremma Sheepdog and a Native American Indian Dog) we have a number who thrive on one-to-one contact and live pretty much as totally indoor dogs. Since both my wife and I work from home, we are able to give this attention on a full time basis and even as I write this, I am surrounded by two very needy formerly abused sled dogs, a paranoid Pointer and a Shar Pei who is my permanent shadow. Sharon has a GBGV and a poodle in tow. We are quite used to dogs that need special attention and we do a pretty good job of making them all feel that they are the centre of attention.

161

We would also ask you to accept that because of the somewhat unusual energies of our pack, we can offer a very healing environment. Even the most damaged and withdrawn dogs that have come to us have undergone massive transformations as a result of being here.

So to sum up, this is an email from someone who you don't know from Adam trying to convince you that an Archangel says that a dog you want to protect above all else is actually an angel in disguise that should come to a home that appears to be unsuitable.

My goodness, that sounds strange.

I guess that this would require a massive leap of faith on your part, a pre-existing belief in the fact that there are such things as angels (or an ability to suspend disbelief), and an acceptance that I am 'on the level'. I doubt if you've ever had a stranger request in all of your experience in rescue?

I can only offer the assurance that this is not a joke and that I am writing in absolute earnest. Were it not for the very specific guidance I received last night, I would not be doing this. I would have been quite happy with your feedback and left you in peace. I have NEVER written a letter like this before.

As it is, and bizarre as the reasoning must appear, I must ask you to accept that there is a lot more going on with this dog than meets the eye and ask that you please reconsider us as a home for her.

Kind regards

Mark

When I told Sharon that I'd not only written, but sent the letter without consulting her first, her immediate concern was that I might have alienated them by my tone or by what I'd said. However, upon reading it, she concluded that it was "a lovely letter".

162

Sadly, the CRN didn't seem to think so. In fact, they didn't even reply. As I had feared, clearly they did think that they'd received a missive from a raving lunatic!

The Great Escapes

Although it was a great blow to be ignored in this way, it was an even greater blow to be considered unsuitable to home a dog. From an objective perspective, we could understand why rescue organisations might have concerns about any dog joining such a huge pack. Yet most in the world of dog welfare know of the benefits of Cesar Millan's multi-dog psychology centre. Although we certainly don't hold ourselves up as the same, subjectively we viewed the environment that we offered as being a demi-paradise for dogs: Loving care, constant attention, a healing pack environment, an excellent diet, a comfortable home to live in and the freedom to play in very extensive grounds. Despite this, if we go back to being objective, we're not always perfect.

When we originally planned the construction of the compound that encircles part of our land, our intention was to protect the outside world from our dogs! Although we only had six at the time, the four Bassett Griffon Vendeens could make enough noise between them to raise the dead. The idea of them giving chase to the local rabbit population was a dreadful thought and although we were moving to a remote location, we didn't want to risk disturbing anyone.

However, it very quickly became apparent that we should also be seeking to provide a safe haven for the dogs. Readers of the first book will recall that the perimeter was tested and breached on numerous occasions by both Emily and Molly, who seemed quite determined to gain access to the local wildlife.

As the pack grew larger, our responsibilities for keeping them safe obviously extended. Incidents of breakouts became mercifully few and most often involved errors of omission with the gate that were quickly and easily corrected. Unfortunately, wicked dogs intent on harassing squirrels and bunnies soon learnt that the metal fencing that formed a skirt around the base of the fence line could be bent upwards, allowing access to the more vulnerable high tensile plastic fencing behind. Due to the undulations of the ground around our property, there were even places where it could be tunnelled under. During the winter, the snow kept the base of the fence line covered from even the most stir crazy of beasts. During summer, Alberta's parched ground could be relied upon to become hard as rock in no time at all, leaving little chance for tunnelling under the fence, although a brief period existed during the thaw where the ground was vulnerable to digging and the Horrible Hounds took full advantage of it! Finding the weak spots was a matter of trial and error and both Emily and Molly were particularly adept at evidencing my ineptitude in providing instantaneous dog proof containment. Only time and systematic repair resulted in penitentiary like conditions.

Up until a certain point, the Huskies were immune to any desire to leave the property other than to go on hikes. Then on one occasion Timba was able to follow Emily and Molly through a hole and found Pandora's box had opened up to him. It wasn't so much the rabbits that he was excited by as the neighbours. He quickly discovered that if he went to any one of a number of surrounding properties and turned up on their doorstep looking cute, they would give him treats. He turned his ability to appeal to all-comers into an art form and developed a circle of local admirers. Fortunately they would all use his fondness for biscuits to lure him indoors, review the writing on his tag and give us a call.

Very quickly, Timba totally outclassed Emily in his ability to find the weak spots in the fence line or create new ones, often in the most unfeasible of places and for a period of around two months we experienced Timba breakouts every week. Each time he would get further and further afield in his venturing and even the onset of drought-like conditions and the impenetrable earth seemed to do little to halt his advances upon the outside world. He obviously enjoyed the pure pleasure of running free and wild, oblivious to the dangers that the environment presented to him. On one occasion he decided to take Idaho with him (or more likely, Idaho tagged along) and after several hours we received a phone call from some kind strangers, six kilometres away, saying that they had the pair penned up and did we want to come and get them?

Idaho wasn't the only partner in crime. Over that period Inara and Zoe also left the compound, only to be found crying outside, wanting to come back in. Sienna too made a break for freedom, only to decide after a few minutes that the outside world was not nearly as nice as it was cracked up to be.

Tristan and I spent many hours hauling huge and very heavy tree trunks from outside the fence line to within its confines. These were used to weigh down the metal skirt to stop lifting or digging. But fifteen hundred feet of fence line is a lot to protect. We would shore up the area of vulnerability and walk the perimeter frequently to look for weak spots. Then with a depressing inevitability, it would only take Timba a few days to suss out another one. He even seemed to develop the ability to roll logs. So we took to putting him on a hundred foot leash every time he left the house. This left him miserable and dejected and eventually we would relent, hopeful that he might have learnt his lesson. And sure enough, he would behave impeccably thereafter. For a couple of days that is.

Finally, Timba managed to get out late at night. This was our worst nightmare. During the day, coyotes were far less likely to prey upon dogs; but as soon as nightfall came, they were fair game.

Sharon and I were on our way back from a pleasant evening out with friends when we received a call from Tristan telling us that Timba had just escaped whilst having his last 'bathroom break' before bedtime! It was nearly midnight and we were still twenty minutes away from home. I accelerated to well above the legal limit, despite knowing that there was little I would be able to do now. But as we pulled up the driveway, Timba was caught in the headlights, racing past the gate at high speed. It was very unusual that he hadn't gone away from the house and my hopes rose that we would be able to capitalize on this.

I quickly put the car inside and raced out of the front gate, flashlight in hand, running in the direction that he had been going. After a few hundred metres I stopped, caught in the moment by an odd noise, but barely able to hear anything above the sound of my own heaving gasps for breath. For a few seconds I was able hold it for long enough to hear a chilling sound. A large number of coyotes were calling, perhaps letting each other know that there was prey to be had. Then suddenly in the darkness, I sensed movement very close and turned my flashlight with the expectation of seeing Timba. Instead there was a large coyote no more than twelve feet away. It was momentarily dazzled by the light, and then it fled. I was shocked because coyotes seldom dare to come anywhere near the fence line. The pack within was far too great a deterrent. Then in an instant it dawned on me that it was Timba the coyotes were hunting. He had been running around the fence line because he was trying to get back in.

In my mind at least, it now became a race to see who would reach him first. Like a madman I tore round and round the perimeter, stumbling over tree trunks and scratching myself on bushes in the process. But after a couple of laps, it became obvious that it was all to no avail. Timba was nowhere to be seen. And every time I paused, all I could hear was the calling of the coyotes, almost as if they were mocking me.

After fifteen minutes I returned to the front gate and went back inside, only to find Sharon calling to me in the darkness. She had just received a phone call from Scott next door. Timba had woken them up, howling loudly outside their house. Tristan had already been dispatched to collect him, but I raced down the hill after him to make sure there was no repeat escape. I need not have worried. A sleepy Scott met us in his pyjamas and handed over a very frightened and shaking Timba. It was shocking to see an animal that is normally so full of confidence in a state of raw fear. Clearly, he didn't want to go anywhere other than back to the safety of the house.

<u>Why was I worried for Timba?</u>

Aside from the obvious – that our precious dog could get eaten by the coyotes(!) – Timba is not an avatar.

Although the nature of the life of an avatar is likely to be every bit as haphazard as that of 'normal' dog, their potential for longevity is likely to be significantly better. Since they only have a one off chance to be here, long life seems to be built into their 'contract'. Although, as many of the stories in this book demonstrate, an avatar may of necessity experience great hardship, they rarely come with the need to experience prolonged illness or unpleasant death, which may be the unfortunate lot of some of their purely canine counterparts.

Although readers may be appalled by this, it is a simple fact that all experience is valuable, no matter how awful it may be. I was once told by a Catholic priest that "a lot of good can come from suffering". At the time I found this incomprehensible; offensive even. It is only with the benefit of hindsight and input from the etheric that I now understand the truth of this (even though I'm not sure it's what he meant!)

Our response to the most negative experiences life can offer, pain, suffering, grief, depression, hardship etc. may be thought of, if somewhat poetically, as fires in which our souls may be forged. Our responses to events are reflections of our learning and our ability to achieve mastery over ourselves: To recognize in the moment the true nature of that which happens to us and place it in the broad context of life and its real purpose.

So often we are overcome by the events of our lives and interpret them as reflections of ourselves and our worth. We lose our vision of our purpose and become like leaves, apparently buffeted by the stormy winds of life.

Yet we are more in control of our lives than we ever realize. Quite apart from the fact that we have planned 99.9% of what happens to us, we ALWAYS have the choice over how we respond. It is a fact that is often forgotten, perhaps because ignoring this allows us to become victims of life rather than masters of it. And this we are most definitely NOT meant to be!

This holds true every bit as much for dogs as it does for humans. It was therefore infinitely conceivable to me that Timba could be facing a gory end. This might have been his choice.

However, had I remembered his purpose in reincarnating (which was to seize the opportunity to achieve balance in a full lifetime with us) I might have felt less fraught. I could also have remembered that had death by coyote been his choice, there is absolutely nothing I could have done about it.

Regardless, I feel very lucky and profoundly grateful that he is still with us.

After that, for some time at least, Timba lost interest in escaping.

However, not everyone had learned their lesson and there remained one weather based condition that we hadn't factored into our protective thinking and maintenance of the fence line. The wind.

It was about three months later that we experienced one of the fairly frequent windy nights, to which Alberta seems quite prone. The next morning, as is our custom after such an event, we checked the fence line for fallen trees, but all was well. The winds carried on throughout the next day, but with seemingly less ferocity.

That evening we were due to go out to a meeting with several other people and were getting ready to depart at about 4:30pm. Every time we leave the house, we have to go through a somewhat convoluted process of getting most of the dogs in. This requires a lot of chivvying along followed by an audit. It can take quite a long time, so I began at 4pm. I can usually rely on certain dogs to come in straight away and others, who are no trouble because they never attempt to leave the compound, to just watch the antics passively. Others require fetching.

So today, like any other, I began calling the co-operative ones. But today, unlike any other, nobody responded at all. In fact the compound seemed oddly devoid of life. Not a single dog was visible.

Immediately a sick feeling developed in the pit of my stomach and I yelled to Sharon and Tristan to come quickly. Something was very badly wrong. Almost instinctively I knew that there had been some kind of mass breakout and told Tristan to run round the fence line to see if this could be confirmed. Sure enough, he quickly discovered at the back of the property in an area that, by sods law, is a part of the fence line hidden from the view of the house, a tree had blown down. Since the fence was actually attached to this tree, a very large section of the fence had been brought down. A lightening audit revealed that every single dog, with the exception of Indy and the geriatrics that remained in the house, had gone. Thirteen dogs were missing. I could have wept.

Instead I asked for angelic intervention.

Within minutes, as if by magic, dogs started to appear. Tristan took the main gate and Sharon the side gate to Scott and Shannon's. The young female Huskies all came back in a rush with their mother Lara, and raced in the front gate. Dougal, Molly and Emily arrived a few moments later. Cinnda and Kachina were discovered standing quite passively at the side gate, simply waiting for it to open. It was Kachina's first time outside of the fence line since she had arrived months earlier and we were delighted (if a little aghast) that the dog we had been warned we would have to watch like a hawk, returned of her own volition.

As I attempted to move the tree, Timba dashed up to me unsuspectingly, perhaps expecting to go on a hike. Instead, I picked him up and heaved him over the fence. A few moments later, Idaho followed him and received the same treatment. A minor panic then ensued as we searched high and low for the remaining two. But as it turned out, Sienna and Daisy had never left in the first place. All was well. Within the space of twenty minutes, everyone had been accounted for. I hauled the fallen tree off the fence line and, instructing Tristan to not let anyone out until we had the chance to make proper repairs the next day, we were even able to make our meeting on time.

Did the Angels intervene to bring the dogs back?

Since the issue has now been mentioned several times in both this and the previous book, it's probably a good idea to explain the nature of the most common way in which beings of the etheric intercede in the lives of incarnate beings.

Although I've referred to it as 'running interference', that's not really what it is. In fact it is quite strictly forbidden for angels to intervene directly in the free will of incarnate beings, despite the fact that it may be for their highest good. In other words, they cannot *make* us do things.

However, they can change circumstances by distorting our perception of situations. Our subsequent response to altered perspectives may (or may not) cause us to change our choices. But their involvement has not directly impacted upon our free will. It works like this:

Beings of the etheric may create the vibration of a specific emotion in the proximity of the one who is to receive it. The being, be they human or animal, receives the vibration, experiences the emotional response it creates within them, and then applies their free will in their response to that feeling. The emotions may include anything in the emotional spectrum.

Such interventions are most often made where the recipient is in a situation where they may otherwise come to harm. Many people can cite occasions when they have received inexplicable feelings of danger or misgiving. Often, they only learn to respond to them by ignoring them and then suffering the consequences. And when they do, it is usually explained as having a 'sixth sense'. Well they do, but it's not necessarily about precognition; it's about their receptivity to messages that are initiated within the etheric!

Some recipients, due to lack of sensitivity or awareness generally, are less likely to respond to those inputs. Therefore, a greater number of angelic beings will be involved in creating the vibration, almost to the point where the sensation they are trying to create and consequent desire to react will become overwhelming. Nevertheless, the feelings created may still be ignored, simply because it is a matter of free will.

In this situation, the dogs were able to use their freedom of choice, so for an angel to have brought them back directly would have required them to surrender their free will. My request for intervention (which would *never* have been ignored), therefore involved their perspective on the experience of being outside the fence line being distorted, as described above. This was most likely achieved via the introduction into their consciousness of anxiety; or that even more powerful imperative for our dogs. Hunger!

As it turned out, the fence was quite seriously damaged. The weight of the tree pushing down upon it had caused the fence to concertina. Even after several hours work, it retained several major distortions for a section of about twenty feet in length. In the short term, there was little I could do to repair this because it would require a new fencing post to replace the tree. I wasn't too concerned though. Although both the metal and plastic fences were bowed inwards in the middle section, the top was still at least five feet above the ground. There was no way the dogs would be able to get over it. Or so I thought.

It was two days later that Aura vanished. I know how she got out because I found Idaho trying to employ the same technique, surrounded by a small band of eager potential followers. They had managed to work out that if they stood on the lower bowed section of the fence which was metal, it was strong enough to support their weight. From this position they could then reach up to the next (plastic) level and pull it down with their front paws. This in turn brought the very top of the fence low enough for the most determined to scramble over. With a drop to the ground on the other side, this was a relatively easy escape route. I watched in momentary awe of the ingenuity of it all before scooping up Idaho and chasing the others away.

At this point I didn't even realize that Aura was gone. Instead I set about using a very thin fallen tree as a makeshift fencepost to straighten out the concertinaed fence. It wasn't until one of the random headcounts, that we do at periodic intervals, sometime later that we discovered she was missing. It caused us considerable disquiet since, apart from the isolated incident a few days earlier, Aura had never left, nor shown any interest in going beyond the fence line. She had always been prone to outbursts of near madness, suddenly running here, there and everywhere, chasing nothing but her own fantasies. She could be as frustrating as she was endearing, but she'd never done anything like this before.

We searched the locale on foot and then I began to drive around, repeatedly stopping to call and listen for any sound. Several hours passed and still Aura had not appeared. Day became night and our anxiety levels rose correspondingly. Still Aura did not appear. Finally at

1am the next morning I retired to a fitful sleep, having left the gates open in the hope that she might return.

The next morning found us listing her on internet lost pet sites, telephoning vets, humane societies and dog pounds and putting up lost posters, prominently featuring Aura alongside our pathetic appeal for the return of our beloved lost pet. I spent many more hours driving around our locale, stopping to enlist the help of dog walkers I met. I was suddenly struck by the futility of trying to find such a small dog in such a vast wilderness and I had to fight back tears.

The day passed quickly, but with no word of Aura. Then at around 5pm Scott telephoned to say that he thought he had seen Aura in the forest, just one hundred metres from the fence line. An instant and extensive search brought no joy, although Sharon now became convinced that she was trying to come home, and was afraid of the rest of the pack.

It was a strange phenomenon we had noted on many occasions that if a dog left the pack for any period of time (most frequently Briony on going to be groomed, but also Timba on some of his more prolonged outings), their return was not easy. The other dogs would be very suspicious and even aggressive towards them until they were sure that this was a bona fide pack member. Oddly, this phenomenon did not impact upon visiting dogs brought by the various guests who visited us. With these the pack are far more accepting and seem to know that they're just 'passing through'. Neither do they respond this way to new pack members.

I wasn't convinced by Sharon's logic but once again that night, I retired having left the gates open. It was at just after 3am that Sharon sleepily got up and went downstairs to let in a dog that had been left outside. The first I knew of it was when her almost incoherent voice asking me if I had forgotten to bring someone in. "No" I replied indignantly. "Then Aura's just come home" she mumbled before falling fast asleep again. And sure enough, forty hours after she had begun her adventure, our most insane Husky had returned safe, sound and, as we were to discover, permanently changed.

Two of our dearly departed. Joe and Saffy.

This is a sample of Tristan's 'Joe Husky' cartoon character, developed partly as a tribute, and partly to help himself come to terms with Joe's passing.

Of course that was before Joe became a tell-tail!

Several cartoon strips can be found on Facebook by searching under the name 'Joe Husky'.

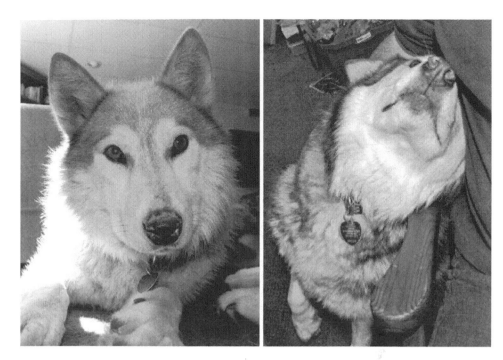

Sienna, who bears something of a resemblance to Joe in colour and food motivation, is very like him in temperament too. Above right, Sienna forces her way under my arm as I'm working on the computer, desperate for attention.

Below, Joe doing exactly the same thing the week he died. It's our last picture of him.

Angie, Diego, Natalia and Valeria finally get their young, white, male, blue eyed Husky. The fact that Madame Ruby La Rue is actually an adult, red, female with blue eyes does nothing to stop her from being absolutely gorgeous and winning their hearts.

Poor Nakita, photographed whilst still living in fear of everything and everyone.

Sharon and I meeting the star of the 1995 'Lassie' movie.
He's a lovely animal, but notice that all of his focus remains upon his trainer.
(And yes, for the sake of size, the dogs that play Lassie have *always* been male!)

Jenny remembering why it's worth coming home sometimes!

Timba at the uppermost of the Headwall Lakes. It was later that afternoon that he had the almost fatal encounter with the toad.

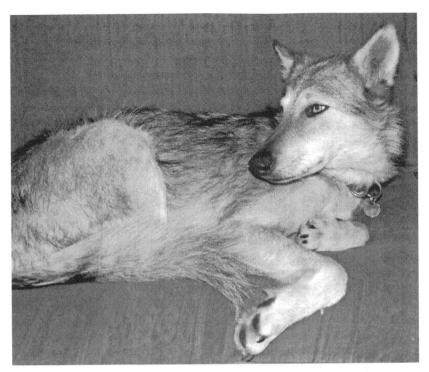

It took a long time before Kachina would even come into the house.
Now she seems to love every moment.

When put alongside a Husky (Timba, left), the physical difference
between canis lupus and canis lupus familiaris is quite striking.

Molly (above) chilled out on our deck seating behind the house, demonstrates her love of the sun.

Daisy (below) hiding in her 'secret' place in the house, demonstrates her love of Philadelphia cream cheese cartons.

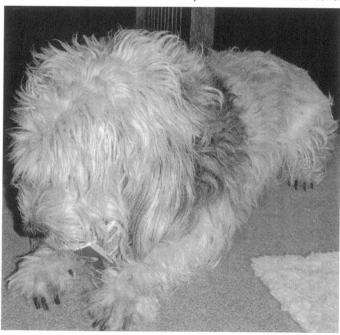

An amazing lady who would become a wonderful friend to us and the dogs.

This is Tracey with her hiking buddy, Timba at
Archangel Michael's Etheric Retreat, the Plain of Six Glaciers, Lake Louise.

Tracey ran there with him!

Sometimes movement around the house can be somewhat restricted.

A series of unfortunate events

The fact that Kachina had returned so willingly to the folds of the pack after the great escape was a major thing for us. It gave us a far greater level of confidence in her and how she would respond to the outside world. In fairness, this was to prove something of a misinterpretation on our part.

Shortly after these events, we were due to take another group to the Plain of Six Glaciers; Archangel Michael's etheric retreat above Lake Louise, to which we lead guided hikes in the summer months. We always try to take several of the avatars because of the impact the energies have upon them and its effect in reacquainting them to some extent with what they really are.

On this occasion, although she is not an avatar, we chose to take Kachina, along with Lara and Timba. Since we had her, she had been too wild to catch and put on a leash. Now that she was calming down and becoming a 'housewolf', we were very pleased to be able to give her the opportunity to get out and about and we imagined that she would enjoy the experience greatly.

Although the two hour journey was fine since Kachina is a very good traveller, she began to show signs of panic the moment we arrived in the parking lot. Walking on the leash, she was very skittish, constantly aware of the movements of everyone around her. She would walk a few paces and then turn her whole body around to see what was behind, then whip back again in case danger now presented itself from ahead. In the process she inevitably wrapped the leash around my legs and very quickly became a complete pain to walk. She was unhappy and very ill at ease.

The response she provoked in others was also very interesting. It was fascinating to watch the look of horror on the faces of some as they realized that it wasn't in fact a tall German Shepard coming towards them. They would give her a very wide berth, as if expecting her to attack them at any moment. Others would gaze with open mouths, almost as if they had been rendered dumbstruck with admiration. A limited few were desperate to somehow connect with this apparently wild beast, but their attempts to make physical contact were met with alarm and a heightening of her anxiety levels. She would go to extraordinary lengths to avoid the touch of anyone who was a stranger; although it was interesting to note how quickly she accepted members of the party as non-strangers.

As we left the shores of Lake Louise and began the climb up to the Plain, we left behind many of the tourists and she began to relax a little. By the time we reached our destination, she was fairly calm. She had even allowed others in the party, who were anxious for the experience, to walk her. She seemed to grow quite fond of one of our party, Carlos, and he walked her all the way back to the parking lot. His gentle manner was reassuring to her and he was very respectful of her little peccadilloes, whilst also being quite protective of her.

Sharon and I concluded that we had made two major mistakes in her first outing. Firstly we had gone to a location where there were too many people for her comfort. Secondly, we had not taken Indy.

The next weekend, we came to do another crystal planting hike to Picklejar Lakes; a gorgeous climb to three lakes far less popular with tourists. This time we took Indy and Timba with us, as well as Kachina.

Sure enough, when we arrived, the parking lot was deserted and Kachina was especially at ease, playfully nudging Indy who was as disdainful as ever of her attentions. We set off with me leading (or rather, Timba leading me) and Indy behind, followed by Sharon and Kachina who was simply happy to be devotedly following her paramour. It was a delightful climb amidst aspens that had recently assumed their fall colours and stunning views of the surrounding mountains. By lunchtime we had arrived at the third lake and we stopped to rest and feed. I have a great photo of Kachina attempting to share Sharon's lunch by raiding her (empty) lunchbox. In the photo you can't see her leash, so from the casual observers perspective, it looks like a sneaky wild creature has crept up on her and is about to make off with her food.

By the end of our break, many other hikers had begun to arrive so we decided to return post haste. We passed a few trippers on the way and Kachina coped quite well. But after about half an hour, we came to a point on the trail where the descent started to steepen and narrow, and by this time, I was holding the leashes of all three dogs. Suddenly, three very noisy young men appeared over the brow of the ridge we were approaching and Kachina was terrified. She lunged to the right, down a sharply sloping grass bank, thickly populated with fir trees. I was pulled sideways and the leash was wrenched from my hand. In an instant, Kachina was gone.

Sharon and I stood in shock, momentarily paralyzed by the seeming impossibility of the situation. "We'll never get her back" I mumbled. "Well let's at least try!" chided Sharon, trying to sound positive. We moved off the trail and down the bank, but Kachina was nowhere to be seen. Calling was futile and after a few minutes we sat down to take stock of our options. The familiar sickening that I always experience if a dog goes missing crawled around the pit of my stomach and I fought with feelings of desperation and helplessness. "Can't you ask the Angels to bring her back?" Sharon asked; but of course Kachina was every bit as able to exercise her own free will as any other being. Angelic intervention seemingly had no effect on her.

Then fifteen metres in the distance we saw a head appear from behind a bush, only to disappear again seconds later. We held our breaths and the head popped out again. A pair of intense yellow eyes fixed us with their gaze and seemed to be waiting for us to do something. Slowly we got up and started to move towards the bush. In an instant the yellow eyes were gone, only to reappear behind a tree, still fifteen metres away. And so began a game of cat and mouse. Kachina would appear and watch us very carefully. But if we tried to move towards her, she was off.

Next we tried to plan a campaign: one of us would try to outflank her and take her by surprise from behind. No chance. She saw that one coming a mile away and disappeared for five minutes after that. Then we tried moving away from her and, sure enough, she moved to maintain the fifteen metre gap. Then we tried coaxing her with food. This seemed to work for about three seconds and then she decided that distance was better than food. So now it was time to bring in the heavy guns. I walked Indy toward her on his leash. This made her stand up and sniff in his direction; but even his undoubted charms failed to elicit the required response. Whatever we did, she would maintain the fifteen metre perimeter around herself. And even if we had gotten close to her, we both knew that she would be as slippery as an eel and impossible to grab hold of. Our only hope was the fact that she trailed a two metre leash behind her.

All of this went on for an hour. Even after the first five minutes, both of us were already conjuring images of being at this game all day without success. Imagining failure in itself was, of course, not a good idea.

Why was it not a good idea to imagine failure?

When people think about manifestation, they think about it in terms of creating good and positive things that they want in their lives. Little do they realize that we can equally well bring about eventualities that on face value, we do not want at all.

The simple act of thinking about an outcome brings an energy to it that the Universe will attempt to turn into a reality.

This is because we are in origin at least, beings of pure light able to manifest whatever we want, whenever we want it. We do not bring this ability here in its entirety when we incarnate in the third dimension (and certainly not when we come as old souls). But we do still have the vestiges of the remains of that ability; and we can learn to use it again.

Intense and concentrated focus upon an outcome (desired or otherwise!) can all too easily bring into being a result. Think about examples in your life where you have thought of something and it has happened. Where you thought of someone you hadn't seen for a long time and suddenly they appear in your life again. Often we say phrases like "I knew that was going to happen." And this is not just because we 'knew' it. It's because we actually made it happen!

The moral? Be very careful what you think about!

178

We tried hard to remain as positive as possible but when, by the end of the hour, we had made no progress whatsoever, things looked to be irretrievably helpless. So we discussed the possibility of having to leave her. Tragic though it would be, would we simply be returning a wild creature to the wild? Was this her choice? Is it what she wanted all along? Could she survive? The prospect of leaving her, however dreadful, seemed to be our only option. Finally Sharon asked "Can't you speak to her?"

Since Kachina had arrived with us, I had only 'played' with my strange ability to communicate with her. Not only was it a physically uncomfortable experience for me due to the pulsing sensation at the back of my skull, it also seemed to be quite unsettling for Kachina. We had conversations when I was tending to her wound after the cougar incident (which incidentally, she refused point blank to discuss); and on other occasions when our needs suited it (such as when, in true wolf fashion, she decided to leave her scent all over the house to establish her territory, and we wanted her to stop!), but she never initiated contact herself and always looked very wary when I did speak to her.

Nonetheless, I thought for a few minutes about what I could say and composed a little speech. Then I focused my attentions on the back of my head and felt the usual band of discomfort and intensity ripple through my skull. Then I began speaking.

Immediately Kachina looked at me, shocked as always. Although I don't remember the exact words I used, what I said was something like this:

"We have to go now. We can't stay here because this isn't where we live and we need to go home. So you have a choice to make. You can either come with us or you can stay. If you want to stay then we'll respect that choice, but you'll never see us again. If you want to come back with us, then we love you and we'd be very happy if that was the choice you made. It's up to you."

As always, it's very easy to anthropomorphise, but I'm sure she looked taken aback or even hurt. Nonetheless, we both got up and started to make our way back up the bank to the trail. After fifty metres we turned around and there was Kachina, now five metres behind. We hardly dared breathe. We just turned and carried on. By the time we reached the trail, she was just two metres behind. We set off downhill in the same formation we had come up, with Timba leading in front, Indy behind me and Sharon making up the rear. Immediately Kachina positioned herself in front of Sharon and behind Indy. We could barely contain our excitement, expressed in the wide-eyed silence of the look we exchanged.

Then, after walking for another two hundred metres, Indy decided that he would go ahead. Kachina accelerated to keep pace with him and she passed me, trailing her leash behind her as she did so. It was too far away to tread on and I'm not agile enough to make a grab for it, so I simply and casually placed the tip of my walking pole in the loop of the handle. I had to extend my arm to do so and because of the angles involved, had Kachina pulled even slightly, the tip would have flipped upward and the leash would have been free again. Instead, before she even placed any pressure on it, she stopped. She looked at me as I stooped to pick up the handle. Our eyes met and once again I experienced the deep penetration of her gaze, accompanied by the throb in the back of my head. "I want to come" was all she said. It was the only time she had ever spoken first.

In my head I imagined etheric choirs breaking out into Handel's Hallelujah Chorus. Massive waves of relief flowed through me and for the whole of the rest of the descent Sharon and I exchanged our feelings of amazement back and forth.

We drove home with a great sense of everything being right with the world and a deep pleasure that Kachina had decided that she did want to be with us.

When we arrived home, we were met with the news that not all had gone well for Tristan and the remaining dogs. Apparently, during the day some bikers had stopped at the end of our driveway. The highway we live on is a mecca for motorbike riders during the summer months. It is written up in guidebooks as a 'not to miss' ride so their presence is not at all uncommon. Stopping on our driveway is. At the time, Tristan was happily involved in a computer game in the basement. The young

Huskies were outside with their mother. They didn't appreciate strangers on their territory and decided to let them know about it. A single Husky can rival any dog for the amount of noise it can make, for variety of sound if not volume. Five irritated Huskies can be heard in the next Province. And so it was that day. By the time Tristan became aware of what was going on, the Huskies had screamed, cursed, yelled, berated, threatened and plain barked at the bikers. They in return were unpersuaded by the efforts of the furry snow dogs to move them on, and even exacerbated the situation.

Tristan related the story with embarrassment and apologies. From our perspective, it clearly wasn't his fault. After all, it was just an unfortunate event in a day of unfortunate events. They all turned out all right in the end. It didn't really matter, did it?

How were we to know that one of the most significant and cataclysmic events of our lives had taken place that day?

The beginning of the end

I could hear the panic in Sharon's voice the instant she called me. A truck with official looking markings had driven right up to our gate and the person driving it had got out and made a cursory inspection of our property. Irrespective of whether or not this individual had tried to gain access, Sharon had 'laid low' and not responded. Instead she called me on the cell phone, full of what would prove to be justified fears. We had been visited by a 'Peace Officer' from our Municipal District.

I tried in vain to combat the sinking feeling that I began to experience and hoped against all odds that maybe it was simply a vehicle from a utility company. But on my arrival at home, a note was inside our moose shaped mailbox. It informed me that we had received a visitation and asked me to call a number. I did so but got no reply. So I emailed and received the following response.

"Protective Service received a call about your property and the noise. Dog Barking is the nature of the noise and it emits from your property. When I attended to your property I counted I believe 10 dogs that attended the locked gate. They were all barking and of course creating quite a racket. The noise echoes through the valley and becomes quite loud. This of course annoys your neighbors and according to the Community Standards By-laws of the MD XXX is a contravention.

On another note you may be contravening the Land Usage By-laws. In the MD XXX a property is only allowed to have 3 dogs on property. If more are needed you must apply for a Private Kennel Permit. If authorized you would be allowed to have up to 10 dogs that belong to you. If you are in the dog boarding business you would have to apply for a Commercial Kennel Permit.

Of course one of the requirements of obtaining either one of these permits is a canvassing of your neighbors where they have the right to say yes or no.

Your compliance with these issues would be most appreciated."

And thus began what has undoubtedly become the most traumatic period of both Sharon's and my life. But before we get into the tale, let's put this into context.

- We live on an acreage that has just less than nine acres of land.
- We don't have 'immediate' neighbours.
- At the time that the MD received the aforementioned complaint, we had been there, complete with all of our dogs, for over three years with no objections, or indeed concern of any kind being expressed by our neighbours.
- We had moved from the UK where we lived with six dogs. Our yard measured forty two feet by thirty five feet and if you exited through our back door, you could touch our neighbour's house.
- The nearest city to where we live is Calgary where there are laws that protect disruption of the peace through excessive noise. But, at the time of writing, there are no restrictions upon the numbers of dogs an individual may own, irrespective of whether they live in a condo or a house with a yard. Acreages basically do not exist in the city limits.
- We had moved from the UK with no knowledge of potential restrictions in our MD (although we knew of such in an adjacent MD).
- We had scrupulously checked out the laws before buying our house, just to make sure that we would be OK with the six dogs we brought across.

And now, here we were faced with this letter from the Peace Officer. It was a very unpleasant surprise to say the least.

With some disquiet I researched the bylaws in an effort to find out what the issue was and was dismayed to find that they had been altered since our arrival. Whereas previously their wording had not precluded our ownership of any number of dogs providing we were not building kennels, now we were only allowed to have three without a kennel licence. We could own up to ten with a private kennel licence, but since we had so many, we would need a commercial licence.

This seemed a little strange since it would allow us to operate a fully-fledged dog boarding operation, which was neither our interest nor our intention. What we actually did, i.e. live with a large number of dogs as family members, in the house, was not included in any of the options available.

Nonetheless, a conversation with the Peace Officer confirmed that we would have to apply for a commercial licence at a cost of hundreds of dollars that would be non-refundable if we were to fail in our application. It was also made clear to us that the consequence of not applying, or being denied the licence, would ultimately result in the necessity to remove all but three of the dogs from our property. And if we didn't do this ourselves, it would be done for us.

The decision of whether or not to grant us a kennel licence would require a public hearing. Paramount in the decision making would be the concerns of our neighbours. Naturally enough, if we were making a nuisance of ourselves, their interests would need to be protected. All those living within half a mile of our property would have a right to object to our application. We followed the advice to solicit their opinions and their likely stance and as we did so, we were pleasantly surprised by the response.

Needless to say, Scott and Shannon, to our north, had no problem at all. Our pack en mass usually made far less noise than their two Bernese Mountain dogs if a coyote came near their property.

Our neighbours to the south had only ever seen Indy and were highly surprised to learn that we had so many. We certainly weren't a problem to them and they wished us well. There were a couple of houses even further to the south that came within the objection zone, but they were so far away that the copious quantities of trees between us and them would prevent the sound from travelling that far anyway.

To our west was the property of the original complainant and we already knew their opinion, so we didn't solicit further.

Just to the north west of them was a couple who themselves had rescued dogs. They knew what we did because we'd had dinner with them on a couple of occasions at Scott and Shannon's and they had expressed their support for what we did. It wouldn't be an issue for them either.

On the extreme north of the zone was another commercial kennel operation; but once again, we had dined with the owners on several occasions, they had been very supportive of 'Some Dogs', Sharon had done energy healing on one of the owners and their animals, and I had begun to do marketing work for them. No need to worry there!

Finally, to the east, there were no houses at all.

So we knew that the only likely source of an objection would be from the one neighbour and our confidence rose. In the immediacy of the moment, the greatest difficulty that presented itself to us was how we would come up with the money to pay for the application, since by now, the seven hundred and fifty dollars required was a minor fortune.

Several weeks passed whilst we scrimped and saved until eventually, there was enough 'spare' in Sharon's account to forward a cheque to the MD. I duly completed the application (although I was somewhat perplexed by what should be entered in certain of the boxes on the form, since we did not actually need a commercial licence) and we posted it off with our hopes on a high.

The cheque bounced.

Unfortunately, rather than cashing the cheque immediately, the MD delayed for some while. In the interim, other payments became due and despite further deposits, the account was just thirty cents short when the cheque was presented. So Sharon's wonderful bank bounced the cheque, leaving us with a substantial penalty to pay, as well as having to begin the whole process all over again. If you're wondering why we couldn't simply deposit the thirty cents (plus bank penalty charges) in the account and resend a cheque, remember that we were living hand-to-mouth by now. Such a large payment had to be filtered into an ongoing stream of outgoings and debt management. The returned money would leave the account bound for other debt destinations within days. We would now have to wait for a build-up of sufficient funds to allow this amount to go out again.

To their credit and our gratitude, the MD was very tolerant of this further delay, and eventually, a few weeks later, a cheque was successfully cashed.

Only for some reason, more money was now required.

Still more weeks passed before we were able to get the additional funds, and finally the MD was able to acknowledge a fully paid up application for a commercial kennel licence.

Sometime after that, a planning officer visited to make a site inspection. Apparently, the commercial application that I had completed made very little sense. Seeing what we did first hand, she was able to understand.

Now it was just a matter of waiting for the hearing. We felt good. After all, with the odds so stacked in our favour, what could possibly go wrong?

A Case of Mistaken Identity – Duke's tale

In the meantime, life went on as normal; or at least as normal as it can be in a home full of avatars, channelling and resident angels! We were acutely conscious that our next instruction from the etheric might come at any moment, and sure enough, very shortly after the MD intervened in our lives so, indirectly, did Michael. But let's back track a little. You have heard what became of Colleen and Nakita, but what about Angie's plight with the fierce and terrible Madame Ruby La Rue?

By the time Angie and the girls got Ruby home, the dog had begun to de-stress. Away from the tribulations of the long journey with so many other dogs, she allowed herself to relax and the family soon realized that she was a big softie whose bark was definitely worse than her bite. Within minutes of arriving at their home, she made herself completely at ease. Totally disregarding her grumpiness, the girls showered her with love and affection as if they understood that it was all an act. The next morning we were delighted that Angie telephoned to say that she was in love with Ruby, that she was everything they had hoped for and that Diego had phoned in the middle of the night (in his part of the world) to find out all about her. He was even trying to come home early just so that he could meet with her.

As with all dogs, there are 'teething' issues. Ruby was initially quite protective of her food, but soon learnt who was boss. She was also initially a little too protective of her new home, but she quickly overcame this. When Diego came back, it was another case of love at first sight for both of them. Her presence in their house was totally 'meant to be' and now, one year later, after a strict diet enforced by Angie (and frequently broken by Diego who was subsequently chastised by not only his wife, but also Sharon, myself and the etheric!) Ruby is a stunning, correct weight, loving house Husky.

Even then, after only a few weeks of things going so well with Ruby, it was no big surprise to me that Angie told us that they would like another dog. So it seemed incredibly fortuitous when, that very evening, I received an email from Karen, telling us about another Husky that

189

needed help. What made this one particularly unique was that it was in Taiwan!

Duke's story was sad, but not unusual for Huskies in this locale. He had been bought as a 'fashion accessory' by a family who found his temperament to be totally unsuitable for their lifestyle. He was put into rescue and over the course of the next ten months, rehomed no less than five times. It may seem incomprehensible to us that any rescue organisation should allow this to have happened since clearly, very poor vetting procedures had been used to select the new owners, on multiple occasions. However, the context needs to be understood.

The regard in which dogs are held in Taiwan is somewhat unusual. Try doing an internet search using the text 'dog show', prefixed by the name of a Far Eastern country. You will find result listings and advertisements posted by kennel clubs and breed groups for traditional dog shows. Try the same search prefixed with 'Taiwan' and you are more likely to find listings for dog swimwear or dog fashion wear events. Now look at the pictures they proffer and you will see that the obsession demonstrated by some Hollywood celebrities with dog garb has been taken to another level in this country.

Add to this the fact that there is a very different system for dealing with strays or 'surrendered' dogs. Overloaded 'shelters' are quick to euthanize their charges or get rid of them in any way possible. This means that pretty much anyone wandering in off the street can walk away with a dog, right there and then. There are no checks of any kind, no paperwork and, of course, no guarantee that the dog is not simply going out of the frying pan into the fire.

Thus it was with Duke. His constant round of rehomings resulted from his adoption from shelters by a series of teenage youths who seemed to know one another. Either their parents disapproved of the adoption, or they found him too much to deal with. A Siberian Husky is a strong minded, independent and powerful animal. It needs lots of exercise and is very strongly pack orientated. It needs company and it needs stimulation. Frequently he was left on his own and became destructive. Or he was simply left to wander freely. So within days, or occasionally weeks, he would find himself back in the pound, only to be removed again by a friend of the previous adopter.

The cycle might have continued endlessly; or more likely have come to an abrupt halt at the end of a needle. So it was a matter of great fortune that he was discovered by a local rescue group run by a German gentleman. It was the objective of these people not to rehome within Taiwan, but actually get the dogs out of the country.

Thus, they had contacted Karen who, in turn, sent an email to all of her contacts explaining Duke's plight and asking if anyone could help. Attached was a link to the Taiwanese site which contained all of his details (slightly unhelpful as my Taiwanese is not too good) and photos (which were unfortunately inaccessible when you attempted to load them). Fortunately, at the bottom of the message Karen had attached several other photos.

When I saw the pictures of Duke I became very excited because the first thing that happened was that I started to get the familiar tingle I get when I'm looking at an avatar. A quick check-out with Michael confirmed my suspicions, but even more exciting in some ways was the fact that the dog I was looking at matched the description of the avatar Angie and Diego had asked me to find for them almost a year before.

As already mentioned, our friends had asked for a pure white, blue eyed, young male Siberian Husky. Here, right before me, was a dog matching that exact description. Not only that, he was stunning! Immediately I emailed Angie, forwarding Karen's email, and was delighted with the almost instantaneous reply. "We want him!"

So we then began a brief process of acting as intermediaries between the rescue agency in Taiwan and Angie and Diego before it was all arranged that the dog would be arriving in Vancouver a few weeks hence. Angie would fly out to meet him at the airport. Excited anticipation was very high in their household. Not only would they now have the wonderful Madame Ruby, they would also be the proud owners of a 'made to measure' avatar.

It was therefore a major shock when on the day of the collection I received a phone call from Sharon who, in turn, had received a call from a very stressed Angie. She had received an email whilst on her way to the airport confirming that Duke had successfully caught the plane and was in mid-flight. Accompanying the email was a photograph of him and an explanation from the agency that they had found it necessary to shave him before the flight for medical reasons. This in itself was not really a problem, although shaving Huskies is a very bad idea. Their coats seldom grow back the same and if a limited patch is shaved, the animal can end up looking quite peculiar. However, Duke had received an all over shave, so no problem, eh?

BIG problem! The dog shown in the picture was brown with no trace of white whatsoever. This, by no stretch of the imagination, was the dog Angie and Diego had been expecting. What had gone wrong?

To me it was obvious. The agency was sending not one, but fourteen dogs to Canada. This was a large scale rescue operation and it was simply a case of them having sent the wrong mailing to the wrong person. I told Sharon to reassure Angie that all would be well and that their avatar would arrive safe and sound at the airport. "Just wait and see" I added with total confidence, not even bothering to check with the etheric.

Of course, the phone call I received a few hours later merely confirmed that Angie had taken delivery of a very large, quite wild and extremely energetic, fully shaved brown Husky with one brown eye and one blue eye. And now she was beside herself; not so much that she had got this dog, but that their precious white avatar was missing. Sharon had tried to console her that she was sure things were meant to be this way and that the dog surely was an avatar. Its behaviour certainly seemed to bear that out. Angie wasn't so sure! And unfortunately, neither was I.

The next day when I arrived home, Sharon had already received another frantic call from Angie. By now she had arrived back in Calgary and taken Duke home. The girls had instantly fallen in love with him; but Angie had not. The comparison between Ruby and Duke was like chalk and cheese. For a start, he was big, agile and very powerful. He was also dominant, slightly aggressive and relatively speaking, very undomesticated. He

192

immediately took their entire home to be a public washroom and even as they were talking, Sharon could hear his boisterous movements in the background. To Angie, this was an *extreme* dog. Needless to say, she wanted to know what on earth was going on and why her expectations had been so badly dashed.

Emergency channelling sessions are something I've become very used to. Many individuals ring up needing to speak with an Archangel or Master at very short notice. Some of the requests are in the most awful of circumstances; some not that desperate at all. But they always seem that way to the individuals concerned and the etheric is happy to respond. Often, even before we leave our house, I am briefed by the etheric on what the situation is. Sometimes I feel that I am unable to help, even though I know the etheric can. I am grateful that Michael will most often (although not always) refrain from pushing me in these situations and respect my feelings.

Why am I unwilling to help if the etheric can?

I have always felt that channelling is a great responsibility. The information that is given is relayed so that the individual who receives the messages may rely upon a higher form of guidance.

For many years I considered, from my personal perspective, that some things were too personal for responses to be given. I did not distinguish well between the information coming from me and from the angels. This wasn't an issue of arrogance, but one of fear, on many levels. Primarily, irrespective of the origin of the message, I was still the messenger (albeit one in a trance-like state). I didn't want to shoulder the burden of responsibility for the outcomes and thus I would warn people not to ask me questions about certain things, (like their health) before a channelling started.

Sharon grew tired of telling me off and reminding me afterwards that it wasn't me who would be giving the answers. So gradually I overcame the fear and began to let go totally. I now place almost no limits upon the questioning.

However, if anyone wants to know the answers to questions about the deaths of family or loved ones, I am still massively reluctant to allow the etheric to answer those questions through me. In other words, I'm auditing what the etheric can and can't say which, from any reasonable perspective, is wrong. It probably goes against my contractual commitments.

When I refuse, nobody ever seems to want to know why, so I don't tell them. The truth is because, when I get asked the question, I normally hear the answer straight away. If it seems to me to be grim, I just don't want to be the harbinger of bad news.

Recently I was asked to assist a lady involved in a missing person case. Her relative had vanished without trace and she had asked for my help in discovering what had happened to her. As soon as Sharon relayed the request to me, Michael commented in a matter of fact way that she was already dead. I paused for a very long time before replying that "No", I couldn't be of assistance. Sharon is a very good-hearted person who would like to help pretty much everybody and she was puzzled by my response. It was a very long time after Sharon told the lady that I could not be of any service that I finally told my wife the truth.

My residual fear relates to the accuracy of the information given. Supposing I gave the lady the news that her relative was dead and she was alive? If she relied upon the information, what untold grief and heartache would she suffer for no reason? And if I told her that her relative was alive and she turned out to be dead, I would have misled her with false hopes and, potentially, caused her even more pain.

There are some things that I regard as too 'big' for me to have complete trust in the etheric over. Sure, if they tell me to get another dog, that's no big deal! But anything that smacks of divination, I am very wary of.

It is a massive fault in me since nothing that we have been told by the etheric has *ever* proved to be wrong.

This however, was a no-brainer. I felt quite responsible for the events that had taken place. I had claimed that an avatar was on the way and now, I was forced to admit, what had arrived definitely wasn't one. An explanation was certainly needed, and to my mind, Michael was the only one who could clarify what had happened. That evening we went round to Angie's to let him do the talking. What he revealed (hugely paraphrased and abridged) was as fascinating as it was informative:

Angie and Diego's delightful daughters, Valeria and Natalia are, as I write this, eleven and eight respectively. Both are 'crystal' children and as such, have amazing potential within them to use a higher order of the energy possessed by their higher selves with a far greater degree of ease than the rest of us mere mortals. Thus far in their lives, this has manifested itself as the ability to see that which does not appear to be there; remote view situations and circumstances as they evolve in other locations; intuitively and empathically sense physical responses in others; have limited amounts of prescience over circumstances that affect close family members and manifest that which they desire. So, all pretty straightforward stuff!

Valeria in particular (who appeared in 'Some Dogs' in a photograph with Joe) has developed a very strong ability to manifest at both a conscious and unconscious level.

After Ruby arrived at their house, both of the girls embraced their new dog filled life with sheer joy and showered the animal with unreserved love. It was in large part due to their attentions that Ruby evolved so quickly. Shortly after she moved in, Valeria suggested that they would most definitely be having more dogs, five in fact. She was already convinced beyond 'knowing' that at some point, the young white, male, blue eyed Husky would be coming their way. This was a little unnerving for Angie and Diego, so several weeks before the Duke incident began, and without revealing this to me, they had asked for feedback from the etheric about the likelihood of more dogs coming their way. "Yes, you have the choice to have five" was the reply. The response wasn't

195

instrumental in their choosing to have Duke; they wanted to get another dog immediately as company for Ruby, as Huskies are most definitely pack animals and need the company. But Valeria hadn't stopped there. She began to conjure with her next objective: A brown Husky with different coloured eyes. And that is exactly what had been manifested!

What is manifestation?

Manifestation is a funny old thing and potentially, as I have discovered, the subject of some controversy. I briefly allude to it in the first book but if only because of what is written above, it's worth exploring a little further. Here's how I spoke of it last time.

Manifestation is the ability to create at will. It is most familiar to people as a result of the bestselling book 'The Secret' although in actual fact, it's no secret at all. We have always had the ability to manifest and create through thought in both a positive and negative way. However, the true extent to which we are able to do this is seldom reached because of the degree of focus that is required.

And here's what I didn't say.

Anyone, at any stage of their soul's progression upon the Ascension Pathway, may manifest. However, the ease with which we may achieve it is in direct proportion to the amount of Higher Self energy that has been brought in with our incarnation.

Baby souls bring in virtually none of this energy as that isn't their purpose or need. Therefore their lives generally suck and they can't get anything they want!

Young souls, anxious to make up for the deprivations of baby soul lifetimes, tend to bring in loads of this energy. Consequently, they can have pretty much whatever they want. These lifetimes are therefore a blast, very seductive and difficult to break free from.

Mid-term souls tend not to bother with it too much and spend umpteen lifetimes wondering why they can't have exactly what they want, and so focus on other stuff instead.

Old souls know they don't need to bring in that energy in order to progress upon their pathway. They understand that they still have it within them to make things happen anyway, with one massive proviso: Whatever they seek to manifest has to be for their highest good and the highest good of all.

To be honest, it's sometimes a little disheartening to encounter old souls who are focused on winning the lottery or pouring all of their attentions into material gain. Usually they've read The Secret and experience frustration with their lack of success in manifesting what they would like. Naturally, I feel obliged to remind them of the highest good proviso.

Funnily enough, they're not usually very happy to hear it...

Because she is a Crystal Child, Valeria has basically the same manifestation abilities as a young soul, whilst actually being an old one. Therefore she has all of the ease of manifestation that comes for the former soul age, but is still subject to the highest good proviso that accompanies the latter.

Michael explained that the power of manifestation was not to be underestimated, or abused. Their current situation had arisen through freedom of choice and subverted the natural order of things wherein Angie and her family could have received the white Husky they sought. The reason that the pictures from Taiwan were invisible in the email from Karen was because if they had been apparent, Angie would not have elected to take Duke since he did not meet her idea of the dog she wanted next. Since Valeria's ability to manifest was way beyond her mother's (who was not even trying to manifest anyway and had simply accepted the developing turn of events with the desired avatar seemingly coming their way), her desire had taken preference.

This then led to one irrefutable conclusion. By implication, having Duke must be not only for Valeria's highest good, but also for the family's highest good. Their needs would be taken into consideration under the umbrella of the 'highest good of all' proviso.

Even though there was a massive message in the channelling of "Be careful what you wish for", Michael was as reasonable and as fair as ever. He made it abundantly clear that they did not have to keep Duke. As humans we live our lives in a constant round of making mistakes. They are simply learning opportunities and the etheric would be content if all parties had learnt from this situation.

After the channelling content had been explained, it all made perfect sense to me; but I still held my breath for Duke. In his current state he was frankly quite unappealing. Whilst you could see the makings of what was actually a stunning animal, the thing in their household was an emaciated, strange looking brute of a beast that acted like he was on crack. Sharon and I understood only too well the ugly duckling nature of rescues. They can be very difficult for months, even years on end when you first get them. We reminded the family that Duke had come from a very rough background. We had no idea of the abuses and hardship he had suffered. Possibly for the first time in his life he was confronted by a group of people who weren't going to cage him, taunt him, ignore him, hit him – whatever it might be. He simply didn't know how to respond in the circumstances and that was why he was as he was in that moment. We assured them that he would come right in the end. Otherwise, how could having Duke be for their highest good?

The family took a vote and unanimously, they decided that Duke could stay. I reflected on how many families would (and do) decide to dump the animal at the first signs of trouble. I know a hundred stories of owners who have turned out their newly acquired puppy because they can't control their bladders the second they walk in the house; of people who get a certain breed of dog and then reject it because it turns out be not quite the same as the one their parents owned when they were children; and of individuals who expect an abused rescue dog to instantly overcome it's fear of new circumstances and return it to the pound for more heartache because it didn't immediately show them love. We left with a tremendous sense of relief that Angie and Diego would not do the same. But we weren't quite out of the woods yet.

Early the next morning Angie rang again. Duke was a nightmare to walk, he wasn't sleeping, he'd turned their house into a urinal, and was jumping all over Ruby and she feared for the older dog's safety. She felt terrible and she was very sorry, but Duke would have to go. No amount of persuading would have her see it any other way.

Sharon relayed the information to me and I felt a great sense of despair. I sat and wrote a long email to Angie. I tried to rationalize all of Duke's behaviours thus:

Duke is a male and males don't behave like females. They are generally more aggressive and have higher energy levels. Any male that you get, avatar or not, is going to be this way unless he is a geriatric!

Pulling: Pretty much ALL Huskies pull on their leads because they are pulling dogs – hence they are good for sledding. The younger and stronger the dog, the more pulling there will be. Remember that when you compare him with Ruby, she does not pull because at the moment she's too overweight to want to exert herself.

He hasn't been taken out for walks for possibly months so it's new and exciting and he wants to run. He will calm down with more discipline.

You have to hold the leash in the right way that I showed the girls. At the moment he's testing you to see who's boss and he's winning. He hasn't gone to any obedience training. This makes a major difference to YOU and the way YOU behave.

Sleeping: He doesn't sleep well because everything is strange and new. He's not stressed BUT he's certainly not relaxed yet. Dogs get jetlag too. He's suffering from jetlag. The times that he would have been used to sleeping are way off line with the night/day hours of Canada.

Toilet: He pees everywhere because he's marking his territory and because that's what males do. ANY new male will absolutely do this.

He's used to being in an impound pen and there, you can pee anywhere. He doesn't yet understand a house vs. a pen. They're both enclosures.

Jumping on Ruby: They're still sussing each other out. It has a lot more to do with play than anything else.

Then I went on to talk of our experience with our dogs at great length. I explained how each one of them, in their own way, had caused anguish and problems for us; some more than others. It was a heartfelt plea for her to give him time and I concluded with an assertion that we would understand and respect whatever she decided.

I needn't have bothered.

She had taken the girls to school that morning and told them how she felt. This was Valeria's response. "I still think we can train him. He is just a baby and I love him". The words haunted Angie and she couldn't get them out of her head.

Then Diego rang Angie from work. He was near to tears. "What if we pay for some training lessons for Duke right away? We could keep him and love him. There is a reason for him to be with us."

Instantly, in that moment, Angie understood that what had happened was a great opportunity to master a lesson of real love and compassion. Even more importantly, she understood that Duke was a part of their circle of love. She didn't need my letter. They'd got it all by themselves.

And so, Duke found himself a full time home with a loving family who understood and accepted his many faults and would help him learn new ways and come into balance.

There was considerable joy in the etheric at their choice. Oddly, it wasn't just because they had decided to take Duke. It was because, as a family, they had just learnt a major lesson that was described to them as "a very significant breakthrough on your journey together".

But what had become of the white, blue eyed Avatar?

Will the Real Avatar Please Stand Up?

When the Duke situation first arose, and before Angie and Diego had decided to keep him, I had contacted Karen. Could she shed any more light on how this had happened and where the white dog was? She was as mystified as anyone because, of course, she could see the pictures of Duke in Taiwan and knew perfectly well what he looked like. She wasn't even able to understand what I was talking about at first, when I started to refer to "the white Husky".

Fortunately she had saved her original email to us and was thus able to go back and check it. However, she could not see any other dog there and so the mystery continued for a short while.

To try and resolve things, I cut the images off the bottom of the original email and pasted them into a new one to send to Karen.

As soon as I did so, everything became clear:

Karen had used a previous email she had sent out as a template for the one regarding Duke. As part of her rescue work, she routinely sends out dozens of emails with information about dogs she is attempting to rehome. Often they go to the same group of people she knows are willing supporters of her work and might be able to assist. This method makes the process a little easier for her. However, she had not realized that these photographs (of a dog she had previously attempted to rehome) were still attached. They were considerably below the text of the Duke email. I had only found them because I could not open the Taiwanese link and thus had kept going down the mail below its ending point, in the belief that there must be some picture somewhere. After all, Michael was telling me that this was an avatar. And sure enough, there was the white, blued eyed, male.

Only the 'he' was a 'she': a two year old stunner by the name of Tasha who was being rehomed, supposedly because she was a frequent runaway and because she had killed a cat.

An avatar killing a cat? Surely not!

It may strike you as bizarre that a creature that is actually the embodiment of an angelic being would kill another creature? Surely angels don't do this kind of thing?

Well firstly, it must be remembered that when avatars incarnate, they rarely have any memory of what they truly are. They may experience some kind of awakening during the course of their lives that allows them to fulfill their purpose; but until that point they are usually ignorant of that which they are.

Experiencing third dimensional reality means *really* being dogs for the duration of that lifetime. That means that they are free to do all of the stuff that canines do, good, bad, funny, gross...whatever!

Secondly, it is the nature of agreements between beings of all species that on occasion, one will actually be *required* to 'terminate' another. In some species, this is an on-going and regular commitment that is an integral part of their experience of being. For others, it is a one-off. The learning comes for both the predator and the prey.

The same thing applies to man. Shocking as it is to us, even a murderer has a contract with his victim. It's easy to see why some would find this startling, if not offensive. If so, consider this: Everyone during one of their lifetimes (or often, more) has taken the life of another and had their own lives taken. It's all just part of the learning process until we 'get' that we really shouldn't do that.

As it transpired, Tasha did not kill the cat, although I only learnt this from the etheric.

It takes a particular kind of person to surrender an animal to a shelter or pound and not feel a heel. If they are able to do it, then they certainly have a lot of learning to do about the nature of their lives and purpose and I can guarantee that they will be making many return visits to the third dimension.

Even more so perhaps, people do not like to look like heels when they are unloading their responsibilities to their animal onto someone else's shoulders; and so they give an account of their circumstances which attempts to put them in a more favourable light.

Most certainly, there are many cases where there are heartbroken owners who are beside themselves with grief over what their circumstances force them to do. They are to be pitied and sympathised with because that surrender is undoubtedly part of a learning contract between them and the animal, which is potentially for the benefit of both. These are deeply sad cases whose outcome has genuine cause. It is not these of which I speak.

There are many hundreds of thousands of animals that are abandoned to their fate each year because, in some way or another, they have become a matter of inconvenience for their owners. In the case of Tasha, there were a number of potential 'inconveniences' she caused.

Her owner's lifestyle was a highly active and social one that such an active dog did not fit into well. He lived in an apartment without a garden and did not have the time to give her the exercise she craved. Her owner lived in California which has a climate that was very much less than ideal for a Husky. As a consequence she shed a great deal and left hair carpets for him. Tasha was filled with an abundance of uncontrollable avatar energy that made her very difficult to live with. Add to this the little matter of the fact that he had discovered that his 'pet' needed over two and a half thousand dollars of surgery. A brand new, trouble free dog would be cheaper than that!

Which one do you think was the greatest inconvenience and the greatest imperative? I'll let you decide!

Yet still, her owner's principal concern was with not looking bad. So he manufactured a very plausible story about how she had killed a neighbour's cat and how he couldn't live with himself, knowing that she could do it again to another poor defenceless animal.

You might think that it's not such a big deal because at least he was good enough to turn her in to a shelter and not merely abandon her on the streets as so many do (although that possibly could have been because she was micro chipped and traced back to him, along with the corresponding fine). After all, it doesn't really affect the dog, does it? Tasha didn't care about her reputation. So why *not* paint a portrait of her as a cat killer? It surely made him appear a lot nicer guy in the eyes of the shelter into which she was dumped.

The problem was that it was a kill shelter he dumped her in, in which she had just two weeks grace before her life would be ended. If nobody wanted to adopt her, then it would be the needle for her! But who wants an animal that has already been branded a killer? Shelters do not conceal information like that from potential adopters.

On the day she was due to be executed, Tasha was rescued by a local rescue group that did not have room for her, but could not bear to see such a beautiful creature put to death. As is the practice with many small rescue groups, her saviours trawled kill shelters to try and help last chance lost causes. A lucky few get to survive, but it is a statistic conveniently ignored by our animal loving societies that in the United States alone, between three and four million animals are killed in shelters each and every year. The years 2008/09 were particularly bad ones to be an unwanted pet in the United States. With the economy biting, people's belts tightening and generosity decreasing, input into shelters went up massively and rescues declined exponentially. Tasha got lucky, but mainly because she was an avatar and had friends in high places. That day the rescue group was sent for her and her alone.

Through a network of contacts and pleas for help that crossed every and all State lines, Karen agreed to take Tasha in. She knew of her need for surgery, she knew of the reported cat killing issue and the problems that would cause in rehoming her; yet still she took her in. Then with the supportive goodwill and selflessness that typifies so many in the dedicated world of dog rescue (of which, by the way, I do not regard us as part) unseen hands arranged for her transportation to the northern States. She made a gradual progression to Karen's home, passing through many hands as she did so, safe at least from the cruelty of a premature death, but becoming increasingly fraught and worrisome.

204

When she finally made it to Karen's, she was a borderline schizophrenic. So many changes without an understanding of the kindness that she was receiving left her confused, manic, and desperate for continuity. Her already overflowing energy could have been mistaken for insanity and now she required leg surgery that would leave her needing months of recuperation to avoid undoing the good such an operation could bring. Without it, she would be crippled.

Karen herself is by no means a rich person. She does what she does out of love for the dogs and sometimes that means that her family almost take second place. However, they are united in their love for the animals and through their own auspices, and with the support of other animal loving contacts, Tasha received her surgery. During the weeks that followed, Tasha nearly drove them insane with her response to being penned up. Again, the kindness of this was lost upon her. When she was healed, then – and only then – would Karen place her up for adoption.

Now, just as we came to know who the real avatar was, we discovered that miraculously, she was still with Karen. Bizarre as it was, this situation was clearly meant to be, if only because Valeria had created it. So the first thing I did was let Angie and Diego know and offer them the chance to take Tasha.

Angie replied that she hated me!

It was the very day after they had made their commitment to keep Duke and it was a cruel irony that the dog she had most wanted was now snatched from their grasp at the last moment. Their living circumstances would simply not allow them to have three dogs. Valeria's vision of the future and a pack of five did not relate to their present home. I felt very sorry for them, but privately very pleased that they continued to honour their commitment to Duke. As, I should add, was Michael!

So the currently recuperating, slightly mad and uncontrollably energetic avatar remained with Karen, oblivious to all of the fuss she had inadvertently caused and totally ignorant of herself as a being of light that was here to fulfill some greater purpose, whatever that might be.

Not for long, however.

Go fetch: Tasha's tale

It was a few weeks later that Michael raised the subject of Tasha again. I was preparing to go to the 'Body, Soul & Spirit' Expo in Vancouver, having exhibited at the same event in Calgary where 'Some Dogs' went on sale for the first time only a month before. At the show I also sold crystal and semi-precious stone jewellery and did twenty minute channelling sessions.

Why were we selling crystal and semi-precious stone jewellery?

Crystals and semi-precious stones are a much undervalued commodity.

Most people are aware that they are said to possess qualities of healing that may affect both our physical and mental states. They do! Wearing them as jewellery can be very good for you since their attributes can then infuse into your own energy field.

However, what people don't necessarily know is how the physical presentation of the crystal impacts its effectiveness.

Across the course of 2008/9 I was increasingly asked by people what crystals would be good for them and where could they get a good piece from. I became frustrated by seeing some of the inert and overpriced crystals that were foisted upon them, and so we ended up becoming suppliers in our own right.

Now, we had been told to do the same thing in Vancouver, and since I was driving over with all of the equipment for the show and the inventory, lots of preparation was required.

So it was quite inconvenient that in the middle of the rush, Michael announced that Tasha was due to be adopted by the wrong person and that therefore we should consider rescuing her ourselves. It wasn't an easy thing to hear as it would take us to twenty one dogs. Readers may recall my scepticism at the end of 'Some Dogs' that we would actually stop at nineteen dogs. But I had thought maybe twenty, maximum.

207

At this point it seemed very foolish to take another dog and I was extremely reluctant. Without mentioning it to her, we discussed taking Tasha and 'holding' her for Angie until their circumstances changed. We knew they planned at some point to move to an acreage. But we also knew that if Tasha integrated with our pack, leaving it would prove a great hardship for her. The knowledge that she would go to the wrong person, whatever that meant, was the overriding factor. We had seen enough evidence of the hardship any dog suffers when it is in the wrong place. So with no resolution to our concerns and no small amount of reservation on my part, we contacted Karen to ask her if we could take Tasha.

I had to leave before she had a chance to reply, but on my drive to Vancouver, Sharon relayed that Karen was delighted that we would take her. She was doubly pleased because another lady she knew had shown interest in adopting her, but Karen had felt that it wasn't quite right. Pressure of circumstances would have forced her to let Tasha go, but knowing that the mad white dog was an avatar, she was relieved that she would be coming to us. See. Michael knows all!

So we set it up that after the show, I would drop south on my homeward drive and meet up with Karen just over the US border to pick up our twentieth dog. It was a major detour for me and Karen could not meet me until the Wednesday after the expo (which ended on the Sunday night); but Karen had already done us such a great service by bringing the three avatars mid-year and we desperately wanted to do whatever we could to make her life easier. Even so, it would mean many hours of driving for her.

The show in Vancouver was not unlike Calgary, but I had no friends to come and visit my booth, as they had done in our own city. Fortunately our daughter Jenny took time off from her studies at UBC and came to help out over the three days of the show. The energies of an event like this are quite difficult to cope with, so as it turned out, by the time it finished I was very grateful not to have to rush down to the US.

What energies; and why were they difficult?

Every form is possessed of a vibration. The majority of that vibration is maintained within them, encapsulated by their auric field. In effect it holds them together. However, some of that vibration inevitably leaves the body. Some of it may be thought of as spillage, some intentional. For instance, a thought creates a vibration that leaves the body, whether we intend it to or not.

These vibrations may be perceived as a form of energy, since they actually create one. You may be able to relate to how the thoughts you have create a feeling within you which (if we use obvious examples like joy or anger) can be perceived within every ounce of your being. This emanates from you and can be described as your 'energy'.

Needless to say, your energies may be positive or negative or a mixture of both. And they may change almost from moment to moment. This effect may actually be captured on film using Kirlian field or auric photography.

When you go to any environment where you encounter people, you also encounter all of their energies, irrespective of whether or not you meet them personally. Their vibrations leave their physical form and bounce around until they eventually dissipate. They have the potential to impact upon you enormously and whether or not this is good or bad for you largely depends upon your state of being in the moment; and theirs.

This is because one form of vibration may complement or counter another. For example, if you go to a concert and the audience is excited and in high spirits, the mood is often described as infectious. Usually, this will be highly positive because the nature of the vibration is high. However, go to a funeral and the sombre nature of what is taking place will cause the vibration of all those present, and the consequent mood, to be much lower. Now imagine the person from the concert suddenly finding themselves in the midst the funeral. How would their vibration change? It would most likely be overpowered by the lower vibration of the mourners.

It almost goes without saying that a high and positive vibration is much better for you than a low and negative one. In the extreme, a negative one can actually create a state of being within your physical form that is contrary to your original form. In others words, you become someone that is not in balance or not at ease with what you truly are. We may describe this as being dis-eased. Or if you prefer, diseased. And that's because this explains precisely what a disease is.

If you are able to maintain a high and positive vibration, you are very unlikely to experience any kind of illness, unless it is one that you have elected to experience before you arrive in that incarnation.

You can create, manage and maintain your own vibration if you know all aspects that have an effect upon it. (In fact this is precisely what Michael instructed us to teach people to do in the Balance Class that we run.) This still does not 'immunise' you when you are faced with the onslaught of energies from others. In these circumstances, actively managing and maintaining your level of balance can be a very exhausting, albeit necessary thing to attempt to do.

You might be forgiven for thinking that the energies at an expo that focuses on matters of spirit would be of the highest and most positive order. Think again. They are bizarre to say the least. In one moment you may encounter a wonderful light filled person whose energies are nurturing and uplifting; in the next, those that are dense, dark and toxic. And that's just the exhibitors! Maintaining your own vibration at a high level can feel a bit like doing battle.

Because I was channelling and surrounded by the crystals I was selling, I received regular top ups of excellent energy not of my own making. Still, with everything else that was going on, by the end of the show I was pretty tired to say the least.

Instead, I meandered along Highway Three, stopping overnight at Penticton and more importantly, visiting the See Ya Later Ranch winery at Okanagan Falls. This was something of a pilgrimage for me. Visitors to www.somedogsareangels.com may know of our great enthusiasm for this winery and their wares. Not only do they, in my opinion, produce

Canada's finest and most consistent chardonnay (along with many other fine wines) they also have a label that depicts a dog with wings that is clearly meant to be an angel. The origin of the name comes from the owner's grief at the loss of a beloved pet dog and his confidence that he would one day be reunited with it. This I could confirm with absolute certainty!

How could I be sure he would be reunited with the dog?

This is not merely a fanciful comment from somebody who already has a number of dogs with whom he'd like to reconnect at some point. It's a basic fact of the true nature of our existence.

As we travel through the innumerable iterations of incarnation, one of the most effective ways of understanding the experiences we go through and thereby fully appreciate the learning that they bring, is to observe our actions from the perspective of others. Only in this way can we truly come to know of the permutations of possibility that exist within the complexities of our interactions with all that is around us.

The need to experience and learn is the province of all sentient things that exist, not merely humans. On a daily basis, we encounter and relate in some way to a greater number of sentient beings than we can possibly begin to imagine. Some of these exchanges are incidental; many are vital to both our learning and theirs. The person you walk past in the store and never see again is unlikely to have much bearing upon your journey; someone you encounter on a frequent basis, be they work colleague, friend, relative or dog(!) may well be a source of reference and comprehension for you; and vice versa. The more frequent the connection within the relationship, the more significance it has later, in the etheric.

That which is meaningless in the moment may be of great significance when viewed from afar. Thus, as already explained, we review our lives and the intricacies of these interactions whilst in transition. In order to do this, we need to re-encounter everyone of significance.

Visiting the winery was a real treat. It was late Fall so I was the only customer there. The beauty of the setting and hospitality I was shown made the visit truly memorable. Despite our hardships, I used some of the expo takings to buy a couple of bottles of wine we had not yet experienced to treat ourselves with upon my return and chatted with the duty hostess. I had noticed that there was a gallery of dog pictures, comprised in part of their own winery dogs and others sent in by customers. Somewhat shyly, I explained my book and its subject matter and asked if they would allow me to leave a copy with them. I was pleased when they agreed and even more thrilled when they gave me two glasses engraved with their dog angel logo as an energy exchange.

The next day saw me arriving in the US and going through the complexity of the border crossing. Unfortunately, I had my remaining stock from the show with me and no inventory. It would have taken an age to produce one, but from the perspective of the immigration and customs people, I could have been bringing it to the States to sell. Fortunately, I had a copy of an email in the car that Jenny had printed out for me in Vancouver. It was from Karen, expressing her pleasure at my imminent arrival and giving me more information about Tasha and her issues. No one could have made up the stuff that Karen had written, so after forty minutes of trying to get over the border, the INS accepted that my purpose was genuine and let me through. As I drove away, I reflected upon what the result could have been but Michael pointed out that I was being looked after. Why was I concerned?

Early the following morning I met with Karen and was introduced to a small white ball of insane, bubbling energy. If her leg surgery had ever been an issue for her, Tasha showed no sign of it now. She leapt in the air and pulled at her leash, showing all the signs of a sled dog in the making. She yelped and made the usual Husky woo woo sound, all at great volume.

On this occasion Karen was on a tight schedule so there was no time for coffee and catch-up. She had already been driving for a long time to reach me at this hour, and she was due back at work in the afternoon;

so our meeting was very brief. There was just enough time for her to observe that as soon as she handed Tasha's leash to me, the dog became peaceful and quiet. She stood shaking her head. "What did you just do to her?" she asked, a big smile spreading across her face. Of course, I'd done nothing. Something inside her had just told her that she was now going where she was meant to be. This was no reflection upon Karen. It was an avatar thing!

On the five hour drive home I was shocked that Tasha was totally relaxed and quiet. At one point we stopped for her to have a bathroom break and another dog owner pulled in behind us. She actually remarked on what a beautiful and well behaved dog Tasha was. So by the time I got back, I had a dog with me that did not match her reputation. At least in most ways.

We rapidly discovered that at mealtimes Tasha becomes the dog from hell. She screeches like an unhinged harpy, and even as she is eating, manages to squeal constantly. It is as if another form of energy possesses her. She certainly becomes torturous! Then as soon as the meal is over, she's as sweet as can be once more. Behaviour can be infectious and after a short while, the other Huskies began to believe that making this much noise was possibly a good idea. After all, it always seemed that we (actually in an effort to shut her up!) fed Tasha first. So now we have to feed her separately from the others. Under these circumstances, she no longer seems to feel that noise is necessary.

Tasha is a dog that loves humans. She is meek and mild and will roll on her back as soon as you are near to her. She is gentle, loving and a real crowd puller because of her looks. But she doesn't take any nonsense from the other dogs. She is surprisingly tough and will not be bullied by them. However, she is also quite fearful and in a pack environment, this is not a good way to be as it leads to tension. If anything, she is the most disruptive influence in the pack and this has led us to ask, several times over, what is her purpose and why do we have her?

Michaels' answer remains somewhat fixed. She was in the wrong place when she was in California. That was not where she was meant to fulfil her angelic role. Her purpose is still to come. She is where she is meant to be. We don't need to know everything that's coming. Do we?

More blessings?

Aura's trip into the great wide world beyond the fence line had both short and long term effects. In the short term, she seemed to calm down greatly after this adventure. We also noticed that she seemed to have no further interest in making forays, quite unlike her bolder father.

Approximately a year later, Molly dug a huge tunnel under the fence line. Fortunately, only she and Aura were able to make an exit before their deeds were discovered. Molly returned immediately, prompting me to wonder why she had gone to so much effort in the first place. Aura was missing for several hours again.

Eventually, I spotted her about a quarter of a mile up the road and made haste to get within her earshot. She was rushing backwards and forwards with no apparent rhyme or reason and seemed highly stressed. But my attempts at recall fell on deaf ears. Instead of coming, she actually ran away and I couldn't even get close to her.

After half an hour of futile chase, she was taking me further and further away from home and the night was drawing closer. As always, for her to be out amongst the coyotes at night was a great concern, so my anxiety levels were rising considerably when I eventually managed to corner her on the deck of a house that was being built. We stood facing each other, about fifty metres apart and she cowered, glancing around everywhere, obviously looking for a place to run to that offered an escape route. I feared that she would make a dash for it so I crouched down and called her name softly. Her response was fascinating. She cocked her head first to one side, then the other, then stared at me intently before racing towards me at great speed, taking a huge leap from a metre out, and landing in my arms with such force that I was sent tumbling backwards. As I lay sprawling (in some pain from the impact!) she covered my face with licks and washed every inch of it.

Bizarrely, it seemed that she had not realized that it was me who was pursuing her. Now she couldn't be happier to be back with me. I attached the leash to her collar and she positively skipped along as I led her back home. It was all I could manage just to keep up with her. But I

215

was also surprised to note that she didn't seem to have any sense of direction regarding which path we had to take, and despite the fact that we were relatively close to home, she was totally lost.

However, as I have already indicated, between these two events, a year had passed and something much more major had happened that may have affected Aura's temperament, and even her ability to receive the telemetry of the natural world. Aura was now a mother.

Upon her return from the initial forty hour excursion into the wilderness, Aura had seemed shaken, even upset by her venturing. As the days passed afterwards, she quickly returned to her normal self, but we became aware that there were other more permanent affects. Principally, we noted that she was far more confident than she had been before; and were we being fanciful that even her appearance changed? The expressions on her face, her coat and her movements all subtly altered. Without any prompting, Michael was able to put everything in context.

Why had Aura changed?

Our lives may be thought of as evolving in direct proportion to the experiences we have that extend our consciousness. The broader the range of experiences we go through, the greater the potential there is for our state of being to expand. The amassing of experience, good or bad, brings about the opportunity for learning, so from the perspective of the etheric, it is a very beneficial thing, irrespective of whether or not the experience is a positive one. Indeed, many lifetimes have as their sole goal the accumulation of experience.

It may accurately be said that we are, to a very large extent, the product of our experiences. The things that happen to us and the circumstances that we go through, when we process them, create for us our beliefs and values as we decide upon their meaning and application to our lives. In turn, these impact upon all consequent choices and decisions that we make.

The more experience we have, the greater the frame of reference we have with which to inform our opinions, thus affecting choices and decisions.

It should also be noted that a broad perspective is not necessarily better than a narrow one, since this will depend upon where each individual is in their state of development upon their ascension pathway. Some lifetimes are meant to be lived without too much opportunity for comparative reference.

In the case of Aura, up until the point of her departure from our compound, almost her whole life had been lived within its confines. On those occasions when she had left, she was always accompanied, and outings had more often than not been to the vets. In experiencing the unadulterated freedom of the outdoors, she had undergone a whole different array of experience, absorbing the wholly new. We may only conjecture as to what occurred during those forty missing hours. Most certainly she passed through totally new terrain, had the possibly uncomfortable experience of having to sleep rough and had to find her own food or go without; but it is also likely that she encountered other dogs, completely new animals and strange houses and people. All of these events may have been met with curiosity, fear, excitement or any one of a number of other responses. These emotions in themselves may have been totally new to her.

What we may be absolutely certain of, irrespective of our ability to observe it, is that Aura most definitely returned a changed dog. This would potentially have been reflected in many aspects of her state of being: Her temperament, responses, character; and even in her physical appearance. We are the products of our experiences.

A few months thereafter, Aura and her two sisters, now mature adults, came into heat. We had heard from many breeders that it is unkind to not let a bitch have at least one season before spaying; other trains of thought suggest that not having a season may result in harmful health implications for the dogs in later life. Despite this, we have always had our dogs neutered as soon as possible. But by now, with so many financial constraints, we had been unable to afford to have the female puppies spayed. Only Idaho had had his ability to pro-create taken away from him.

During their season, Indy, as the only intact male, was driven to a frenzy by the prospect of creating a dynasty. We went to extraordinary lengths to ensure that he and the junior Huskies never encountered one another and became quite adept at sealing him behind one closed door whilst they passed through another open one. Finally, at the end of a fortnight, his interest in them waned, and we were grateful that the strain of enforcing their separation was taken away from us.

It was richly ironic that a couple of weeks later, a friend offered to pay to have them spayed on the basis of a 'value exchange' arrangement, and we were very pleased to accept. Sharon duly made the appointment and we set off to see our vet, Ingrid, with the ladies in tow. However, we had not gone far when Michael advised me to have them scanned before the procedure began. And now you can write the rest of this paragraph for yourself!

The discovery that Aura was pregnant was a shock and, if I'm honest, a major humiliation. I am only too well aware that a vast percentage of those dogs that find themselves unloved and facing a sorry end are the products of unplanned matings. Hereto, I had critically viewed the carelessness of owners who had allowed these breeding transgressions to occur. Despite the fact that we now fell into that category, I wasn't about to change my mind about this particular sin. I berated us for our negligence and lack of care, whilst still being in awe of the fact that Indy had somehow managed to have his wicked way with the Husky! I also offered thanks that he hadn't managed to get to more than one of them. It was with grim fascination that we watched Ingrid reveal first one puppy and then another. We asked her to stop after three had been located. Clearly we weren't going to go ahead with her operation today!

That afternoon I gloomily reassembled the home made whelping box that had been the scene of Aura's first minutes and days in this world. In a strange coincidence, my father rang at the very time of its construction, exactly as he had one year earlier and I broke the news of our impending arrivals. Now very familiar with the strangeness of our extended dog family, he asked if they would be avatars and I replied with a resounding "no". "You'll be able to move them on then!" he asserted, and I readily agreed.

In the brief few weeks that followed, I shared my embarrassment over the impending births with several other people and was gratified to find that many people wanted to have one of the puppies from this illicit pairing. In truth, Indy had become something of a minor celebrity since 'Some Dogs'' was published. Having literally been the poster boy for the book, he had now gained quite an extensive fan club and word spread rapidly of the arrival of his progeny. Even unsolicited interest began to flow in, and our emphatic declarations that the offspring would not be avatars did little to quell the enthusiasm of others. By the time the litter arrived, we could have rehomed them three times over. Although we made promises to none (deciding instead to wait for etheric guidance about where the best homes for them would be), it was a tremendous relief to us to know that we would not have to cope with extra dogs beyond a few weeks.

Prior to this birth, I had sought Ingrid's advice regarding both Aura's youth and the potential size of the puppies. She reminded me that, as had been the case for her mother Lara, giving birth at a year old would not be an issue for Aura. The size issue bothered me more. Indy is at least three times the size of the Husky and Aura is smaller than Lara (who herself, is a fairly small example of the breed). I well recalled the enormous puppy I had collected from Germany, and assumed that the puppies Aura was carrying would be similarly huge. Would the birth be difficult? Should we arrange something with the vet in advance? Ingrid was very reassuring and counselled that all would be fine; but gave me the after-hours telephone number just in case. In all of this, I forgot that Aura was an avatar.

Why did it make a difference that Aura was an avatar?

Although avatars are by no means immune from pain and suffering, Michael reminded me that because of the uniqueness of opportunity that incarnate life presents for them, avatars will seldom place themselves in situations where anything can threaten their lives. For them, this is a matter of deeply imbedded instinctive response. Consequently, they may be seen to be far less careless with their lives.

For instance, it would be very unusual for one to be run over since they would exercise a far greater degree of caution in managing even something as apparently simple as their day-to-day movements.

In maintaining their safety, they are also surrounded by far more angelic beings (than would be common for an earthbound dog), whose role would be to provide the highest levels of protection for them. Such 'guarding duties' would be quite popular since vicariously, those in the etheric would seek to learn from their colleagues experiences, perhaps in anticipation of theirs to come. Their ability to comprehend what their incarnate brethren go through would be greatly accentuated by the higher vibration possessed by the avatar. Therefore the relationship would be highly synergistic and beneficial to all parties.

If something does happen that threatens an avatars existence, they will cling onto their lives with an extraordinary degree of tenacity (far greater than that demonstrated by a normal dog) recognising at an instinctive level the one-off nature of this existence. They truly appreciate the preciousness of their life.

They are also not interfered with by the actions of their higher selves (an element of their existence that you may recall was discussed in 'Some Dogs') so there is no unseen element that will have a bearing upon whether or not they are whisked away from their earthly presence.

Aura would know that giving birth to puppies would not threaten her at all.

The actual birth of the puppies came with practically no warning whatsoever. One moment Aura was outside playing with her brother and sisters; the next she was in the whelping box giving birth. She was considerably more co-operative than her mother and remained within the safe confinement of its laminated wood walls, giving birth with relative ease to four very large and almost identical puppies. As with Aura's own birth, I played midwife and was once again enthralled by the experience of the coming of new life. Because she also chose to deliver at a very convenient time, starting at midday, Sharon was able to share the experience this time around. We spent an exciting afternoon watching their staggered arrivals.

Despite the joy of this, we resolved to remain aloof from the proceedings in the knowledge that these miniature beings would not be remaining with us. Attachment would not be a good thing, so we were fairly reserved in our enthusiasm. Normally we would have decided upon names, but even this aspect of ownership was missing from our thinking. It was perhaps fortunate that the four were almost indistinguishable. Although closer inspection revealed that two pups were male and two female, only the first born had any attribute that could mark it out from the others, possessing a tiny white tip to its tail.

With the miracles of modern computing, digital technology and the internet, I was able to post pictures on the Some Dogs Are Angels Facebook fan page within minutes of their arrival. They were even decent enough to allow a sufficient interval between their births for me to process numerous pictures. Perhaps those who saw them and had requested ownership felt hope as they saw their potential pets flash up on their screens. If it was so, their hopes were soon to be dashed.

About ten minutes after the forth and final puppy arrived, Michael announced that every single one was an avatar. Moreover, it was his 'recommendation' that every single one should stay with us.

Here to stay

With this revelation, I didn't know whether to laugh or cry.

Our adjustment to the knowledge that we were to keep them took a matter of minutes. We went from "Oh no" to "Oh, alright then" with an ease that was borne from the barely concealed knowledge within both of us that in the final analysis, giving up any dog would be the most awful wrench.

Nonetheless, this did not stop me, over the coming weeks, from suggesting to Sharon on numerous occasions that we move some or all of the litter on. For me at least, they created many conflicting emotions.

Prior to their birth I had become quite used to the idea of giving up the puppies (who I had deliberately depersonalised in my thinking). I felt genuine relief in the knowledge that they would not be with us for long. Perhaps my feelings of guilt for this aberration in our dog ownership practices led me to feel this way.

On the other hand, I was loathe to part with any puppies born into our vastly extended family. Having witnessed first-hand the intricacies of the relationships between Timba, Lara and their puppies, and the obvious affection and caring that existed between them, it seemed almost cruel to separate this new brood. Conversely, I was very well aware of how well puppies do get on when surrounded by a loving new family.

For me it was the avatar element that was the real clincher.

Knowledge that there was a purpose in them being with us in itself created something of a sense of misgiving. Were there to be further disclosures regarding more purposes that lay ahead of us that we were as yet unaware of? We were totally cognoscent of the fact that if an avatar came to a household, any household, there was a reason for it being with the occupants. So what now?

Michael was resolute in his insistence that we did not need to know this at this point, since the information pertained to our future. He also reassured us that it was a matter for rejoicing, not concern. We were moderately mollified.

Things were a little different for Sharon. Almost from the moment they were born, she found this brood particularly captivating and felt a deep attachment to them. The knowledge that she 'should' keep them was something of a relief since she found the prospect of letting them go traumatic. Her affection for them would undoubtedly have extended beyond their departure from our household and spanned years of subsequent concern. Her pleasure at keeping them was evidenced by the speed with which she embraced welcoming them into our home as permanent pack members. It was little short of astounding. Immediately she commenced the search for names for these new pack members and there was an instantaneous switching of mindset that encompassed them in her thinking about them as members of the pack as a whole. Perhaps her notional comfort with giving them up had been a self-deception all along? It was certainly one I could understand.

For a little while we struggled with what to call them from a generic perspective. Since their father was a Leonberger and their mother a Husky, did we call them LeonHuskies or HuskBergers? We settled on the latter as we thought it funnier and it was certainly better than mongrels!

As with Lara's litter, we wanted a common theme for the puppy's names. After two days of intense search and much debate, we agreed that all of the designations should stem from some association with the US State of Indiana, in homage to their father. That seemed reasonably straightforward until Sharon remembered that Michael Jackson was from Indiana. Sharon has been a fan of his since childhood and now lobbied hard to call one of the puppies MJ. In response I threw in the complication that to be thematically compatible, all of the puppies would have to be called after Jackson family members. That meant that one of the boys would have to be called Randy, Marlon, Jacky, Tito or Jermaine; and the girls had to be Janet and La Toya. I am eternally grateful that this, coupled with the discovery that MJ didn't really work too well as a name anyway, meant that Sharon backed down.

Eventually, we settled upon place names. The boys would be called Henry (after the County) and Brice (a community in Jay County). The girls took as their names Hope (a town in Bartholemew County) and Belle Vista (a community in Allen County) which we abbreviated to Belle. Only once we had chosen did we notice that we had picked two 'H' names and two 'B' names. This was not intentional. And then we were struck with the realisation that the H/B names had been given to what we had pronounced to be HuskBergers!

Even at birth, compared with the Husky puppies, this lot were fairly huge and it soon became apparent that their size would rival that of their father. Despite their similarity at birth, each rapidly developed a particular look of their own with a curious likeness that could easily have had them mistaken for other breeds. Henry, the first born with the white tip to his tail, was very like a Leonberger and had his father's powerful forehead; Brice bore a striking resemblance to a Rhodesian Ridgeback – without the ridge(!); Belle had the intense look of a Mastiff; only Hope had the look of a bona fide cross breed, but had the sweetest face and the most gorgeous gentle eyes.

Once again it was beguiling to watch the family relationships as they developed. For several days Aura would let no dog near her brood other than her mother who, with total acceptance of her role, immediately assumed the position of grandmother and maid. In Aura's absence she would stand in as fierce protector and comforter of the whining young ones. As a surrogate mother, she would clean and tend to the pups as if they were her own. I often found myself wondering how much tougher her role as parent had been without her mother to help her. After the second week, Aura allowed Inara and Zoe to help and occasionally, we would find all three sisters washing, grooming or just generally being with the puppies. At three weeks, Aura allowed her father Timba to come and inspect his grandchildren. He wasn't too impressed but at least he showed an interest. And that's more than can be said for the idle father, Indiana Jones Vom Erlau.

The first time Indy set eyes on his scions, he turned tail and fled. For weeks he avoided being in the same room as them and was masterful in his avoidance tactics. He was the epitome of an absentee father, which is to say that he was plain bad and totally useless. Only in the second week did he venture a quick sniff and then ran again, seemingly horrified at what lurked in the basement. While Aura struggled bravely with these rapidly growing and powerful bundles of fur, Indy had a blast enjoying the snow and getting up to his usual carefree activities outside. For all intents and purposes, you would definitely have concluded that he was in denial that this lot had anything to do with him!

At three weeks after their birth, Aura and her Husky siblings had opened their eyes. After eight weeks, they were only barely able to clamber out of the high sided whelping box, but clearly sought to explore the wider world beyond its confinements. Yet at two weeks, the Huskbergers were already sighted. At four weeks, they could come and go from the whelping box pretty much as they pleased. In fact, to try and contain their movements in any way whatsoever was a joke. So we just gave up and allowed them to mingle freely in the adult world around them.

At this point, all of the interactions between the dogs began to change as the puppies learnt their place in the pack order. Most specifically, Timba and Lara moved from being doting grandparents to playing the more assertive role that was reflective of their place in the order of things. Lara now became the strict disciplinarian that she had been with her own children and seemed to take great pleasure in exercising maximum control over the youngsters. She would be ruthless in her treatment of them and have no truck with anything that she regarded as inappropriate or lacking in respect for her status. Although from our previous experiences with her very effective parenting of her own puppies, we knew and accepted that this was all for their own good (since it would ultimately result in calmer and more balanced growth into adulthood), we nonetheless nicknamed her 'Bad Grandma'. Timba was more lenient with his treatment of his grandchildren than he had been with his own offspring. But even his occasional lapses of tolerance could not compare with Lara's mercilessness.

Aura herself was a much more forgiving mother than hers had been. She doted on the puppies and was highly stressed if they were out of her sight for too long. She played with them gently or roughly as befitted their state of tiredness and allowed them to use her as an uncomplaining toy (all at the same time!) even when they were nearly as big as she was. No bullying of one another was allowed and if they offended the bigger adult dogs, she would have not one second of hesitation in defending them from their aggression. They, for their part, seemed to respect her motherly instincts and would always back off when faced with her fearsome challenge, even when it is Aura who would definitely have come off worst in any confrontation. She was absolutely fastidious in her attention to their cleanliness and despite the fact that her puppies were weaned considerably earlier than her and her siblings, she tried to feed them by regurgitation for weeks after they had lost interest in her stomach contents. We were surprised by how excellent a mother she was.

As for Indy, at the point at which they fled their whelping box, they became an inescapable feature of his reality. Each and every one insisted upon forcing their way into his life and we would regularly observe the hilarious sight of his huge and lumbering form being pursued by beings intent on claiming paternity. As the weeks passed, his gruff and growled rejections of any claim they held upon him gradually turned to begrudging acceptance that perhaps, they were something to do with him. Oddly, in the face of repeated rebuffs and anger, they all made it obvious that they adored him. Comparatively, they took their long suffering mother for granted. They would rush to his side as soon as he appeared, oblivious to his grumpiness and attempts to scare them away. They would delight in washing his face and cleaning his teeth with their perpetually eager tongues and compete to see who could get nearest to him when he lay down to sleep. Particularly touching was the sight of either Henry or Brice, lying back to back with their father, a feat they were only able to achieve if he was insensible to their presence. As frustrating as the scene was poignant, was my inability to capture these moments on camera. The slightest disturbance would alert Indy to the travesty of what was happening and cause him to flee like a celebrity who does not wish to be caught in flagrante delicto. Only a grooming brush seemed to hold more fear for him.

Despite their size and total acceptance by the rest of the pack, they were surprisingly lacking in confidence in their dealings with people and didn't act like any of the other dogs in many other respects. To notice what the specific differences were, you would have to study them carefully. They weren't gregarious, attention seeking or even concerned with their interactions with others. They played happily with their aunts and uncles but preferred the company of one another. At the same time they were very much individuals and each was content with their own company, seeming not to need the pack association that the others thrived upon. Not exactly inexperienced in the ways of puppies, we were nonetheless surprised to find that more than any of the other dogs, they displayed sensitivity to emotions and an eagerness to please. A harsh word or rebuke would send them into paroxysms of guilt and self-recrimination. The observation of sadness or any less than happy emotion in Sharon or I would bring unlimited amounts of attention and evidence of attempts to lift our spirits. And then there was also the way they looked at you. Many dogs can have a knowing look. These four looked as if they possessed the knowledge and wisdom of the entire universe and when you stared at them, the constant gaze that was returned would have been positively unsettling if it wasn't comforting instead.

As the weeks passed, it became obvious that it was Hope who was the smartest and most confident; Belle was the most aloof, yet a big softie, despite the cross look her 'mask' suggested; Brice, having initially been the boldest of them all, rapidly became the nerviest, but a great guard dog; Henry, at first my devoted acolyte, transferred his affiliations to Sharon, maybe when he figured out that she needed protection more than I did. This allegiance prompted Sharon to invite him to sleep in our bedroom one night, as he seemed so distressed to leave her. And of course thereafter, it was only a matter of days before all of them began sleeping in our bedroom, relishing the abandonment of the dog room, the traditional puppy sleeping quarters, months earlier than their mother had.

By the time eight weeks had passed, Sharon was so enamoured of these strange souls that to part with them would have been unthinkable for her. Perhaps it was their avatar state of being; perhaps it was just that they were all so connected to her. At the very point where we might have been releasing them to their eagerly awaiting new owners, our home was filled by the irrefutable presence of four gangly beasts with colossal appetites that already rivalled their mother in height, were into anything and everything and emanated an energy that was so palpable you could almost see it. And we, for our part in it, were none the wiser as to what their purpose with us could possibly be.

We Stumble. We Fall.

If all felt bright, light, right, and as it should be with the puppies ensconced in our midst, we were entering an even darker period in our finances. We had learned to cope with the perpetual dread of unpleasant phone calls and letters from debt collection agencies, banishing the fear and discomfort they were intended to cause. Now an even more serious prospect arose. For several months we had not been able to make mortgage payments, and the patience of the bank was rapidly running out.

From an outsider's perspective, I guess it must have seemed irresponsible that we were prepared to take on more dogs. Yet throughout we maintained an (almost) unfailing confidence that we were doing what we were supposed to be doing. Only in the very darkest depths of anguish and feelings of futility would we rail against the bizarre purpose that we felt had been 'foisted upon us'. One or the other of us would refuse to go on or even make outrageous comments about divesting ourselves of the pack.

Only after venting spleen, when we had ranted and become calm again, were we able to put things in perspective. Nothing was foisted upon us. Everything had been our choice and we totally accepted that our commitments had been made prior to our incarnations in this lifetime. There was also the inescapable knowledge that whilst our acquiescence to requests from the etheric had been at great cost to us, financial and otherwise, it had brought more happiness and wealth of other sorts than can be imagined or fully explained within these pages.

Despite all of this, one day, as if out of the blue (but in reality, very far from it!), there were 'no wheels on our wagon'!

When the repossession notice came, it hardly took us by surprise and even the depths of depression that it plunged us into only lasted for a few hours. We could discern no way out and had no prospect of coming up with the tens of thousands of dollars required within the four days we had remaining. There seemed to be little point in worrying about what had now become an inevitability.

That day I spoke with my parents on the phone. They could hear the dullness in my voice and instinctively knew that something was wrong. There seemed little point in denying it, so I explained the situation. I had once taken pleasure in my achievements in the business world and relished the success I had achieved. It had felt like a payback for their investment in me and I knew that they had experienced considerable pride in what I had accomplished. As work dried up and my services to the etheric became more in demand than those to the business community, embarrassment at my situation had turned to humiliation. It had been a long way to fall and I seemed to have been falling for an awfully long time. In the face of all of this, they had been unquestioning in their support. They had far less of a problem with what had become of us than I did and had already bailed us out financially on numerous occasions, eating into their own hard earned savings and going without so that we could go on.

Now, as I explained what was happening, the dullness in my voice came from the grim acceptance that what would be, would be. I was passed shame and I also had the advantage of having had Michael explain to me the nature of parents and parenting. This helped a lot!

<u>What is the nature of parents and parenting?</u>

We choose our parents before we incarnate because of the learning that we will get from them, or they will get from us. The direction in which the learning flows is often a matter of soul age and many children are older in soul terms than their parents (particularly those who are 'indigo', 'crystal' or 'rainbow' children).

However, the notion that a parent is committed to a child simply by virtue of the fact that they decided to have a baby is an illusion. In contractual terms, a parent *may* have fulfilled their obligations simply by having the child. Thereafter, it may be their lack of intervention or involvement in the life of that child that is important to the learning of both.

In fact, the whole 'blood is thicker than water' myth is highly misleading. From a societal perspective, the integrity of the family appears to be of great importance, so many maintain familial relationships even though

230

they actually find them damaging and draining. From an etheric perspective, it should be recollected that ascension may only be achieved by ourselves, for ourselves. Feelings of familial obligation are damaging and have the effect of holding us back.

This is not to say that either parental or familial relationships may not be happily maintained through choice; and it *is* the case that many of those with whom we share these relationships are fellow members of our broader soul families.

It is worth noting that if we extend the concept of family to a broader group, as is the case in certain animal societies, we create a more harmonious and caring society.

How then did this help me with my parents?

Principally in the area of understanding that my beliefs about my own shortcomings or failure meant little to them. They hadn't pegged their sense of achievement or fulfilment to anything I did. Neither did they judge me or feel that I had let them down.

From a slightly different and more unique standpoint, Michael had also made me aware of the nature of my contractual agreements with them and vice-versa.

As those brief few days flew by, Sharon and I were in something of a daze. It was like waiting for a bomb to go off and accepting that there is no escape.

We both wept with joy, profound gratitude and a colossal sense of relief when my father telephoned to say that they had paid off our arrears. At least for the time being, we had a reprieve.

The Act Of Kindness

With at least one wheel back on the wagon, we were able to keep rolling along. My efforts to get a job were tireless but as futile as ever. Those needing channellings, clearings and whatever continued to beat a pathway to our door, though it did not stop us from wondering where and when the next crisis would arrive. It was not long in coming.

When individuals have more than one of anything, be it dogs, cats, cars or children, I am always somewhat sceptical when they claim to love them all absolutely equally. I believe that it is the nature of our emotional processing that we like some things more than others, even if it is only in the instant. Although our ranking of everything may change from moment to moment, and the differences in our responses so slight as to be almost imperceptible, we do nonetheless love some things more than others.

When you have a house full of dogs, all of whom are immensely lovable, this 'stack ranking' (as the relative value of employees to the organisation is termed in the corporate world) can change on the basis of who has just done what. Even a much favoured hiking companion can fall from grace if they suddenly decide that your sofa is a washroom; the cutest puppy is not so popular when it's just chewed a hole in your goose down comforter. The change might be momentary, but it happens nonetheless. Few manage to be faultless and you grow to love them as much for their imperfections and moments of naughtiness as anything else. Only hindsight allows us to view our animal companions as sainted, usually when the pain of loss blurs all remembrance of anything less palatable to our preferred memories.

This being the case, Ktuu was somewhat unique in that she seldom if ever fell from the very high position in Sharon's stack ranking. Known to us affectionately as 'Kitty', this ancient Alaskan Malamute was rescued from a tragedy in Athabasca when she might otherwise have met an untimely end, and she wouldn't have been everyone's choice for a favourite dog. Readers may recall her positively toxic breath that resulted from a mouth full of ulcers and rotting teeth that could only be corrected by surgery within days of us taking her. The operation was very successful, and a revitalized, almost youthful dog returned to us that held its head high and relished life once more.

At all times, Kitty was good natured and sunny in her disposition. Both her ability to give, and her pleasure in receiving affection was without measure. She was a master of the notorious 'Malamute lean' for which the breed is well known, placing the full weight of her body against yours so that you simply couldn't ignore her. She would gaze into our eyes and, of all of our rescues, always seemed to express the most profound gratitude for the comfort and love that she now received. Despite her considerable age (she was fourteen when she came to us) she still maintained a great dignity and grace in her movement. On occasions she would run, and her great bounding strides were a beautiful sight to behold. We found ourselves wondering what she must have been like in her sled pulling prime. Awesome, was our conclusion.

Sadly, her operation provided only brief respite. All too soon a second expensive surgery was required from which she returned to us an almost toothless wonder. Her gums were once again in too poor a state for sutures to be applied. As before, she experienced considerable relief; but it rapidly became obvious that the issues with her mouth were a manifestation of something far more insidious. The noxious breath and pain in her mouth returned with no way of correcting it. She began to suffer occasional nosebleeds, which suggested that she might even have a brain tumour.

As with all those who have appalling breath, be they human or canine, she seemed to have the unfortunate habit of sticking her face really close to mine. Her most favourite moment for doing this was at mealtimes when she would stand between my chair and Sharon's, hopefully awaiting stray food that might come her way. Her excitement and enthusiasm always caused a great deal of heavy breathing and exhalation of fumes that I would swear, on occasion, were of a green colour reminiscent of a chemical waste disaster. These would be liberally distributed in my direction; whereas when she turned towards Sharon, I was convinced that she held her breath. I lost count of the number of times I would encourage her to go elsewhere, but she was quite determined to share her internal outpourings with me. Perhaps it's something I attract? Sharon was convinced that she was providing me with a learning opportunity to exercise tolerance and forbearance.

Her trips outdoors became less frequent. All too soon we arrived at a point where she simply couldn't run. The space beyond the front door, once so sought after and cherished, became a place where frailty would be exposed and she could no longer participate in the frolics that took place there. She seemed content to become a full time housedog.

Then as with so many dogs, her back legs began to fail her. Daily doses of steroids kept the nosebleeds and pain in her mouth at bay, but this was a new feature for her to cope with. With increasing frequency, she would suddenly lose control of all four legs simultaneously and 'pancake' on the floor. Thus splayed out, she was unable to lift herself without our support. It was a pitiful sight. Sharon was able to provide support for her by giving her energy healing and she would go from immobility to walking reasonably comfortably after a half hour session.

Anyone who has owned a dog that is coming to the end of its life will recognize the symptoms. Failure of the back legs is often the augury of the beginning of the end. It was increasingly clear to us that she could not go on for too much longer.

Despite her rapidly increasing decrepitude, she continued to be a major personality within the pack. It was interesting for us to note that the respect the other dogs maintained for her was without question. They would not try to steal her food or disrupt her in any way, even as she became increasingly weak. Even during the pancake incidents, they kept their distance as if allowing her to retain some semblance of dignity.

Throughout, we remembered everything that Michael had originally told us about why it had been suggested to us to take her in the first place. It was an 'act of kindness' not simply because she was an old dog that nobody wanted, but because she was an old soul who would have the chance to ascend living in our household. Although we had not fully comprehended the meaning of these words at the time, we now understood that this might well be dependent upon her passing naturally, without our intervention. It was this that we would notionally allow her to do, when in her previous circumstances, she would have been disposed of considerably sooner than even the point she had reached now. Her surgeries alone with their substantial cost would have warranted her killing.

Over the weeks and months that passed, Ktuu was a tower of strength in the way she bore the discomfort of her passing physical faculties. Throughout, she remained cheerful and happy, and clearly continued to enjoy both our company and the attention that was poured upon her. She had good days, bad days, and disastrous days. On many occasions she would seem to be at death's door, only to rally when Sharon gave her healing. When even this seemed to have no impact, Sharon would insist that I channel more powerful infusions from the etheric and whilst this did the trick on a couple of occasions, we could both see that they merely prolonged the inevitable.

What 'more powerful infusion'?

At one point I had retired to bed, only to find Sharon, who had gone upstairs some hours earlier, writhing with pain. She had done something to her back and was now suffering the consequences.

She is the healer, not me. Although we are told by the etheric that anyone may heal, to be effective (in my experience) requires the highest of intentions and purity of purpose, coupled with a propensity for considerable patience. Sharon has this in abundance, I don't. At least, not the patience bit! In fact for some reason, I don't really feel comfortable with the idea of me healing at all.

So when she asked me to see if I could do something, my response was somewhat reluctant.

"I'm not asking you, I'm asking the etheric!" she said.

I asked if I could do anything and was surprised to hear "Yes, you can". Still somewhat disinclined, but wanting to ease her pain, I walked round to Sharon's side of the bed, threw back the comforter and placed my hand on her back.

In that instant it felt like a ripple of electricity passed through me and almost as soon as I put my hand there, I took it off again. The experience was a little debilitating and I felt quite giddy. "That's all I can do" I said, expecting to have been totally ineffectual.

"Oh my goodness" was her reply. She sat up, totally free of pain, looking at me with a mixture of gratitude and admiration. "How did you do that?"

"Well, it sure wasn't me and I couldn't do that again" was my response. And sure enough, I couldn't. On several occasions thereafter, she asked me to repeat the performance for lesser ailments, with no success whatsoever.

Michael explained that in that moment, Sharon's need had been very great. I was therefore allowed to channel a more powerful infusion of energy from the etheric. Need did not warrant its repetition on subsequent occasions, other than to provide relief for Kitty in her most dire moments.

Like I said, I'm not a healer.

I guess that many would have dispatched their dogs weeks or months before we even gave this thought consideration, relying on the 'alleviating suffering' argument to justify this final action. There might be many of you reading this now who think critically of us for not acting. But knowing what we knew about the nature of ascension, assisting her passing through euthanasia was a thought we tried to push away. We were constantly aware of her pain level, which with the steroids, never rose above the standard aches and pains of old age. Until one day it did.

The end came very swiftly. Having been her usual self the day before, we awoke one morning to find that Ktuu was unable to stand, even with assistance. For the first time, she whimpered in pain. A thin trickle of blood ran from her nose, a reoccurrence of the nosebleeds that we had not seen for months. When we helped her up, blood also trickled from her rear end. Despite all of our resolve, it was clear that she was now suffering and we could bear it no longer.

Once again, within my terms, we would be found wanting.

Within minutes we were on our way to see Ingrid who mercifully relieved her of any further pain. I watched as the blue tunnel opened and she was collected, not as a dog but as a being of light. It should have been fascinating to see, but I was too teary at loosing Ktuu to care in that moment.

Ingrid could not have been nicer or more caring. Even if she were not already a superb vet (which she undoubtedly is), those few moments of unparalleled sensitivity on her part would have earned our undying loyalty and gratitude. But it did not prevent us from leaving under the cloud of despondency and grief that accompanies any loved ones passing.

Then like a moth irresistibly drawn to a flame, I did the dumb thing. I asked if Ktuu would ascend.

There was a lengthy pause before Michael replied. Clearly some consideration was being given to either the answer itself, or how to break it to us. It was the latter:

"No. Your actions have denied her the opportunity and she will now have to return for another lifetime so that a further opportunity to ascend might present itself".

We were devastated. A dog's life can be harsh and cruel and we bore direct responsibility for ensuring that Ktuu would have to go round again. A round of self-recrimination and railing at the injustices of the situation followed. Michael was quick to intervene and because I needed to understand it fully, I recorded the response to listen to over and over. Here it is, transcribed:

"A being that has chosen to incarnate in this form [dog] accepts in totality all that will befall it in its lifetime. It is a part of its pathway that it will be subject to the choices and decisions of other beings to whose auspices it is subject. This may include the manner of its passing. The choices that you have made were not made easily nor without consideration of what would be for the highest good of the dog. Under these circumstances there was conflict between what was for your highest good and what you believed to be for the dog's highest good.

You allowed your need to take preference. For this, there is no need for blame or reproach. The exercise of your free will in all things is your unassailable right. The being that was your dog embraces you for the joy you were able to offer it. It feels nothing but gratitude for your love and accepts totally that you acted the only way you believed you could.

In circumstances such as these when the predominance of one choice exists over another, it is the intention of the being that affects the learning that is taken from a situation. Were you to have acted with different motivation then there would be much else to say in this regard.

As it is, rejoice in the life you have shared and be grateful for the synergies that have been created. Do not allow yourself this despondency. Recall all of your understanding and take comfort in the knowledge that you will encounter this form again shortly. "

I wasn't too perturbed by the 'shortly' reference, since I know how little time can mean in the etheric. But I knew what was coming next from Sharon and I already knew the answer: "Can we get her back?"

"No."

It was short and simple.

<u>Why couldn't we get Ktuu back?</u>

A soul will only try to return to the same place if there is more learning that can be achieved as a result of reprising the relationships that have been part of a previous lifetime.

Ktuu wouldn't derive much benefit from us because, quite frankly, given the same situation, we'd do the same thing again and spoil her chances of ascension a second time. We were no longer good bets from her perspective.

So then, naturally enough, we wanted to know what would become of her. We were told that Ktuu's next lifetime would be a relatively brief one, lasting only a few months. It would not be pleasant but it would present her with a slightly easier opportunity to ascend, since the 'kindness' that we had extended to her would not be repeated.

Too much information. I wished we hadn't wanted to know. But Michael was again quick to point out the failings in my logic and reiterated the points made to us so many times that even lifetimes of great suffering can result in great learning and therefore great opportunity.

The information was comforting and it certainly helped. It stopped us from beating ourselves up too much, but I had to go over and over what he'd said to come up with an unequivocal version that I understood with regard to pet euthanasia.

If it helps you, here's what I came up with. I had to check it out with the big guy with wings to make sure he approved it first and he did. If it makes you feel uncomfortable, don't read this bit.

Mark's simple guide to pet euthanasia

Any time we euthanize a pet, it has the POTENTIAL to impact upon their progression upon their ascension pathway. And ours.

The act MAY be what was agreed to for them in that lifetime. If this is the case, it's for *your* learning and not theirs.

The decision to euthanize should NEVER be based on convenience.

The ONLY justifiable reason is the suffering of the animal.

Standard old age issues do NOT constitute suffering. An animal can still enjoy its life with creaking joints, no teeth and poor eyesight. You could.

Don't kid yourself when it comes to making the choice. If you lie to yourself, it's YOUR progress on the ascension pathway that suffers. You are accountable for the decisions you make.

For Sharon, it was a little different. In her personal stack ranking of our dogs, Ktuu had always vied for the top spot and even though her breath was disgusting, she adored the geriatric Malamute. Now she was heartbroken and discovered that although the departure of a Husky leaves a big hole, a big old Malamute's can be even bigger.

And holes must be filled, mustn't they?

Art imitates life

You may have realized that I'm a total movie buff. I try to keep my references to a minimum in case the reader hasn't seen the movie, but if you have looked at the movie and book recommendations page on www.somedogsareangels.com, you will have seen a number of dog related movies that I consider to be essential viewing.

One of these is 'Eight Below', a Disney movie that stars Paul Walker giving (to my mind at least) a career best performance. As I remark on the website, the movie does an excellent job of portraying not only the resilience of our four-legged friends in a worse than tough situation, but also the angst of the caring and loving human, for whom nothing is more important than the protection and safety of his dogs.

I won't spoil the movie for you in case you haven't seen it; but I will tell you that the basic storyline involves a team of eight Huskies that, of necessity to their human masters, are left in the Antarctic. It's not your usual Disney movie and is even disturbing in places; certainly for dog lovers. It has a moderately happy ending, but it's still a major weepie.

What some don't realize is that it's actually based on a true story. And not only is it true, similar things can and do continue to happen, all be they under slightly different circumstances.

It was about a month after Ktuu's passing that we heard about the so called 'Eight Above' rescue operation that occurred in Rimini, Montana. A gentleman who owned eight very large and very elderly Malamutes had died. They were left stranded seven and a half thousand feet up the mountain where the man had lived, with no one to look after them. A distant neighbour was able to provide some food for them, but with the onset of heavy snow, travelling the considerable distance between their homes was no longer an option. Eventually, the neighbour was contacted by the owner's son, and together they contacted Moonsong Malamute Rescue. This group was based in Idaho, but Montana does not have a similar group; and since they are contiguous States, the volunteers at Moonsong readily agreed to help, calling upon other volunteers from Wyoming to assist them.

243

Between them, they devised a plan to rescue these poor souls. As soon as they were able and in the face of extremely difficult physical conditions, the rescuers went as far up the mountain as they could by car, until snow drifts blocked their way; then were forced to revert to snowmobiles and cross-country skis in order to make the rest of the ascent.

After a further three miles of arduous climbing, they arrived at the home of the Malamutes with no idea of what to expect. What they found was uplifting and heartbreaking all at the same time. The dogs, which by now had not been fed nor had access to water for a very long time, were all still alive. To do justice to the story of what happened next, I will turn to the description given by one of the volunteers who was actually there, Liz Copp.

"Five dogs were chained to trees near dilapidated plywood dog houses. Each dog had beaten a path around their tree the length of their chain. While some dogs barked at the volunteers, others would not even peer out of the dog houses where they hid. Although nervous, eventually all of the Malamutes warmed to the volunteers. The dog houses did not contain any winter bedding, such as straw, and the only water available was from the surrounding snow. Frozen urine and feces ringed each dog house. Discarded building materials thrust through drifts; a new wood stove, plywood, a door. Two travel trailers were partially drifted over. A frozen mixture of noodles and pinto beans filled a five-gallon bucket near the door to the trailer that had served as the former occupant's residence. Scattered along the counter inside the trailer were half-full veterinary prescriptions. The team marvelled at the random assortment of materials accumulated on nearly every flat surface of the trailer. This trailer served as "headquarters" for the team and their gear.

The MMR team needed to catch or trap the three loose dogs before moving any of the other dogs off the mountain. Their fear was that if the loose dogs were not captured before the chained dogs were removed, the loose dogs would abandon the site and perish. The team set one baited live trap near a packed trail the loose dogs had created. The odour of green tripe wafted through the forest. Nervous tension crackled on the chilly mountain air. Amazingly, a volunteer was able to approach and leash Tank, a red and white male, who was loose. Dolly, an unchained, sweet older gal, wandered out of her dog house. She was cornered just off the trail in deep, powdery snow. Two volunteers attached a collar and leash to Dolly and then secured her to an unoccupied dog house. Dolly appeared to be fragile and it was decided she would need to be crated to transport down the mountain. Unfortunately, that meant leaving the tenacious little survivor on the mountain another night.

Meanwhile, Sweet Pea, the last free-range Malamute cautiously approached the trap and started to step forward. The wind caught the band of fabric covering the trap's lever and flipped it towards the female Malamute. The dog bolted. A feeling of defeat washed through the MMR troupe as the afternoon waned toward evening. A team member hit on an idea to capture the flighty Sweet Pea. He suggested the team use the same technique used to capture Dolly; that the dog be herded toward deeper snow to restrict her movement. The group formed a loose line around the Malamute cutting her off from the packed trails. Two members moved closer, driving the dog into the deep snow. The Malamute dove into the snow and floundered. Sweet Pea was tethered and lead to stable ground! A small cheer erupted from the rest of the onlookers; they had captured all of the loose dogs!

It was impossible to ski down the steep trail without risking injury to the dogs or to the volunteers. The MMR team decided to remove Tank and Sweet Pea by snow shoeing with them downhill three miles to where the vehicles had been left and return for the last six "Eight Above" Malamutes the next day. Before Tank and Sweet Pea could hike out, giant ice balls had to be removed from their feet. The ice balls attached to long hair surrounding their pads and made walking painful. The dogs were muzzled and the ice was carefully cut away from the dog's feet. Both Tank and Sweet Pea were patient and allowed the impromptu grooming without fuss.

With the ice balls removed from Sweet Pea and Tank, they began their three-mile journey down the steep mountainside. The Malamutes tried several times to turn back to their mountain home, but with treats and affection were soon trotting alongside the two volunteers escorting them. That both were senior malamutes became clear as the volunteers and dogs navigated several of the vertical snowy slopes on the trail. The

245

pace was slowed and mini-breaks were taken to revitalize both animals. Dusk fell and time was counted by the number of steps the dogs could take before they needed to rest. Both dogs slowed further, but still plodded alongside their rescuers. Nearly two and a half hours later the two handlers loaded Sweet Pea into a crate which was secured to a sled and she was pulled down the road towards the waiting vehicles and other team members, whilst Tank continued on foot. After watering both dogs, the team loaded them into side-by-side crates in a truck and they were taken to safety, warmth and food."

The next day, the team completed the rescue operation, successfully recovering all eight Malamutes. At the time of writing, Liz's full account of this remarkable story may be viewed at the Moonsong website at: http://www.moonsongmals.org. It is a tremendous testament to the compassion of the volunteers, their selflessness and their dedication to saving the lives of these helpless animals.

I first came to read the story because the Moonsong site was one I visited regularly, having first been directed to it in the search for an avatar a year earlier. Although I had not taken a look at the site for some while, my thoughts had been very much about Malamutes since Ktuu's departure and I found myself engrossed in the story. What was not recorded, but was obvious to me and to those wonderful souls at Moonsong, was the enormous difficulty they would now face rehoming these eight ancients. It is a sad fact of life that if elderly dogs find their way into rescues, their chances of ever finding their way back into 'forever' homes are slight. Very few recognize the true worth of a more mature companion, and so never get to experience the joys of their devotion to those who free them.

The 'Eight Above' group presented a sorry prospect to any potential adopter. In their prime, like Ktuu, they must have been remarkable to behold. All were big, heavy set animals with long coats, and several of them were a very unusual orange colour. One of them was even named Pumpkin as a result! The YouTube videos that provided an excellent marketing tool for them also betrayed the fact that many bore serious and disfiguring scars from what must have been intra-group fighting; or even possibly encounters with wildlife in their remote location. Because of their age, many were obviously suffering from severe arthritic conditions that affected their walking. Some had nasty skin conditions. It didn't take a genius to work out that as a result of the terrible deprivations they had just managed to live through, that other even worse physical prospects probably lay just beneath the surface of their appearance. And all that was to say nothing of how potentially emotionally scarred these poor creatures would be.

So all in all, it was quite clear to me that one of them would be absolutely perfect for us.

One Above: Sweet Pea's tale

Of course, Sharon agreed. Immediately her heart went out to them and our path was set to welcome another decrepit Malamute into our lives, despite the nagging concern that its tenure could be even shorter than Kitty's. Frankly, we'd have taken them all if we could.

Several weeks of discussion, vetting and arrangement later, I drove down to the US border to pick up our new charge, Sweet Pea. I was met by a lovely lady called Katy who had been part of the rescue team. With her was a very beautiful and very dignified (if somewhat confused) senior citizen who instantly melted my heart. As I led her round the parking area at the border to allow her a little time to become used to me, she looked anxiously at Katy. Her whole life in recent months had been one disruptive and unsettling episode after another. She had evidently formed an attachment to Katy, yet here I was, about to drive another wedge into her comfort zone. Sweet Pea was clearly disturbed by the whole procedure.

To ensure that our new pack member would be welcomed with open arms, I had taken the precaution of bringing Indy with me. As alpha male, his acceptance of another dog was basically a make or break thing for newcomers. Although he had never rejected anyone, we recalled how he gave Joe a hard time. While our incumbent house angel had totally forgiven him and dismissed his dastardly deeds as mere aspects of his doginess, we wanted to guarantee that such a delicate old being as Sweet Pea would have no repeat of his growly greeting experience.

I introduced the two dogs in the car park and to my great relief, he was instantly accepting of her. Michael was later to explain that this was a feature of something that I had only suspected previously. Not only did Indy respond to her age with something approaching respect; he was also aware of the experiences she had been through. At the very least he was able to empathise.

In spite of her misgiving, Sweet Pea was very acquiescent and between us, Katy and I lifted her considerable bulk into the back of our SUV. Before I departed for the long drive home, Katy explained that the dog's names had been given to them by the rescuers. They had no idea of their original names, and although some veterinary records had been discovered, exactly who was who remained a mystery. However, they were quite convinced that Sweet Pea's real name was 'Bo Peep'! So that was it. Sweet Pea she would remain!

On our journey home, my more elderly companion was perfect in both her manner and restraint. She lay in the back without uttering a single complaint and when we made a stop for a toilet break, she was compliance itself. Only afterwards did she attempt to 'do a runner'; but this in itself was a sadly comical sight to behold. Her physical shape was a far cry from how she perhaps still imagined herself to be. It took no effort at all to catch her and I reflected that even since the time of Liz Copp's account of the rescue, her condition must have deteriorated considerably.

When we arrived home, our usual carefully orchestrated 'meet and greet' with the rest of the pack became an impossibility when Sharon was overpowered at the door by the seething masses. They all raced outside in a barking melèe, and then stopped dead in their tracks as they saw Sweet Pea. Even Poppy, usually the first to give everyone and anything a hard time, was oddly silent. Instead they took it in turns to walk around the Malamute and were as respectful as you can be when you are sniffing someone else's backside!

Sweet Pea bore the inspection patiently, and when they'd had enough, she wandered off to see the rest of her new surroundings. When, after twenty minutes she hadn't returned, I went in search of her and was dismayed to find that having gone down the hill to the back of the house, she couldn't get back up. She was obviously very weary and was just standing half way up the hill, unable to go further. Huffing and puffing, I carried her up the slope and was very relieved when she then decided to explore the indoors.

For the first few days, whenever she went outside Sweet Pea was accompanied by Poppy who seemed to act as both guide and guardian. It was like watching a youngster helping an old lady cross the road and Poppy was very attentive in her care of the geriatric. However, as with many of our rescues that come from more extreme cases, Sweet Pea

250

rapidly developed a great fondness for the warmth and comfort of the indoors and basically became a house dog. Just like Kitty, she eschewed comfortable beds and was quite content to lie on the floor and watch the world moving around her.

However, not all was immediately 'happy ever after' for Sweet Pea. Although she rarely asked to go outside, when she did her behaviour was unlike the other dogs. It quickly became obvious that she was searching for something and she would pace backwards and forwards, looking off into the distance in the apparent expectation of something or someone emerging over the horizon. When she slept, her sleep was fitful and full of dreams that seemed to cause her some distress. She would whimper and wake up suddenly, then immediately want to begin a search around the house. After a few days of this we began to suspect the cause: she was looking for the rest of her pack.

Within days of returning with Sweet Pea, we had begun discussions with Moonsong about the possibility of taking Pumpkin, believing that our old girl would value the company of another of her original pack members. We had repeatedly watched the YouTube video of her in the rescue and noted her very friendly interactions with her kennel mate, Pumpkin, whom she clearly regarded with some affection. We had opened a dialogue with the individual who was now fostering Pumpkin and all seemed to be going well. Then without realising the implications of what she was telling us, Katy dropped a bombshell: It wasn't Pumpkin in the video at all. It was Tank.

She went on to explain that Sweet Pea and Tank had gotten on so well together that there had been speculation amongst the rescuers that perhaps they had been mates. It was possible that at least some of the other Eight Above dogs may even have been their puppies. Suddenly everything became clear. Sweet Pea was not looking for the rest of pack; she was pining for Tank.

Joe was able to confirm this and we kicked ourselves for not having asked for his input before. He also requested that we take Tank as a matter of urgency (although he didn't explain why), so we immediately put in a request with Moonsong via Katy. However, since he was with a different fosterer, the process of applying began all over again. Katy warned us about incontinence issues he had, but I assured her that this was of no consequence to us. Then we sat back to wait...

After about a month we heard that Tank had been taken for x-rays. Apparently there was something more seriously wrong with him than incontinence. Another two months passed before we heard from Katy again. Tank had not been doing well and got to the point where he wasn't very mobile. Then he stopped eating. He had lost a lot of weight and the fosterer decided to let him go. He was dead.

We were devastated because we knew exactly why he'd stopped eating. His mobility was probably just about on a par with Sweet Pea's, but we knew with absolute certainty that his self-starvation was caused by his grief at not being with his mate.

Consider their situation. The two of them had most likely been together for their entire lives. Sweet Pea was at least fourteen, which in 'dog years' would put her somewhere in her human nineties. Even if she met Tank in her twenties, they'd spent the equivalent of seventy years together, then suddenly been torn apart. They didn't have the knowledge of one passing, which might well have been easier to cope with. Instead, it was as if she'd gone to one nursing home, and he another. There was no means of communication and no means of knowing what had happened to the other. The tragedy of the separation must have broken their hearts. It certainly did his.

I asked Michael if I was being fanciful in my interpretation of what had happened and his reply was quite revealing for humankind generally.

<u>What was Michael's answer?</u>

"The notion that beings of another kind are lacking in emotion may be seen as an indictment of those that hold such a belief.

All beings experience that which is around them and process their experiences. This is a necessary part of their sentience.

Although the emotions may not be identical, or have similar causes that evoke them, they are nonetheless an inextricable component of existence.

For those beings that share relationships in common, between whom there is a pre-existing agreement to share synergies within a lifetime, the correspondence of experience becomes more acute.

A dog that has, as part of its ascension pathway, such a co-existence will experience a very high level of overlap between those emotions that may be regarded as unique to their experience as a dog, and those which a human would undergo.

To deny that emotions exist in other beings is a fundamental misunderstanding of the true nature of the world around you.

Although scientists and those who study other beings go to considerable lengths to avoid any tendency to anthropomorphise in their assessment of the animal kingdom around them, their fear should instead be of failing to recognize those common elements that bind different species, their experience of emotions being first amongst them.

Within your understanding of the impacts of these emotions, you may correctly conclude that Tank died of a broken heart."

What was worse for us was the realisation that we could so easily have prevented these sad consequences. If only we had... But we both knew that it served no purpose to add recrimination to the tragedy.

In truth, Sweet Pea had by now stopped looking for her departed mate. Perhaps she knew he had gone. Perhaps she'd forgotten him. I doubted it, and instead accepted the more palatable belief that she'd decided to move on.

Right from the moment we first got Sweet Pea, little peccadilloes began to surface which demonstrated just what a character she is. After a matter of days, I have to confess that I tired of using two words to call her (isn't that lazy?) and abbreviated her name to Sweep, or Sweepy which, to my mind at least, only added to her persona! (If any readers have ever seen a British children's TV programme called 'Sootie and Sweep', you'll know exactly what I mean)

Physically, she was in as good a condition as could be expected from a dog that had endured the hardships she had been through. Although her coat was thick and luxurious, it was dry and brittle and her skin beneath suffered from major dryness that made it shed surface tissue like colossal chunks of grey dandruff. Her backbone, like Kitty's, was bony and obvious due to the depletion of muscle around her hindquarters. She had a tear out of one ear, obviously the result of a much earlier confrontation; but more disturbingly, the left side of her lower jaw was completely missing. Although it was almost too painful to think about, this too was likely to have been torn out in the most terrible of fights.

The consequences of this latter imperfection are simultaneously both sad and amusing. From the perspective of her appearance, Sweep seems to have an endearingly perpetual smile on her face, with her tongue almost constantly lolling out of the left side of her mouth. But this is simply because there is nothing to keep it in her mouth.

When she drinks, she drinks a whole bowl full of water. But for every drop of water that enters her mouth, ninety five percent of it finds its way onto the floor, literally cascading, waterfall-like, out of the gaping hole left by the missing jaw.

Food is restricted to what she can get down her with as little chewing as possible, since one whole side of her mouth is incapable of adding any value to the eating process. And the other is almost devoid of teeth. Nonetheless, she will still willingly tackle bones. When she has a meal of rice mixed with raw liver, kidneys and kelp (a favourite of hers), the rice shoots everywhere and the other dogs have a field day after she has left the scene as there's almost a second meal for them.

On the subject of food, Sweep is the only dog we have that telegraphs her desire to eat in the most physical way possible. If she's hungry, she sticks out her tongue! She has a most particular way of doing it and both

Sharon and I recognize the signal instantly. Needless to say, it laps out of the hole, upwards and outwards in a manner that is highly amusing and very obvious. Bring me food. Now!

When the food comes, she will never eat if you stand next to her. She eats lying down, basically because she's too unsteady on her feet to stand for too long, and will only commence eating once she is alone. Although the circumstances of her rescue suggest that the care she received was not as good as it might have been, this looks like the residue of a learned behaviour. If other dogs come near whilst she is eating, Sweep can produce a very menacing growl that sends them scurrying away, even though she would be absolutely incapable of following it up, and they must know it. I take this as another example of their respect for the elderly. It might also have something to do with what formidable dogs Malamutes can be when in their prime.

For the most part, Sweep tolerates the rest of the dogs without being integrated into the pack structure. We still believe that she would enjoy the company of one of her previous pack and still hope to get Pumpkin at some point in the future. However, time works against the Eight Above dogs. Sadly, two others apart from Tank have also passed since the rescue took place. On a happier note, Sweep has formed a friendship with Cinnda. Readers may remember her as our unwilling sled dog rescue who hates stairs. She still hates stairs but she likes Sweet Pea a lot. They hang out together almost all of the time and are content to lie very close to one another.

Sweep's most major peccadillo is that she seems to love music. From the moment she first walked in our house, she was attracted to the sound that came out of the almost perpetually playing iPod docking station that resides in our lounge. As you may imagine, we play music that assists in maintaining personal balance and although many would disparage this as 'spa music', we, and Sweep, love it.

255

Music is one of the most obvious examples of something which comes into existence as a result of vibration, since vibrations are precisely what music is comprised of.

The vibration of any piece of music impacts upon our own individual vibration. It can be harmonious with it, or it can have a jarring affect. This impact goes far beyond simple like and dislike. A piece that you love can potentially damage your vibration and one that you hate, enhance it. This is because the affect is both active and ambient.

If you fully understand the way this comes about, you can enhance your vibration and consequent state of mind on an on-going basis just by having the 'right' sort of music playing. You certainly can pick up 'good vibrations'!

Her favourite place to lie is next to the iPod where she soaks up the vibration and relaxes totally. We leave it on for her at night, although we did discover that if we accidentally forget to put on her favourites after playing something a little more upbeat earlier in the evening, she doesn't get nearly as much rest. Of particular interest to her are the works of Dan Gibson; but she also enjoys anything by Fridrik Karlsson, and is just starting to get into choral music too. And if you think I'm joking, think again!

All in all, Sweep now leads a very sedentary life and spends most of her time chilling and listening to the 'good vibrations'. As the rescuers discovered on that cold mountainside many months earlier, she adores attention and will not let you stop scratching her ears once you start. She isn't nearly as mobile as Kitty was. Her back legs are strong some days and she has a good wander around the grounds; but on others they are very weak and she does not stray too far. She has to wait for one of us to go to her for the attention she craves, but she waits patiently and is always grateful for whatever she gets. She is typical of the joy-filled bundle an older dog can be. And it goes without saying that she is adored by both of us, but Sharon especially. The funny thing is I'm not sure that Sharon would like a young Malamute; they can be quite a different kettle of fish. But perhaps caring for a crusty old geriatric Malamute is a form of preparation for dealing with me in a few years' time...

Me and Jenny at the Vancouver 'Body, Soul & Spirit' Expo selling crystals and copies of 'Some Dogs Are Angels' just after it was first printed.

Sales of the book were disappointing at the show, but on the way back, I collected Tasha... Or was it Duke?

Sharon offers her powerful energy healing to Ktuu who has 'pancaked' on the kitchen floor. She rallied almost immediately, but time was running out. Below is one of our most cherished photos of her.

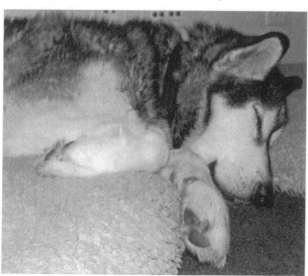

If you've never seen one before, here's what a newborn Huskberger looks like!

Not a picture of the mother fussing with her offspring, but Aunty Inara (left) and Grandma Lara (right) doing some babysitting three weeks after the birth. Aura was taking a desperately needed break from looking after these giants.

In 'Some Dogs' there's a great photo of all four Huskies lined up along the edge of the whelping box. It was impossible with this lot. Here are Belle, Hope and Brice at a mere three weeks old. They were nearly ready to come and go as they pleased.

Belle and Hope battle for dominance over a cuddly monkey, whilst Henry decides that discretion is the better part of valour, and watches from a distance.

As I posted on Facebook, probably to some people's consternation:
That's what I call a *nice* baby!
It's Brice who's enjoying the tummy rub.

Here are what we think of as before and after shots, showing the adorable puppies alongside the fabulous adults they became.

From the top: Henry, Hope, Belle Brice.

These two photos were taken during the 'Eight Above' rescue operation. Sweet Pea was initially muzzled because of fears of how the dogs would respond. When it became clear that she was gentle, she was led down the mountain unrestrained. In the right hand picture Sweet Pea is seen with the tragically fated Tank and a snowshoeing rescuer.

Me on the day I collected Sweet Pea at the US border.
This picture is always puzzling to me because she looks so much smaller than she actually is.

Sharon is immediately besotted with the crusty old Malamute. It's not surprising. She's a wonderful dog who has adapted very well, despite all of the anguish and heartache she must have experienced.

If only we'd have known then what we came to learn of later...

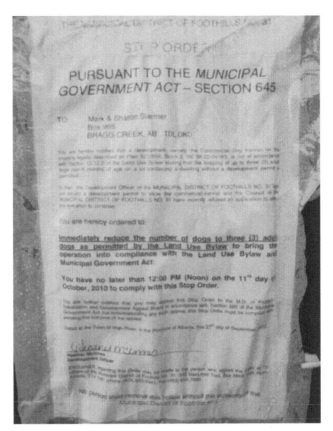

The piece of paper that changed all of our lives.

The way we were. Pure joy.

Channelling laid bare

OK. Let's be honest. She doesn't have to wait a few years. I'm crusty right now.

It has not escaped my attention that people expect that someone who is a channel will be of a certain type and that because I represent a gateway to beings in the etheric, that I must be in some way sainted. Oh dear me, no. Far from it. I'm always very uncomfortable when I hear that having read the book, people want to meet me, since I know that I will most likely disappoint and confound their expectations. It would be fair to say that Sharon is far more in conformation with who they imagine they will meet than I am.

Whilst many of the people who have approached me after reading 'Some Dogs' have simply wanted to share the stories of their dogs with me, there are a small number of individuals who have wanted to understand more about channelling; some have even asked me to teach them to channel. So in the interests of satisfying curiosity about it, here are a few explanations that address the most commonly asked questions. If this aspect of the story freaks you out, skip this chapter!

What is the difference between channelling and mediumship?

This seems to cause a lot of confusion.

Oversimplified, a channel does not 'do' dead people!

Better explained, both a medium and a channel connect with the etheric, but with different purposes and making different connections.
A channel's raison d'etre is to relay information from beings who are full time residents within the etheric, rather than those who are simply passing through it. A channel connects with angels and Ascended Masters.

A channel relays information regarding general aspects of our purpose and attempts to convey understanding of our place in all that is. This is of most benefit to old souls who are ready to receive such information.

Technically speaking, an Ascended Master IS a dead person, but since they have earned the right to proceed onward from a fourth dimensional state of being, they are no longer classified as such.

A *real* medium's purpose is to connect with the higher selves of those who are transitioning from one lifetime to the next and thus relay messages from them.

A *real* medium helps others recognize that there is more to their lives and deaths than they had previously realized by giving them proof of life after death. Although of value to anyone, this is of most benefit to mid-term souls since it can help them overcome dogmas relating to their understanding of the meaning and purpose of life.

Mediumship also tends to have a great appeal to old souls, since those in transition are able to relay information about the future. However, this information relates to *possible* futures and not absolutes.

A key difference between channelling and mediumship is the fact that full time beings of the etheric will not give information about the future because of the potential for the individual to then distort their freedom of choice to make a particular future happen or not happen.

Is channelling the same as being psychic?

Definitely not! Neither is being a *real* medium.

A psychic has the ability to receive those messages that emanate from another being by picking up on the vibrations of their thought waves. This is of course, telepathy.

True telepathic ability involves being able to receive and transmit. Everybody naturally transmits, whether they are conscious of it or not. Skill in telepathic communication requires sufficient awareness of the vibrations that fly around the ether and being able to control them i.e. receive when it is desired and transmit when it is desired. This ability is latent in ALL, but mastered by few.

A psychic has the ability to receive the thought vibrations of others, irrespective of their intentions to transmit them.

Some who pass themselves off as mediums can do no more than what is just described. When they are visited by clients seeking to connect with departed loved ones, the client's minds are full of thoughts of their dearly departed and thus, the vibrations that emanate from them are full of these thoughts, which are easy to pick up on. The so called 'medium' then relays aspects of what they receive (which is not coming from those in the etheric at all) which is usually enough to convince the client of the genuineness of the connection. This is better described as 'psychic mediumship'.

Often, the individual who has learned this form of mediumship genuinely believes that the connections are with departed. They do not seek to deceive or harm. But they are not *real* mediums.

Mediumship is an ability that is innate to a soul and is part of an individual's contract, often spanning multiple lifetimes and running in families.

All of what is written above would be endorsed by the World Council of Mediums, made up of those who are born with this 'gift' and not those who have learned it.

What is it like to channel?

Uncomfortable!

The actual physical act of full-body channelling involves a complete surrender of yourself to whichever being desires to be channelled. Although principally this involves the utilisation of the vocal chords, I have to be absent mentally too so as to avoid 'contaminating' the message by the intervention of my thoughts.

When I first started to channel, there was huge fear associated with doing this and it took me a long time to trust and a long time to leave! Now I can do it in seconds and I'm much more relaxed about it.

The uncomfortable bit is coming back as it's a bit like being shoved back into your own body. It's slightly giddying and disorientating. My mouth is usually very dry and my voice croaky. I can't see properly and if I look at people, I see them as their true selves. This means that they appear very bright (and actually quite painful to look at) and some change their appearance totally.

Another amusing but nevertheless uncomfortable aspect of channelling in public, is that when I do 'come back', the audience is often staring at me, the room is in silence, and there's a shocked air about the atmosphere. This is really embarrassing!

Relay channelling, which may be likened to simultaneous translation, is a lot easier physically. The only problem with it is that I am unable to blink as I'm doing it. At the end of an hour, my eyes are raw and painful. Wearing dark glasses helps, but I look a bit strange doing it that way!

What happens to you when you're channelling?

Once I leave my body, it's anybody's guess!

In recent months there has been a trend for me to be driving. It's totally vivid and just like the real thing, but I repeatedly drive the same section of road many times over and it really annoys me.

Sometimes, it's like being asleep and I come out of a channelling bright and refreshed.

Most often I view scenes related to the person I'm channelling for. I see them in silence as an observer, and seldom remember too much detail afterwards.

Who or what can be channelled?

As I've already mentioned, angels and Ascended Masters. But what constitutes an Ascended Master is something that can cause confusion.

It may be a natural conceit that humans may regard themselves as the only life form in the galaxy. In actual fact, there are more different types of being than we can conceive of.

On several occasions now I have channelled what we would think of as 'aliens' in public forum. The sessions, which were recorded and transferred to CD, are wild! The beings sound very different from humans and there is one in particular that is unbelievable to listen to as it basically speaks with a growl. When I listened to it afterwards, I tried to emulate its sound and had to give up after a few seconds as it was so painful. Yet the channelling had gone on for twenty minutes. I was awed that I could still speak after that session.

Before one of these sessions I was contacted by a lady who expressed her hope that I was only channelling 'good' aliens. I could write a whole chapter about how we choose to interpret the word 'good'. But what this lady had forgotten was that the beings I was channelling were all Ascended Masters, irrespective of where they'd come from.

Aren't you worried that you'll get 'interfered' with?

Readers of 'Some Dogs' will recall that Dougal's original purpose in coming to us was to prevent such things from happening as I was learning to channel. Interference is a real prospect for anyone channelling and some spiritual teachers are very negative about it as a result, giving their pupil's dire warnings about the consequences.

I would endorse this totally. The type of channelling that I do is not so much of a choice as a vocation. For this reason, I am no longer subject to concerns of this nature. But if it isn't a vocation, the individual who is attempting to channel is very vulnerable.

Why don't all channels say the same things in the same way?

The etheric has to communicate through the 'veil' of the individual who is the channel. The being that is channelled uses the channel as a temporary source for their own faculties, and therefore uses their language and their references to express their message. Inevitably, there is an 'overlay' of the channel's own interpretations of the being.

Therefore, one channel hosting Archangel Michael is unlikely to sound like another.

The messages themselves are always appropriate for the group to whom they are delivered. People are drawn (angels will make sure they get there!) to a particular channel whose message they are 'meant' to hear, or a channel who will deliver the message in a way that is palatable for them.

However, this is not always the case. Sometimes people will come to a channelling out of idle curiosity, and are often horrified at what they find, particularly if they have expectations of what channelling should be.

Many seem to expect a very reverent person who speaks softly and in hushed tones, dresses in flowing clothes, has an ethereal quality about them, inspires awe and might float away at any moment.

As I've already made clear, this is definitely NOT me.

I understand why people need/want/like those qualities in a channel, but frankly, in my experience the beings of the etheric aren't that way. They are practical, down to earth and often 'in-your-face'. If that's what comes across from my channellings, I'm happy.

How much of a channelling do you remember?

If I'm full body channelling, next to nothing. My recollection is usually limited to the pictures I've been shown.

If I'm relaying, I recall fragments, and again, I see scenes related to the channelling. These can be incredibly vivid and it's like being there.

What do other people perceive as you are channelling?

It varies enormously from person to person.

Some can actually see the beings I am channelling, usually behind me and much larger than me.

Some see lights around the room.

Some experience temperature rises.

Some see me physically transform during the channelling.

Some notice that my eyes are very different after a channelling.

Some see nothing at all.

The only truly common feature is that people only ever seem to hear about thirty percent of a channelling. This is why we record them and make CDs. It is a general feature that people find the sessions somewhat overwhelming.

None of the experiences are ever reported as unsettling. In fact, they're quite the opposite.

How can you prove who it is you're speaking to?

I can't.

Neither do they seem to be interested in proving who they are. If you ask an angel for proof of who they are, they'll tell you straight that your belief is not their concern. You may choose to accept their presence and their message or not.

Those Masters who are 'well known' are often concerned to correct misconceptions that we have about them. Angels are also interested in correcting our misinterpretation of them and their roles.

I've had a session with another channel. Is what they told me true?

I HATE being asked this question, but I do get asked it a lot.

It calls into query the veracity of messages and therefore the channel themselves.

Frankly, I have come across those who seem more concerned with telling an individual what they want to hear rather than relaying the truths that may be offered by the etheric. When I ask Michael about this, his answer is usually something along the lines of: "What an individual hears at any moment may be what they wanted to hear".

How do you get to be a channel?

If you are destined to be a channel, it is an inescapable feature of your life. No matter how you fight it, it will find you.

Some are only channels for one being in the etheric, usually because they have some form of special relationship with them.

An open channel is available to pass on messages from any being in the etheric.

Channels are pretty much born, not made.

I believe that I already channel. Do I?

This is the number one most common question.

There's channelling, and there's channelling...

Everyone absolutely *had* the ability to channel their higher selves. We are born with the ability to do so, but lose it (often very early on) as we grow up.

It may be thought of as a communication link that gets broken; but one that may be re-established later in life if we are willing to develop that link.

Meditation as a practice came about simply so as to enhance our ability to re-create and utilise that link. That was its purpose, however it may now be 'sold'.

Once the link is re-established, vast amounts of wisdom may be accessed from the higher self, and it is certainly possible to connect with the higher selves of others too.

If the personal vibration is raised high enough, communication with angels and masters is possible.

But to answer the question directly: It varies greatly from person to person.

What I will say is that unfortunately, many who believe that angels are communicating with them may not even have reached their higher selves, and instead have connected with the first and easiest thing that we hear. The ego.

Often this stems from desperation on the part of the individual to make the connection they know is possible. But the ego can be very misleading and allows us to believe that we are in touch with the etheric, and it must be overcome to establish a true link.

Then, between the ego and the etheric comes the ether, which is full of vibrations and thoughts that can all too easily be mistaken for channelling angels.

To tell a person that they're not actually channelling in the way that they would like to is difficult because a negative response from me will simultaneously defy both their expectations and their desires. Unfortunately, on occasion the reaction from them is somewhat unpleasant and involves a denial of my ability to discern their true ability. When faced with this, I wonder why, if the person doesn't believe what I can tell them, did they bother to ask me in the first place?

It's much easier to keep quiet when asked this one. It causes way too much grief.

Can you teach me to channel?

No.

I have no idea what it takes to be a channel or how I learned to be one. In fact, I don't think I did; it seems to have been in me all along and was kind of 'brought out' by the beings of the etheric referred to in 'Some Dogs' who were instrumental in getting me to the point where I could let go.

After 'Some Dogs' came out, I received a letter from a person requesting that I teach them to channel. They explained that they had studied mediumship with a well-known figure in the New Age world that they admired and respected greatly. However, this person actively discouraged channelling ("as she believes that it can be dangerous to allow any being to use any part of your body for any purpose") so could not help my correspondent fulfill this desire.

I replied that I was unable to assist, if only because I didn't know how to teach somebody to do something that I don't know how I do!

I received a very rude and damning response, accusing me of basing my answer on ego and not wanting to share my 'gift' with others.

In my considerably more polite rejoinder, I pointed out that all I was doing was endorsing what her greatly admired and respected teacher had already stated. Funnily enough, she had no retort for that one.

As I've said, if you are meant to channel in the way that I do, it's coming to you as surely as an unstoppable train and you don't need me to assist you at all.

And by the way, if you want to be a channel, I think you're crazy! Do you want your life messed up and your faculties played with? Read biographies of people like Madame Blavatsky and Edgar Cayce, and you'll think twice about it. Can you see the running theme when you look at what's happened to our lives! Being a channel is a vocation that some were dumb enough to commit to. Don't wish it on yourself; it's not nearly as cool and sexy as you think it is.

Most certainly, try to develop your communication with your higher self in whatever way works for you. That's a really good and useful thing to do. If you're meant to be a messenger for the etheric, your service contract will catch up with you when it's meant to.

Finally, there's one thing I'd like to make very clear. Being a channel does not make you in any way special or better than anyone else, wiser than anyone else, or more advanced than anyone else. It's just something you agreed to do in some other place. And that goes for me too. If anyone expects any more of me, they'll be disappointed!

On with the story!

On the other side of the fence

Of Timba and Lara's puppies, Zoe, to my mind, is by far and away the cutest. I remember her birth well because it was a difficult one for Lara. She was unable to bite through the foetal sack and so I assisted. She didn't seem to breathe for the first few seconds, but was quickly licked to life by Lara. I also happened to have the camera right by me and so was able to photograph her straight away.

Her manner in dealing with the other dogs is not so polite and she can hold her own in the rough and tumble games that they all play. On occasion, the others gang up on her, perhaps because she is the smallest of the Huskies, but she has a hiding place that only she can get into underneath the front porch.

In common with her siblings, she has experienced the freedom outside of the compound, but came back very quickly and has never shown signs of wanting to get out since that time. In fact, she actually fights shy of being taken out hiking, preferring to get her exercise racing around the outer perimeter, chasing her sisters.

However, she is the only one of our pack (that we know of) who seems to have established relationships with animals that live outside the compound. And I don't mean domestic ones!

It is pretty standard behaviour for the majority of our dogs to get very excited and protective if there are any wild animals that come calling, which has the advantage of being a very powerful deterrent for coyotes and (sensible) cougars. Our land outside of the fence line bears evidence of regular visits from animals great and small, with well-worn tracks and scats clearly demonstrating that they are wary of coming too close.

Most either know, or have learned to steer clear of the fence line, but on the odd occasion when one decides to come take a closer look at what's going on inside, the dogs feel it is their duty to hurry them on their way. I'm quite sure that we would have many more coming to visit with us at close proximity were it not for the abundance of canines, but maybe it's not such a bad thing that this isn't the case. The previous owner of the house had a photograph of a black bear looking in through the glass window of the kitchen door!

So it was a great surprise to me when, a few weeks ago now, I discovered that not all wild creatures are *that* wary of what lurks within.

For several nights Zoe had been going outside mid-evening and not returning. Normally at this time, all of the other dogs are sprawled across the beds in the basement, to which we retire after our dinner and theirs. We had thought nothing of it, but I was becoming increasingly irritated by the fact that when the others went out for their final washroom visit before bed, she did not come back in with them. Instead, I would have to go and find her, walking around the fence line, flashlight in hand, in an effort to stumble upon her. Searching two acres of undulating and dense forest in darkness can be a very difficult thing to do. However, usually she was to be found at some point next to the fence, on the perimeter. It just seemed to be my luck that if I began to search for her at a particular point, I would ultimately discover her only a few metres from where I'd started, having circumnavigated the fence line in the wrong direction!

She seemed to have no favourite spot and there seemed to be no rhyme or reason behind where I might find her. Then again, on some nights she just didn't want to go out at all.

There came an evening where she was crashed out and sleeping peacefully like the others, when suddenly and for no apparent reason, she leapt up, whimpering and desperate to go out. Assuming an upset stomach, I rushed to let her out and she disappeared into the night.

A little while later I had gone upstairs to get a drink and remembered that Zoe was still outside. It was a beautiful clear evening so I decided I would go and have a look at the stars. I went out without turning the outside lights on so as to avoid light pollution. Enjoying the starlight filled darkness, I had been staring upwards for several minutes and my eyes had become quite accustomed to the darkness, when I heard a commotion coming from the fence line. I moved towards it and was amused to see Zoe running at breakneck speed along the perimeter. She got to a certain point, did a 'play bow' and then raced back the way she had come before repeating the process again. I watched her do this for a while, wondering why on earth she was behaving in this way but assuming it was one of her mad moments. Suddenly I saw a flash of movement and caught a glimpse of something beyond the fence that was obviously the object of her attentions.

My first thought was that it was a coyote trying to lure her out, so I moved towards where the chase was taking place. As I did so, I triggered the sensor of a motion activated outside light and the scene was bathed in near daylight. There I saw, nose to nose with Zoe, a red fox.

Dazzled by the light, the fox made the briefest of retreats, and then careless to any potential danger, restarted the game. Off they raced together, backwards and forwards, but now moving away from the lit up area. In the darkness I could hear them running and crashing through the undergrowth, permanently separated by seven feet of high tensile plastic and wire, but nonetheless, clearly enjoying a cross species friendship.

This strange relationship has continued for months now. It became bitter sweet to observe when on one occasion, Zoe became very excited in the house and made it obvious that she wanted Lara to come outside with her. This behaviour was so unusual that I followed the two of them and watched as, in the twilight, Zoe led her mother down to the fence line, repeatedly looking back to ensure that she followed. It took only a few moments before her foxy beau appeared, and I watched in awe as Lara sniffed him through the wire, clearly being introduced to her daughter's boyfriend for the first time! But rather than showing the interest one might have anticipated, Lara turned tail and bounded back up to the house without so much as a backward glance. A rather crestfallen Zoe was left watching after her. Her lovely face is so expressive that I was sure I could see traces of sadness. Mother did not approve!

By itself, perhaps this is not so strange. However, just three evenings ago as I write this, Zoe had again made her mid-evening exit. We assumed that her fox boyfriend was out there waiting for her in the gloaming. Unusually for that time of night, Sharon and I were on the main floor and I had just finished channelling an Ascended Master for Sharon. Looking over my shoulder, her eye was caught by movement near the front gate (which can just be seen in the distance from our lounge). Zoe was running backwards and forwards along the fence line and Sharon was a little bit alarmed that someone appeared to be standing there. When you live in the middle of nowhere as we do, this is a somewhat surprising occurrence; so I was dispatched to see what was going on.

I could see nothing and no one; but Tristan, who was outside taking a stroll, whispered to me that there was a moose near the front gate. What Sharon had seen and mistaken for a person's legs were actually the front legs of the moose that was peering through the fence, with Zoe parading in front of her. It was largely in darkness, hidden by the density of the trees in this area, but you could just make it out. Just then Zoe decided to go to the front gate, which is in an open area where there is enough light to see clearly.

To my delight, the moose followed her out and stood on the other side of the gateway, staring down at the dog which, in comparison with her colossal size, appeared miniscule. The top of her head was well over seven feet tall but she repeatedly lowered it to the ground next to the fence, trying to sniff Zoe. Every time her head went down, Zoe would jump backwards; then when she lifted it again, Zoe would rush up to the gate once more. After a few moments had passed, the moose looked to her right, and out of the trees, as if given the OK to do so, two calves emerged. Then all three began the game of trying to sniff the petite Husky. The calves themselves stood over five feet tall and the dipping heads of mother and children was quite something to behold.

Both Sharon (who had now joined us) and I love moose. We stop the car when we see them and never tire of watching their extraordinary laid back gait. They are awkward and graceful at the same time and we find their oddly angular features quite beautiful. So it was enormously thrilling to see this threesome.

As we watched, awestruck, I remembered Scott's dire warnings about how protective moose can be of their calves. Despite being on the other side of the gate, I wondered if they posed any threat to Zoe? I quickly dismissed the idea. If anything, they were being extraordinarily considerate in their attempts to connect with her. There was absolutely no sign of aggression whatsoever. It was as if they wanted to make some form of connection with her. It was Zoe herself who was concerned, and not them. Clearly they could see that she presented no threat.

Somewhat emboldened, Sharon and I made our way down to the gate. The moose were not in the slightest bit concerned and were far too interested in the dog to worry about us. So there we stood, six feet away from these huge and powerful creatures, foolishly relying upon high tensile plastic to protect us, but in reality, at no risk whatsoever. They exuded calm and gentle energy and seemed perfectly content.

After a few minutes, Zoe's concern got the better of her and she bolted away. The moose watched her go as if disappointed that she was too intimidated to take the friendship they offered. They turned their attentions to the young trees growing to the side of the gate and began to munch on them. Sharon and I remained with them for a further ten minutes before the mother decided that it was time to move on.

A few days later the family returned, this time at the back of our property. Zoe was indoors but many of the others, including Kachina, raced down to inspect them. Rather than bark or attempt to intimidate them, the dogs sat in a row and just looked at them, seemingly transfixed. The moose in return paid no attention to them whatsoever, despite the fact that they were literally inches away. Instead they kept lifting their heads and looking towards the house. Was I being fanciful in thinking that they were hoping that Zoe would come out?

In observation of these incidents, I was offered what I found to be magical experiences. On each occasion, some form of communication seemed to be taking place between our avatar and these wild creatures. I wonder what Zoe made of them? And I am also left wondering why they both involved Zoe?

In The Great Outdoors

If nothing else, Zoe's chase games with her foxy beau provide her with more than her usual level of exercise. Not that she needs it. We are often asked how we manage to walk twenty five dogs. It's easy to see why people find the idea of taking so many for a hike so daunting, when fitting in a daily outing for one dog can be a challenge in the lives of busy people. Fortunately, the amplitudes of the compound provide endless opportunities for carefree gameplay for the dogs and they regularly run themselves ragged. If you've ever taken your pet to a dog park and watched the canine interaction for half an hour or so, you will know how energetic their play can be. Now imagine that the dog park is outside your front door and you haven't taken your pet there for a half hour treat: it actually lives in the dog park. That's our home. All we have to do is open a door and the wild fun begins.

The only restrictions we place upon the dogs relates to noise. For the most part, they play almost soundlessly. Only Poppy has the inclination to disrupt the peace, barking when she feels that the others boisterousness is getting out of hand. If she starts, we are outside as quick as flash to ensure that peace is restored, although unfortunately for Poppy, this usually results in her retiring to the basement with one of us. Of course this does not stop her from doing her amazing psychic dog tricks and barking indoors to let us know what's happening outside!

Not all of the dogs are willing or able to participate in the frivolity. Some, like Kaiti, are too old to do much more than take a sedate stroll around the grounds, which they prefer to do when the younger ones are indoors. Others, like Indy, simply don't 'do' play. He has mastered the art of casually ambling around with an air of aloofness, often followed by the other members of what we refer to as the 'Big Dog Club'. This consists of a very select clique (Kachina, Poppy and lately, Sienna) who like to hang out with Indy; or to be more precise, are Indy's 'hangers on'. Perhaps it's strength by association or some dog reasoning unbeknownst to us that causes them to follow his every footstep. They form a line behind him and go wherever he goes, always in the same order: Indy, Kachina, Poppy, Sienna. Eventually he tires of them dogging his footsteps (sorry!) and will turn and chase them away. Then after a few minutes more, they'll start following again. When he is outside with them, Kachina and Poppy will not play together, almost as if they have to maintain some semblance of dignity whilst in his presence. If he goes indoors however, the madness begins.

When we do guided hikes to Archangel Michael's etheric retreat, or Earth Healing hikes, participants always seem to appreciate the presence of the dogs so we bring several along.

What's an Earth Healing hike?

We'd already been doing guided hikes and crystal planting for over a year when Archangel Michael requested that we do an Earth Healing hike, at which I would be channelling Archangel Sandalphon. We made the assumption that its purpose would be as the name suggested. We would somehow be doing something that assisted in some form of planetary healing. Not so.

As we were to discover, the healing referred to the participants receiving healing energies from the earth and not vice versa!

It is most often the case that on these occasions, we take a mixture of Avatars and non-avatars. The dogs love meeting new people and the people benefit from the dog's energies. They particularly like to walk them, so responsibility for handling the dogs that day falls to individuals who sometimes vie for who will have what dog. Rotas are often necessary. I'm sure some people come back just to see the dogs again.

With so many dogs to choose from to bring with us, we can pretty much guarantee to introduce our guests to new animals on each occasion. However, in reality, there are some dogs that don't actually want to come hiking, even though they are well are capable of doing so. If this seems strange, consider that for the rescue dogs, our home offers a safe and secure haven in which they have found their first peace of mind. By contrast, the outside world may represent a place of fear, hardship and suffering. On many occasions we have tried to coax some of the more damaged dogs to leave with us, only to lose our resolve when we see

278

the anguish (or in some cases, raw terror) in their eyes. They are content to stay.

Consequently, we pick from a relatively short list. This always includes Huskies, but despite having nine of them, only Lara, Timba and Tasha, (who positively insist on attending every hike possible) join us. Cinnda and Sienna, both of whom have previously come on hikes with us, now hate to leave the compound and refuse to get in the car. Lara and Timba's puppies run away from the car if you try to put them in, perhaps associating the ride with trips to the vet clinic, injections and invasive thermometers. Their lack of enthusiasm is not such a bad thing as hiking with Huskies can be a nightmare. Being sled dogs, they are inclined to pull like mad things. This is great when you're going uphill, but on relatively flat ground, or particularly downhill, this is not good news. They can hike for a whole day, ascend three thousand feet up a mountain, cope with a difficult scree section, find themselves forced to jump amongst rocks that are almost too much of a challenge for humans, and still be ready at the end of the day to start all over again. Their energy is boundless and they are hard work for whoever holds the leash. So if you're wondering why we haven't trained them not to pull, the answer is simple: six of them are either at, or just coming up to the age at which they will be able to (safely) pull a sled, and we don't want to discourage their natural instincts.

On guided hikes, Indy is a great favourite. Although he can be quite stand-offish at first, everyone seems to love to meet him. Perhaps this is because of his cover-dog status, having adorned the front of "Some Dogs', or perhaps it's because he's a generally majestic and awesome creature. Most are quite disappointed that you don't really need to walk Indy. He prefers to stay in close proximity to me on a hike and since I'm usually at the front and he never runs away, he's seldom on a leash unless it's strictly necessary. Sharon is usually making up the rear, and so every few minutes, he will dash to the back of the group to make sure that she's alright, and then come charging back to me. This can sometimes involve a return trip of a quarter of a mile or more if the group is spread out. His hikes are always a lot longer than ours.

That leaves the Huskies for others to lead, or rather, be led by. Many an unwitting volunteer has enthusiastically offered to have a Husky with them during a hike, and later wished that they hadn't. In fact, to date only one individual has been able to fully cope and even apparently relish the challenge they present.

On one hike to the Plain of Six Glaciers, we were joined by a fairly large group that included a previous hiker who had returned with two lady friends. As introductions were being made in the parking lot before we set off, I very briefly made the acquaintance of a lively and enthusiastic individual called Tracey. Getting ready for the numerous channellings that occupy my time during the day, I like to begin the day as we walk around the edge of Lake Louise by myself; or at least with only a dog for company. So I set a furious pace that most can't quite keep up with, and by the time the far end of the azure waters are reached, I'm usually good to go with relaying whatever the etheric desires for that day.

It was therefore quite surprising to me that on this particular day, despite employing my best rapid walking techniques, and even having Timba with me to make things even easier, Tracey was able to remain right next to me as if it were just a Sunday afternoon stroll. And what was more, she was able to talk almost non-stop, without needing to pause for breath, asking endless questions about the dogs with which she was obviously fascinated.

When we reached the end of the lake (which that day was in record time), Tracey asked if she could take Timba. "Sure" I replied, happily surrendering over the leash before I turned my attentions to the rest of the group, who were just beginning to arrive. Timba would surely provide a more able distraction for her than I. But she wasn't done yet. "Is it OK if I run with him?" she queried. "If you want to" I said, a little warily. I knew that the Husky was on finest pulling form today. If my pace couldn't wear her out, he surely would. So off they went.

The ascent from the Lake to the Plain is considerably harder than the preamble and depending upon the overall fitness level of the group and the number of etheric interventions that go on, it can take some considerable time to arrive at. For me, it can get a little exhausting since I am usually talking almost non-stop. I walk, in turn, with each individual member of the group, relaying messages and answers for them. As we climbed, today was no different. But every time we would reconnect with the group as a whole in order to change message recipient, Tracey would be notable by her absence. Finally, concern prompted me to ask if anyone had seen her and I was surprised to learn that everyone else had seen lots of her. Apparently she was running backwards and forwards, up and down the difficult and (reasonably) steep trail, with Timba, having a whale of a time!

Eventually, when I finally caught up with my delinquent dog and his surrogate mistress, they were taking a brief rest at the tea shop near the Plain, both looking as happy as could be and not in the least bit tired. As the day wore on, the pattern continued. Tracey could occasionally be seen in the distance, galloping off with Timba gallivanting alongside. And when, at the end of the day and after around nine hours of being in the outdoors, I found them back in the parking lot, they both seemed ready to do it all again.

Who we meet, when we meet and how we meet them can often seem to be the most casual of events. At the time, I thought very little of our meeting with Tracey. Later, she bought many copies of 'Some Dogs' as gifts for others, clearly loved the dogs and signed up to take the Balance Class. Often she would hint that she'd like to come round and meet the rest of the pack, but we kept her at arm's length. Michael had some interesting feedback on the nature of our relationships generally.

What was Michael's feedback on relationships?

On many occasions we had received feedback and guidance from the etheric regarding the implications of one beings' ability to affect the vibration of another. Principally this had come about as a result of the fact that prior to the publication of 'Some Dogs' (when I had first begun my 'public' channelling career) we had some experience of finding those who sought us out ultimately being damaging in their intentions. We had developed circumspection about entangling our energies with those of others too readily.

We had even sought Michael's advice in specific instances and been advised to have no further dealings with particular individuals.

Tracey was so insistent in her desire to be friends with us that we asked for guidance and Michael explained that the energies of all individuals are in a constant state of flux. Their compatibility with our own may not be in one point in time what they are in the next. Thus our reservations about the nature of her connection with us were justified.

He then went on to begin a description of the way in which our lives affect one another's, that would continue evolving in the intricacy of the explanation for over a year. Here's the basic version.

The interactions between beings are like the movements of cogwheels whose tines have the ability to propel one another forward. They may also jam and seize up, causing us to falter in our progress. Sometimes, the separation of tines causes fractures or breaks within the tines that may seemingly affect the motion of the whole cogwheel, although this is in fact an illusion. If we do not move forward as a result of the encounter with one cog, another will come into play but we may halt our own progress through not detaching from an unmoving cog. Sometimes we journey through a whole lifetime being constantly moved by certain cogs, whilst other cogs that could or should benefit our propulsion do not connect with us due to their own movements. Although they are the same size, different cogs may be thought of as greater or smaller depending upon the ways in which they will propel us forward. Some are therefore minor and relatively insignificant (though nonetheless providing propulsion needed in the moment); others are almost inconceivable in the impact they create.

The whole imagery for this process should be seen as a three dimensional model, the cogs being spherical rather than flat and the tines too numerous to mention.

Michael made it clear to us that Tracey was a powerful cog within our lives but from the perspective of what was to come, not in the moment.

At this point we had no concept of the fact that Tracey was destined to become one of our pack's greatest and unfailing supporters, and in many respects, our saviour.

Timba may have met his human match but the wilderness could still throw him a curved ball. When we go out to do crystal planting hikes, we always take avatars with us out of necessity, since they are an essential part of the process. As the earlier story about Kachina's escapade illustrates, these can sometimes take interesting turns but misadventures seem only to occur when non-avatars are involved.

On another occasion we had done a rather unusual 'planting' that involved hurling a beautiful piece of clear quartz into the middle of a lake. This was the first time we had been asked to do such a thing and when I queried it, Michael explained that the effect of this strange interment would be upon the whole of the watercourse, infusing it with a positive vibration. So doing as we were instructed, I flung the crystal as far out towards the centre of the lake as I could. What followed amazed us. The resulting impact as the crystal hit the water did not form the concentric rings one would normally expect to see. Instead, a raised line approximately thirty feet across spread out from the point of its entry, remaining visible for around forty seconds before disappearing. Whilst we reflected upon this physical impossibility, Michael suggested that we take some of the water in one of our empty containers, which I duly did.

On our return to the car, several hours hike away, I led the field as usual, being dragged along by the endlessly energetic Timba. At one point, suddenly and without warning, he leapt forward and with lightning speed, pounced upon something that his very finely honed prey instincts had detected moving. He closed his strong jaws over whatever it was and it was instantly no more. Unfortunately, he had leapt before he'd looked and what he had bitten into was a very large toad. The poor creature lay dead but it had already wrought its revenge upon its murderer. Timba's mouth immediately began to foam and froth streamed from all sides. As the poison from the glands on the toad's back took hold, he began to wretch and stagger uncontrollably, evidently going blind and experiencing great pain. Hideous strangulated sounds came from his mouth and I was certain that he was dying. I had read about incidences of this nature on the internet and knew that dogs could die if they bit toads, depending upon the type of amphibian and the amount of poison ingested.

I was helpless. There was nothing I could do or administer and we were still at least an hour from the car and two more from any vet. I was in a state of considerable panic as he was getting worse by the second. Michael however, was quite calm (and quite loud!). "Give him the water from the lake."

I wrestled to get the container out of my back pack, only remembering that it was there when he mentioned it. I pinned Timba down easily as he was now so weak and flushed out his mouth, clearing away the odious foam. Then I poured the rest of the infused water down his throat.

The effect was instantaneous. As soon as I released him, Timba jumped up, steady as a rock. He shook his head and looked around him, seeing again for the first time in a few minutes, and adopted his usual grinning expression, evidently eager to go on and acting as if nothing had happened. He was totally cured!

As we continued our journey, I offered thanks that Timba was still alive. Although I remonstrated with him for his foolishness, the experience did not stop the silly ass from trying to do exactly the same thing with something else unseen a mere five minutes later. Fortunately this time I was ready for him.

Hearing The Worst

The day before the hearing for our kennel licence application was due to be held, both Sharon and I felt confident about our likely success. We knew that our dogs caused no problems as far as noise went and that the incident that had caused the complaint had been an isolated one, never repeated.

We knew that the original complainant would object, but we also knew that the Council would take a broader view of the situation. From a certain perspective, anyone rehoming dogs alleviates some of the financial burden upon locally funded shelters. It made no sense to shut us down when potentially, that would mean that the MD themselves could then become responsible for twenty two dogs.

Even when, by way of preparing us, the MD forwarded the objections raised by the complainant, we were not too concerned as it read something like a mad list. The objections are filed and available for viewing as a matter of public record in the MD archives but I have recorded them verbatim for your interest, and possibly amusement. They included the following assertions:

"For approximately a year and a half we have been faced with incessant barking/pack howling day and night to the point where we have not been able to enjoy quiet time on the deck or in the yard. It has been impossible to sleep with windows open unless we resort to the use of ear plugs."

This sentence expressed what might have been the heart of any real problem, if there was one. In point of fact, it was a rather ridiculous fabrication. If this were even vaguely true, why had they waited until the biker incident to complain? Surely other neighbours would have complained? And how on earth could we as the owners of these reprobate animals possibly sleep? Their property was a long way from ours so if they couldn't sleep without ear plugs, we must both be deaf! By the time this was written, all of our dogs were sleeping indoors and even Kachina, whilst outside, was utterly silent. It was nonsense to say that they could be disturbing anyone apart from us, and we slept very well thank you!

If there was incessant barking, we'd have been the ones complaining! We too liked to enjoy our deck and didn't appreciate noisy dogs. Ever since we had arrived, we had gone to extraordinary lengths to ensure that if any of our dogs started barking, they were rapidly quieted. At the first sound of a dog barking, one of us would rush outside and "sshh" them, and bring the offender inside.

What we are aware of is that we live in an area where there is a large coyote population. They certainly howl, sometimes all night long, in an unearthly but rather beautiful way. There are also, as Zoe's story illustrates, foxes and they do bark just like dogs. There are also neighbours who *do* keep their dogs outside, and they can occasionally be heard barking at night, probably at the coyotes! We can attest to the fact that even sleeping with the windows wide open, as we do in summer, it is not a problem because everyone lives too far from each other for it to be an issue.

The other thing about the area in which we live is that it's all dense forest. The origin of any sound can be a confusing thing because of the interference the trees create.

If there was any element of reality in this aspect of the complaint, there was one thing we were absolutely sure of. Whatever was disturbing the neighbours wasn't coming from our house.

"He doesn't appear to have a proper facility to shelter these dogs except for his house and garage."

True! Is a house an improper shelter for a dog? Clearly they thought that a garage *was* a proper shelter. We certainly don't. None of our dogs has ever been left in the garage.

"We know that the Applicant has boasted to others in the area of housing up to nineteen dogs combined with a breeding operation."

Well neighbours, I wrote a book about it, but I certainly don't 'boast' about it! But doesn't that in itself illustrate that we weren't trying to hide anything? As far as we were aware, we weren't doing anything wrong.

And where does the 'breeding operation' come from? This is what you call the activities of those who breed dogs for sale and profit. We've never sold or even given away a dog.

"...the applicant was away for the long weekend and had left his children to care for the dogs. A cougar attacked the dogs and apparently one was almost killed. How can this be a safe, responsible care and rescue facility if the dogs lives are in jeopardy of predators in the area? Cougars are common in our area and will be more enticed to visit with an increased dog population."

Some silly and major factual inaccuracies: The cougar incident happened months before the dogs barking at the bikers. The two were utterly unconnected. (By now it was becoming clear that they were spouting nonsense based on hearsay from a source we had not yet discovered.)

Potentially, any dog in a forested rural area is at risk from predators, particularly coyotes and cougars. We have heard many local stories about people having their dogs taken by both. However, as anybody who is knowledgeable about wildlife will tell you, predators are discouraged when they smell anything that may present a threat to them. We have been told on several occasions by individuals involved in wildlife and game occupations that the sheer number of dogs we have would be a massive deterrent to predators. They would, apparently, give our house and compound a wide berth since the dogs all scent the perimeter. In all likelihood, our property would be a deterrent to predators, not just for us but for the whole area. In fact, since we arrived, there had been no reports of pet deaths within a considerable distance of our property. Indeed there was some incredulity from these same wildlife experts regarding Kachina's altercation with the cougar, because it had been stupid enough to come inside the compound. (This contributed to the conclusion that it was an inexperienced youngster.) And of course Kachina, the *only* 'dog' involved, had not *'almost been killed'* at all.

"On two occasions we witnessed high bred Husky dogs running through our property… It appeared to us dogs could be escaping from the Applicant's property because soon after the incidents, the fence on the applicants property was raised. And please note, the fence appears to be temporary construction fencing."

We had to laugh at this one for several reasons. Firstly, we couldn't understand what a *'high bred Husky'* was! Was that a pure bred Husky, or a hybrid Husky? And in either case, what was the significance? Thereafter, we have always referred to them as our 'high bred Huskies' and it still makes us smile.

The second reason was the notion that we had 'raised' the fence after an escape. As readers of Some Dogs will recall, the fence was put up before the dogs ever even arrived here. Or did they mean we increased the height of the fence? And if so, how did we manage that? It had always been seven feet tall and never heightened. I also wondered how Benners, the manufacturer of our seven and a half thousand dollar, high tensile wire, invisible from fifteen feet away, very high quality deer fence, would feel about their product being described as temporary construction fencing?

"After discussion with our neighbours, we are very concerned about the conditions that the Applicant's children are living in and the health of the Applicant's dogs. Nineteen dogs is a lot of dogs to be housed in a home with children. Which raises questions as to how animal waste from nineteen dogs has been handled to date! An unclean environment can result in disease, parasites, smell and out of control rodents."

Hmmm. Interesting. Was this a suggestion that we weren't looking after our children? Did they realize that the comment was borderline defamatory and would allow us the right to sue them? This aspect aside, we wondered how many dogs could a child live with? Did they think this would be a bad thing? Had they spoken with Jenny or Tristan? What had the neighbours been telling them and who were they? Only Scott and Shannon amongst our neighbours had ever been invited into our home. They loathed these people for registering the complaint in the first place, but even if they had ever spoken to them, they would certainly have told them that both of our children were very happy living with so many dogs and that Jenny, now at university, relished her vacations for the opportunity they provided to be surrounded by them all again.

If we look at the seemingly rational complaints: Clearly they didn't know that if you feed dogs the bones and raw food diet, their waste has almost no smell, dries to chalk in a couple of hours and disintegrates to dust in days. It's one of the major benefits of the diet (from a human perspective!) and almost all our dogs eat it. Those that don't have their deposits dealt with as any dog owner deals with them. Did they really think that the dogs could produce enough waste to create a smell in the neighbourhood? Or was that just their kindly concern for the children?

We wondered how on earth we were still alive with all these diseases and parasites that our dogs must create. And as for the rodents... Were they not aware that dogs are just about the greatest deterrent to rodents there are; even more so than cats? Oh, and by the way, Alberta is known for being pretty much rat free.

The remainder was a series of statements about how we would single-handedly affect land values in the area, put off prospective purchasers and *'depreciate what we have worked toward building equity in'*. Then they made comments regarding the name of our house and its inappropriateness and asserted that granting us a licence would increase highway traffic, which *'could be a potential concern for traffic accidents'*.

Then they wrote what perhaps they had assumed would be their coup de gras in swaying the minds of the council members.

"We would also respectfully request that an inspection of the premises be conducted to determine what kind of conditions the Applicant's children are living in".

Up until this point, I had accepted their right to their beliefs and even their speculations. I had understood why someone would object, if one half of the assertions made in the document had been true; I 'got it' that ridiculous distortions of the truth were their attempt to get their way; I even imagined that they might believe these falsehoods. This however, was beyond the pale and moved them into the libellous category.

Our indignation was interrupted by another email from the MD. There was a second objection, and this time we were caught off balance. It was from the neighbour opposite Scott and Shannon's who we had dined with who shared the boundary with the complainant. Clearly, he was not only the source of the hearsay that had been relied upon, but had been utterly two faced in his previous contacts with us. So much for their being enthusiastic about what we did. His objection was relatively brief, and basically stated the following.

"I am very concerned about the increase in barking/howling that will come from this commercial operation if the applicant is allowed to 'legalize' the keeping of a large number of dogs. As it stands there is an inordinate amount of barking that does come from this property."

He went on to express, in several paragraphs, his concerns about having a second commercial kennel in the area. He made reference to this kennel saying that *"the noise from this operation makes it less than enjoyable..."* This was understandable, since they are practically next door to his property. But he also made the curious comment:

"I have serious concerns about the motive of the applicants to start a commercial kennel. As there are already a large number of dogs on this property, I believe (no proof) that this is an attempt to legitimize the keeping of all these dogs".

I wasn't sure if he realized how contradictory this was. His concerns were that we wanted to start a commercial kennel; yet he didn't believe that we really wanted to start a commercial kennel. The funny thing was that he knew full well we didn't want to have a commercial kennel; we'd discussed it over dinner. And the MD knew full well that our application absolutely was *"an attempt to legitimize the keeping of all these dogs"*

It was odd, but not too worrying. Most of all, we were upset by the comment *"As it stands there is an inordinate amount of barking that does come from this property"* since this was a barefaced lie and one which, it would eventually transpire, he was well aware of making. Clearly our apparently friendly acquaintance with them had been an illusion. And by the way, why would there be an increase in barking/howling if we had a licence? Would the knowledge of our newfound commerciality inflame the dogs and set them off on a frenzy of pent up barked anger?

As the day wore on, our discomfort in receiving these missives subsided; but there was one more to come, even more shocking to us. This is what it said.

"We own and operate a commercial dog kennel approximately quarter of a kilometre north of the Starmer property. Our kennel is the sole income for both of us. If another kennel was to open within such close proximity, it would have an effect on our business.

Our kennel has had no complaints of noise or disturbances of any kind. Having another kennel in such close proximity may have a bad reflection on our kennel if any complaints are received to them.

Even though the Starmer's may not use their kennel licence to run a commercial business, if the property is approved of this application, and the property sells, the new owners may wish to open a commercial kennel business. Again, we need to protect our livelihood and there is no need to have two kennels within quarter of a mile. As we too are great supporters of dog rescue, we support rehabilitating and rehoming rather than keeping such a large number of dogs in our house."

Quite apart from the fact that (as you may notice) our properties got further apart as the letter goes on (they're just under *half* a mile apart as the hearing subsequently demonstrated) and the fact that the Canadian free enterprise business culture meant nothing to them, this letter was more hurtful to us for the personal implications than the damage it would ultimately do to our licence application.

Unlike the writer of the previous objection, we had genuinely considered these people to be friends rather than acquaintances. We had socialized with them on several occasions, and been invited to their house only two weekends before this took place. They had been grateful for Sharon's healing work and appreciated my marketing work. At least one of them claimed to have been reading 'Some Dogs' and was supposedly enjoying it greatly. They knew with one hundred percent certainty that we did not want to start a commercial kennel and that it was only the licencing laws that forced us into this situation.

It was obvious now that either the friendship had been an illusion or that to them, personal relationships were a secondary consideration to business interests. Perhaps we were merely being naïve. Perhaps we just had a different personal code. But if we were going to do that to someone, we would have had the guts to tell them up front and have discussed the issue with them. Had they done so, we would have given them any assurances they needed, legal or otherwise. And I could have put them straight on the laws regarding the transfer of licences and the ways in which they may be divested, so that they need have had no concerns. The fact that they chose this rather insidious route was both a huge disappointment and a major blow to our application.

Worst of all was the last comment. It was unnecessary and hypocritical when placed in the context of our previous discussions. We were left reeling, our confidence, to a large extent, shattered.

Trials and Tribulations: The Hearing

It would be fair to say that in the lead up to the hearing, we had regarded its outcome, positive or negative for us, as something of an inevitability. Whatever would be would be. We approached it with sanguinity and didn't worry about it. Since its outcome was a feature of our future, the etheric would reveal next to nothing about it lest that distort our freedom of choice.

On the morning that it arrived, we set off, each of us with unpleasant feelings of disquiet deep within our stomachs. Jenny, home for the long summer vacation, remained at home with Tristan to watch over the dogs. She had been utterly incensed by the libellous comments regarding our children's welfare and had wanted to come to be able to reply to the accusers face-to-face. We knew that if she did so, she would really want to give them a piece of her mind. We doubted that she would be able to control her tongue given how inflammatory she found the comments; Michael also concluded that her presence would serve no purpose.

When we arrived, it became obvious that the hearing was to be conducted very much like a court case, and we were immediately presented with another last minute piece of 'evidence' submitted by the complainants. This was even more puzzling. It was a review of 'Some Dogs Are Angels' posted on-line that they had apparently found the night before. It said the following.

"I have just bought a book called 'Some Dogs Are Angels'. I want to recommend it very strongly to everyone who reads this.

It is a beautifully written true story about an English businessman who discovers that he can hear and communicate with angelic beings. This is disruptive enough, but when he is told that one of his dogs is the actual physical incarnation of an angel on earth (an avatar), his life, and that of his family, is turned upside down. Eventually they end up moving to Canada and owning 19 dogs, most of which are rescued and have amazing, funny or very moving tales of their own.

As well as the story itself, the book is full of wonderful information from what the author calls 'the angelic realms'. At first I was a bit sceptical about this, but by the time I'd finished, I was a total believer. It answers a lot of questions for me and I'm sure it would be a great help to others who search for answers about life, the universe and everything!

Somewhat embarrassingly, I have to admit that initially I was drawn to the beautiful picture of one of the dogs in the story that is on the cover (and I'm not even a dog lover!). But I was unprepared for the full impact that the story had upon me. As I read it I laughed and cried in equal measure, and when I'd finished it (which I did in one sitting, only going to sleep when I'd finished it at 5am - it's compulsive reading!) I started reading it again the next day. I'm now on my third time going through it.

At one point the author makes the rather bold statement "If you're reading this book, it's because you're meant to." I really believe I was meant to read it. I was drawn to it and once I'd started it, I couldn't put it down. It's full of light and love and hope and it has messages we could all learn from. I don't usually recommend books because I think that reading is such a personal thing. I'm making an exception here because I truly believe that if more people read 'Some Dogs Are Angels', the world would be a better place.

My only gripe is that I wanted to buy more copies for Christmas presents and I was a little disappointed that I couldn't find the book on the Indigo website. Neither have I managed to find the book in stores apart from the one in Bragg Creek where I bought it. But there is a website called www.somedogsareangels.com and it is available for order there.

If you read it, you will most certainly not regret it and it could even change your life!"

Why they felt that this was evidence of anything other than the fact that the writer had enjoyed the book, was beyond us. Did it prove something that they thought we would deny? Did it prove I was insane? Perhaps in their eyes, that was it. A man who openly admits that he can hear angels, surely *must* be mad and therefore shouldn't have a commercial kennel licence. Did they believe that the ability to talk to the etheric was a criterion the council would be considering?

Just then, we observed those whom we assumed to be the progenitors of this interesting line of thought, talking to a planning officer in the distance. We weren't one hundred percent sure as we had never seen them before and from that distance, we couldn't even make out their features. It was an odd energetic thing. A vibration we sensed from a considerable distance. They deported themselves with what seemed to be somewhere between anger and self-righteousness.

Before we could conclude one way or another, a voice behind us said "Hi you guys" and we turned to see Scott and Shannon's neighbour from across the road. "I think I should tell you that I'm not exactly here in support of your application" he smiled, evidently expecting that this would come as a surprise to us. "Yes, we know" I said. "We had your letter of objection emailed to us yesterday". He visibly paled. Did he really think that it would be a secret? "Well, there's no hard feelings" he said, "It's nothing personal". And he placed his hand on Sharon's shoulder.

I have known Sharon for twenty five years and we've been married for twenty three. She is still probably one of the nicest and mildest people I've ever met and certainly one of the most accommodating you could come across when it comes to other people, but I have never seen such a face on her as this very physical contact provoked. A look of absolute contempt came over her as if somebody had just deposited something of unspeakable disgust on her body. I was momentarily stunned by her expression and the icy vibration that came from her was palpable.

Nobody spoke and the tension was broken by our case being called. We followed a planning officer into the council chamber. Ahead of us, the angry couple moved towards the chamber too. They certainly were our neighbours.

As perhaps befits adversarial situations such as this, we were seated at different sides of the chamber which, as I had expected, looked very much like a courtroom. It was a little different from the almost antiquarian Royal Courts of Justice in London that I had visited as a fledgling lawyer, but the gravitas of the place and the formality of the situation was obvious. We had the benefit of observing another planning hearing before ours; so the process became apparent to us.

We, as applicants, would have the right to make a statement. The councillors could then question us if they desired. The objectors would then have the right of reply and they could also be questioned. We could then make a final statement and the council would give their decision within a fortnight of the hearing.

If you have ever been involved in a court case in any capacity, you will certainly be aware of how intimidating a situation it can be. I was grateful that my life experience had equipped me well for this type of event, if only because Sharon certainly had no wish to speak. Nonetheless, I had never been in a position where so much that was so deeply personal to me depended upon the outcome. I found my mouth drying up and a feeling of butterflies in my stomach, which was most unlike me. Michael, as always, was very reassuring and asked that when the time came for me to speak, that I simply channel what was said. I readily agreed.

Thus it was that in presenting our 'case' for being allowed to have the licence, I was clear, concise and passionate. I refuted, without any direct reference to them, the accusations levelled at us by the objectors and countered their arguments. Overall, I was more than usually softly spoken and on occasion I sounded overly emotional and appeared to be on the point of breaking down. I had to pause to master the feelings that welled within me as I spoke of our love for the dogs. Later, when Sharon justifiably criticized my performance for these aspects, Michael countered that it was exactly the way he had wanted it to be. There was, he said, more purpose and method in my delivery than we knew.

The Council member's questions were fair, balanced and reasonable and I was able to reply with ease and with more composure. Then it was the turn of our neighbours, and a fascinating thing happened. Sharon's 'shoulder toucher' stood up and spoke with little cohesion to any line of thought he presented. Normally a confident and urbane fellow, he spoke in non sequiturs. He summed up his entire argument with the statement that "Well, I don't think it's right that people should be allowed to have that many pets".

Then it was the turn of the angry couple. The husband was clearly nervous and although I was listening very carefully, I personally found

296

his statements almost unintelligible. He muttered some things about 'high bred Huskies' (we had to supress our smiles), and cougars; and then he sat down.

Then his wife stood up. She was a lot more together in what she said, but was quite brief. At the end of her statement, very loud and very clear, she expressed her view that Child Support Services should be sent to our house because of the conditions in which we kept our children, the slander there for all to hear.

The council seemed to not even register the statement. They asked a few questions and then I was allowed to make my final statement. I used the opportunity to refute their accusations regarding our children's welfare, pointing out that our daughter had wished to be present and of her love of coming home. I also explored the irony of their comments since they had never even seen us before that day, let alone had opportunity to gain intimate knowledge of our family circumstances. I explained that my previous successes in business had allowed us to have a home of considerable comfort. Finally I made it clear that our intention had never been to harm or cause distress to anyone.

The Council chairperson then asked if any of the members had any more questions and there was a brief pause before one of the panel members, who in the introduction had been described as a lawyer, asked us the following. "So, according to the statements made, you have been living here, with these dogs, for four years. Is this correct?" We replied affirmatively. She turned to the objectors. "And this complaint was made after they had lived here for how long?" Nobody spoke. Then she turned to Scott and Shannon's neighbour and said "And you seem to have had no cause to complain before this licence application was submitted? Is that right?"

There was silence from all of them. No answer was given and in the silence, the implications spoke for themselves. The hearing was over.

Aftermath

Our application was refused.

By the time we'd arrived home there was a message waiting on our answering machine from the MD letting us know that as a matter of policy, it would be inappropriate land use to have two commercial kennels in such close proximity. The fact that we didn't actually want a commercial kennel seemed to mean little. However, the council members wanted us to know that they had been sympathetic to our cause, and that they would be prepared to allow us some time in order to rehome our dogs. Nonetheless, in order to comply with the ruling, we had to get rid of twenty two. So for us, it came down to this: Lose your dogs or lose your home.

The choice took a millisecond to make. We had to move home!

Not for an instant would we be prepared to let even one of the dogs go, so we immediately began to consider our next move. However, we now found ourselves in a difficult situation with trying to get any new home since our impecunious circumstances and my lack of full-time employment meant that we could not get a mortgage. What remained of our once substantial equity in the house would be next to nothing after debts had been repaid. It might just be enough for a down payment, provided I had a job. Irrespective, the ever mounting debt dictated that we needed to sell our house but there was no way we could do this with twenty five dogs in it. So we couldn't stay but we couldn't go until we had somewhere to go to and we couldn't get somewhere to go to until we'd gone. Nice!

Around this time I redoubled my efforts to get a job, simply by casting the net much further afield. We did some pretty detailed research into the different Provinces based upon MD responses to multiple dog ownership vs. job availability and discovered that The Maritimes would be a pretty good bet for us. We all liked the look of the place (Tristan was particularly enthusiastic) and I was surprised by the number of jobs that came up in my field. In the weeks that followed I began to get very favourable responses, including numerous telephone interviews. This gave us new hope and a confidence that we had not experienced for quite some time now. It was like finally seeing a glimpse of light at the end of a long and dark tunnel. Although taking a job there would have been a matter of free will, we still thought it prudent to ask Archangel Michael whether or not it would be for our highest good to be there. He confirmed that this was the case, referring to the very pure energies of this place, which are assisted by the presence of whales.

Why did the whales help?

Not everything that is on the planet is quite what it seems to be.

Whales are in fact Ascended Masters that support the energy fields of the planet and are of great service to both it and to the human race. This makes their wholly unjustifiable slaughter all the more unconscionable.

With so many positive auspices, we began to warn people that we considered it likely that we may end up moving east. It was quite moving to receive responses from almost everyone that they would prefer us to stay here and many said that they would put it on their manifestation agenda that we remain. Although this was touching, we imagined that it would be of little impact if going east was for our highest good. What we hadn't considered was what would be for the highest good of all and when we asked this, we were more than a little surprised to be told that it was for the highest good of all that we remained in Alberta. Hereto, we hadn't even imagined that there could be a conflict between our highest good and the highest good of all?

Why was there a conflict?

It is all too easy to imagine that what is for our own personal highest good is that which gives us the easiest life and fulfills our needs in the moment, allowing for a minimum of hardship. This is an erroneous belief since in actual fact, personal highest good is formed by the opportunity to experience all that we should in order to make progression upon our ascension pathway.

300

In younger soul lifetimes (baby, young and mid-term) it is difficult for individuals to do anything that does not serve the needs of their highest good since these lifetimes are only about fulfilment of relationship and experience contracts. This also means that souls of these ages have a far greater degree of self-determination with regard to what they do, where they go and how they live their lives. The learning agenda may happily coincide with the erroneous belief.

Old soul lifetimes are somewhat different since the soul has amassed the vast majority of the experience and learning required. The definition of what is for our personal highest good now changes subtly, since there is an emphasis on applying that knowledge through the exercise of discernment and free will so as to stay in balance. Old soul lifetimes are also encumbered by service contracts. In the exercise of free will there is an onus of responsibility to do that which is for the highest good of all or that which is above and beyond the personal need. The two *may* be happily in correspondence with one another, or they may not.

Putting it plainly, it seemed that our service contract was to be played out in Alberta where we would be serving the highest good of all; yet for our own personal needs we'd be better off elsewhere.

Bummer!

Needless to say, this left us in something of a state of confusion and wondering to what extent we would actually be able to exercise our free will if it conflicted with the highest good of all.

Many of our friends had begun to question why, if we were following the instruction of the etheric, were we struggling so greatly? They were incredulous that people who were able to receive guidance so easily could be unemployable, effectively bankrupt and borderline destitute. Why weren't we being provided for and why were our lives plunged into so much uncertainty? Us aside, why weren't the angelic looking after their own? We had all these avatars so surely they, if not we, would be taken care of? Some were even angry with the etheric. It raised a number of issues that are worth explaining since the answers affect one and all.

Why were we struggling so greatly?

Basically, it was our own fault because we *hadn't* followed the instructions we received from the etheric.

This book is a snapshot of our lives and not a comprehensive blow-by-blow account of all that befalls us. There has however, been one major omission that I have chosen to make until now; an untold story that seems to be nothing and on face value, hardly merits a whole chapter.

Shortly after we got Kachina, in response to a friend's request that we find her a 'second hand' avatar, we were driving down to the US border once again to meet with Karen and take a dog from her. As we did so, we were driving through a particular area of countryside when Michael suddenly spoke and said "You should move to this place". I didn't say anything to Sharon, but by a curious coincidence, she began to express how unappealing she found the area. Amused, I informed her of what Michael had said and she scoffed at the idea. We didn't speak of it again and it was now more than a year and a half later.

Nevertheless, the implication was clear. We were *meant* to move.

Had we acted upon the guidance, our circumstances would undoubtedly now be massively different. Our struggles had come about because we hadn't listened, not because we hadn't been warned!

People receive guidance on an almost daily basis, particularly with major issues that occur in their lives. On one level, we simply don't look for this guidance. On another, our ability to accept it and act upon it is often a matter of trust, or rather lack of it. That which we may perceive as our instinct is therefore ignored, often to our great cost. Much of the prescience that we receive in the moment as a feature of our supported state of being, later becomes confused by (or encapsulated within) what we then think of as the wisdom of hindsight. It's a lot more than that.

Why weren't the angels providing for us?

From everything that has been written in this book, I hope it has become clear that we *were* being provided for. Most certainly, the methods were unconventional, but the wagon, albeit it on one wheel, was still rolling along. The involvement of our family, friends (and even well-wishers who had read 'Some Dogs' and wanted to help) was more support than we had any right to hope for.

Some of our friends seemed to think that the etheric could do more and I had to remind them that they are angels, not fairy godmothers with magic wands! The parameters and limitations of their interventions have already been explained. There is little else that they are able to do that would not constitute direct involvement, and therefore interference in our lives. We had no doubt that they had done and continue to do as much as is possible to effect the most positive outcome for us. Even so, all lives are subject to the vicissitudes that uncertainties cause.

It is nonsense to believe that we can be provided for materialistically by the etheric. It is actually quite disheartening to hear people stating the belief that money would be the resolution to all of their issues. For old souls, money actually makes it harder to see what's what. It can be a major distraction from our true purpose and even stop us from pursuing our service contracts.

<u>Why was there so much uncertainty?</u>

Our lives are always subject to the interventions of the free will of others and thus, nothing is ever certain. In all the possible outcomes that we pursued (only a few of the many are hinted at here) we found ourselves buffeted by other people's choices. That's the way life is and although it was inconvenient, it would have been folly to expect otherwise.

On a day to day basis, our lives were no more uncertain than they had ever been. The only difference was that those aspects of our lives that were being affected were somewhat 'larger' than most people face in such a concentrated fashion.

In actual fact, one of the constant reminders that we received was that things were progressing as they were supposed to!

Why weren't the avatars being looked after?

From the etheric's perspective, the avatars were absolutely fine right where they were. They knew that whatever happened to us, we would ensure that our charges would be well fed, well looked after, loved and protected. They'd even sent people to help us with them specifically.

Another question that frequently came up from locals related to the energy line that formed part of the area's light city. The avatars presence was in large part responsible for charging it. If we were going, what would happen to it?

What would happen to the energy line?

The charging of the merkaba, the geometric shape that formed the boundary of the light city of which the energy line was a part had been a role played by the avatars ever since our arrival in the area.

The light city was a dormant energetic formation (best explained in a channelling I did in 2009) that had its functionality rapidly rekindled by their presence. With the birth of our Husky litter it had received a massive infusion of energy, and was now effectively restored and, to a certain extent, self-sustaining. Its maintenance would now seem to fall to a single avatar (the one referred to in the previous box) whose sole responsibility it would be to 'run' the energy.

Ours were now required elsewhere to perform another service, hence the imperative that we *must* move.

You may wonder how we now fared with our neighbours. Although we saw nothing of them, it did not stop us from being the recipients of further interesting experiences of them. A mere two days later, I received an email from our 'friends' at the kennel asking me to do some more marketing work for them and offering us some raw chicken for our dogs that they did not want. It was quite clear that they did not anticipate that we would know anything of their involvement in the hearing and were still prepared to pretend to be our supporters. I think I managed to remain balanced in my response.

Thanks for your message. We appreciate that you thought of us with the chicken. However, at this point it would seem somewhat hypocritical of us to accept it from you. We were made aware of the content of your objection letter regarding our kennel license. We have been reeling from its implications ever since and it is this that now colours our response.

We greatly value being up front in our dealings with people. We were really disappointed that you didn't feel able to discuss your objection with us. We would have assured you that we would never seek to profit from selling our property with the license attached. We would have done nothing to harm your interests. We would have made any legal commitment you wished in order to reassure you of this. Perhaps then you may even have felt able to support our application. It would have helped. Instead, we now face a choice between our dogs or our home. Naturally, the dogs win every time!

Thus, we will be leaving the neighbourhood (maybe even the Province) and, apparently, not in a position to help anybody with anything. We were greatly saddened to learn in your objection that you disapprove of what we do with our dogs. We honestly thought that you understood and accepted us and our motivations. We had been looking forward to a long and enjoyable friendship with you. However, we do not feel that your actions reflect the friendship that we thought was coming our way. Therefore, our personal values prevent us from accepting your, nonetheless, generous offer, for which we thank you.

A week afterwards, we were to learn that Scott and Shannon had been talking with their neighbour's partner, who had not been present at the hearing. She had explained to them that she had been very opposed to his joining in with the objection and they had quarreled over the issue. She revealed that they *never* heard our dogs and that his representations had been somewhat less than truthful. We weren't surprised but felt no rancor. We were also very grateful that this lady had the courage to tell the truth. A few weeks later I met with her at our gate. She had found our errant white Husky Tasha on their land and was returning her. I was touched and very appreciative when she expressed her sorrow at what had now befallen us. I was also very pleased for her that in the face of what must have been uncomfortable opposition, she had maintained her integrity.

Many of our friends asked us for the etheric's take on their behaviour. The answer from Michael was fascinating in its import.

<u>What was Michael's answer?</u>

If you look at the bizarre chain of events that had led up to our current circumstances, it goes something like this: The bikers stopped. The Huskies barked. The neighbour complained. We had to make the application. The application was refused.

The fact that the bikers stopped at the end of our drive was in itself highly unusual but it was the Huskies barking that was the trigger for the complaint. The neighbours were absolutely within their rights to complain. The council members would never have allowed the licence not only because of the land use issue, but because we were meant to move on.

In all of these interventions, there was prior knowledge and purpose. Each played their role as had been agreed in the etheric. Beyond these relatively simple and unconnected actions, there was no need for anything else to occur. The original complainants had in many respects done us a favour being the catalysts for our move which was, for the reasons previously explained, now essential and a matter of some urgency. Without their intervention, we would not have shifted the avatar energies that were now required elsewhere.

However, in then making objections that were comprised of wild misrepresentations and falsehoods, the original complainants had gone too far. As for the others, they had 'chipped in' with their wholly unnecessary interventions when there was no need for them to be involved at all.

Michael explained that for each and every action that we take we put in motion vibrations that have consequences for our lives and the lives of others. For some actions there are just and reasonable causes that are proportionate to that which has instigated them.

With what was ultimately to transpire in this situation (as will be seen) this little group of people had become participants in causing vast amounts of misery and heartache without any justifiable cause.

We now began a waiting game to see what would happen next, unsure even as to when the MD would impose their ruling upon us, since no timescales were mentioned.

In the meantime, life went on. With so much drama resulting from these events, the other aspects of our lives could almost be considered tame by comparison. After all, being a mouthpiece for the etheric and doing such simple things as taking people on guided hikes could never produce traumas like these, could they?

High Drama!

Guided hikes take plenty of planning and it's necessary to have a familiarity with the route you're taking well in advance of departure, if only so as not to appear foolish in front of your guests! This entails walking the route in advance, which I do accompanied by dogs. When we lived in the UK and had only six dogs, I could walk all of them together with relative ease. The scent hounds would strain at the leash, but they did not possess the sheer power of the Huskies. So if I take these pulling machines on my own, I can just about manage two. This is only possible if they are tethered to a very strong and sublimely comfortable handmade walking belt that I got in the U.S. some years ago. It doesn't make for an easy hike so I will often press-gang Tristan into coming along to share the load but he isn't too enthusiastic about being dragged up the side of a mountain. I therefore considered myself very fortunate when a few months ago, I persuaded my father who was over on a visit, to join us on a hike.

It was a Thursday and we were checking out a route for an Earth Healing hike that was due to take place on the following Saturday. It was a comfortably warm and sunny day but certainly not hot. The climb we were making was classified in the guidebooks as 'moderate'. We were taking Timba, Tasha and Indy with us and we left home bright and early, knowing that the relatively short hike (around 8 km) would allow us to easily be home by 4:30 pm. As we began our ascent, it became clear that the pathway had been affected by recent rains. It was rutted and difficult underfoot, constantly crossed by rivulets and occasional stronger water flows that forced you off the track if you wished to avoid the quagmires that they created. The gradient was somewhat steeper than might have been anticipated.

Nonetheless, it did not produce too much of a challenge for Tristan or I, he because of his youth, me because of the frequency with which we hike. It was a little bit different for my father however. In years gone by he had been a keen hiker until his enthusiasm for walking gave way to a passion for cycling. However, that passion was overcome by a love of sailplane gliding that took away much cycling time. His pursuit of raw physical activity had therefore markedly decreased in recent years and the effect of the climb showed. Frequently, he would pause to catch his breath and his stops to regard the ever more magnificent views afforded by the climb became longer.

After a while I noticed that Indy, normally at the front with me, was making up the rear with Dad. I was quite pleased that he had apparently stayed behind to look after him, or at least provide company. However, after some time, it became apparent that his motivation might be a little different. He seemed to need the breaks every bit as much as my father. At first I thought nothing of this. Indy is only four years old and had done many long, hot and strenuous hikes with us before. This one was a push-over by comparison. So even when he began to breathe in a very curious manner when we reached the top of the mountain, I thought little of it. From that point onwards we did a very easy ridge walk to our destination and then stopped for lunch. Indy's breathing was back to normal and he drank well from his portable water bowl before choosing to sit right in front of Dad (wearing his most alluring doggie expression), as he ate his lunch. Having achieved minor success with his begging he proceeded to relax while we enjoyed the fine view. After forty minutes or so, we retraced our journey back along the ridge and then paused briefly at the start of the descent. It was at that point that Indy's odd breathing started again.

Within minutes it had intensified to huge heaving sighs and gasps, strangulated sounds and intense fits of gagging. He brought up bile and weaved backwards and forwards drunkenly. Then he would suddenly race forward, almost unseeingly, only to collapse a few metres ahead of us and begin the process all over again. After several repetitions of this cycle, he seemed to recover and his breathing became almost normal. Even so, we had to coax him to go any further down the mountain. Whilst Tristan looked after Tasha and Timba (who had suddenly become very subdued), Dad and I took turns in supporting and encouraging Indy to go forwards. After a hundred metres more, the scary breathing began all over again. He made one more effort to go forward and totally collapsed, unable to move and too heavy to lift.

By this time I was fighting panic. I had seen nothing like this before and assumed that since he had been drinking normally and it wasn't hot, that it must be poisoning from something he'd eaten en route but knew that Indy seldom touches anything whilst out hiking. Even his water has to be taken from a bowl, unlike the others who drink from any old stream or puddle. This was certainly not a re-run of Timba's toad attack.

We stood around rather helplessly for half an hour, vainly hoping that he would make a recovery. We were around three kilometers from the car, so we debated ways of carrying him down the mountain; we soon realized that any attempts to do so improperly could easily damage his spine or bodily organs, to say nothing of the effect of his not insubstantial weight upon us. We were significantly out of cellphone range so there was only one thing left to do. Someone would have to go and get help. I wasn't about to leave my precious avatar alone on the side of a mountain, so somebody had to stay. I wasn't comfortable with Tristan remaining and Dad is not insured to drive my car, so he had to be the one. I felt bad about this, since this had been meant to be a pleasurable day for the three generations but he didn't seem to mind.

Tristan and I literally ran down the mountain. Once out of the presence of their ailing alpha, the Huskies perked up again and were only too pleased to play their part in assisting us to descend as quickly as possible. We got back to the car in about twenty minutes, parked on a very good road devoid of other traffic. At that point I had no idea of what form of help I could get, or how far I would have to drive to get it, so I put my foot down. I drove like someone possessed, surprised to notice that although the needle on the gauge had stopped when it showed 180 kph, we were still accelerating. I was only able to focus on the need for urgency, certain that Indy was probably dying, constantly glancing at the cellphone to see if we had a signal. After fifteen minutes we burst into an area where the indicator bars flickered into life. I braked hard, pulled into the side and phoned Sharon, my voice breaking as I told her that Indy had collapsed.

I asked her to call our vet in Black Diamond and ask if they had a stretcher and if they could give us any advice. I would await her return call. Long minutes passed and Sharon did not respond. I was aghast when a frustrated glance at the phone showed that there was no longer any signal. We screeched off down the road again and it was another five minutes before we left the dead zone and I was able to reconnect with Sharon. To my immense relief she told me that a stretcher was waiting for us at the clinic and that Ingrid would be on hand to give me whatever guidance she could. Even better, she and Shannon were going to come out to help us carry Indy down the mountain and they were setting out as soon as they had their things together. All I had to do was get there and at this rate, I could arrive in fifteen minutes.

The stress of the next minutes was unbearable for instead of making the rapid progress I had expected to Black Diamond, I drove straight into roadworks upon re-joining the main highway. Fifteen minutes became forty. But true to their word, the stretcher, a thermometer, calm guidance, and even a syringe for certain eventualities awaited me in Black Diamond. I felt much more optimistic. There was a slight hint of disquiet in Ingrid's voice as she outlined the likely causes. The biggest indicator would be Indy's temperature. It sounded like heat stroke and that was better than some other options. She refrained from saying that even heat stroke wasn't that good.

We chose a different route to get back to the mountain so as to avoid the traffic hold ups and I rang Sharon to give her specific guidance of what to do when she arrived. I had already let her know the name of the day use area where we were parked, so now I warned her of the road works and told her an avoiding route to take that she was familiar with. "Go to the end of the range road then turn right and keep going". They couldn't miss it and by now their helping hands would be only twenty minutes behind me.

Some thirty minutes later we arrived back at the day use parking lot and I gave Tristan instructions to relay to his mother. He would need to point out the trailhead and ask them to join us as soon as possible while he would wait in the car with the Huskies. Then I set off to climb the three kilometres up the mountain for the second time that day. I'm not that fit so running was probably a bad move. Nonetheless I did, arriving virtually exhausted, more than two hours since I'd first left but delighted to find that Indy was alive and that Dad was fine.

The Leonberger had moved a little since I'd departed and had kept trying to make his way down a thickly wooded slope off the side of the track. Anxious not to be led away to a point where they would become invisible to me upon my return, Dad had managed to lead him back and now Indy was collapsed in mud amidst the forest shrubbery. An unresisted insertion of the thermometer revealed that he did indeed have heat exhaustion, and it became obvious that the dog had been trying to do exactly the right thing. Some way further on down the slope was a crystal clear stream. He wanted, and desperately needed, to cool off in its icy waters. Now he was too weak to get there by himself and the slope was much too steep and perilous for us to carry him down. Instead we decided to sit and wait for the cavalry, in the persons of Sharon and Shannon. Between the four of us, carrying the stretcher, (which had six handles) would surely be a relatively easy task.

My calculations that the ladies were about twenty minutes driving time behind me had not taken into account the likelihood that their ascent to meet us might be somewhat slower than mine. So after half an hour I got the stretcher out and we decided to see if we could position Indy on it by ourselves. He was like a limp rag and resisted nothing that we did, but he was too big for the stretcher! At full length, depending upon how we positioned him, either his head or his legs hung over the edges! We got around this by having him lie with his legs at right angles to the stretcher so that they hung over the sides and not the end. This would make carrying slightly more awkward but with the four of us it shouldn't be such a problem.

With our patient ready for transportation, Dad and I decided to lift him back up on to the path so that we could at least get a feel for the weight. With a fair amount of huffing and puffing we lifted one hundred and fifty pounds of deadweight dog back onto the track. As we did so, the fully flexible material of the stretcher sagged under his bulk and for a moment I feared that the handles might come off. Only later did I discover that it could have held the weight of several large dogs!

After a few minutes more waiting for our female saviours, it began to rain. We decided to try and carry Indy down a little further with just the two of us. This would serve the purposes of giving us something to do as well as saving time by getting closer to them; furthermore, there was a point lower down where the stream crossed the path. We could lay him in it to cool off. As we picked the stretcher up once more, it became evident that because of the steep gradient, one of us would have to walk at the front either going backwards or with their back to the stretcher and their arms behind them, whilst the other at the back would not be able to see the ground beneath them as they walked forward. Neither presented a good position. Dad was less confident about not seeing what was beneath his feet so we adjusted our positions with me taking the back, and off we went.

It's easy to say but it wasn't easy to do! The strain on our backs and shoulders was instantaneous, the pathway rapidly became slippery and treacherous beneath our feet and the near comatose patient rapidly developed a tendency for suddenly moving on his mobile chaise longue, causing the weight and balance to shift, and even more stress and strain on the stretcher bearers. On a good 'lift' we might manage to walk fifty feet in two minutes, but then need five to recover. After the first ten minutes we looked back up the mountain and it was disheartening to see that we could still see where we had begun from. In fact, we hardly seemed to have made any progress. The burden was awkward and mighty. This was clearly going to be a nightmare. Thank heavens help was on its way.

Eventually we arrived at the stream, laying down the prostrate and immobile dog in the middle. The waters ran over the stretcher and all around him but it was not deep enough to have too much effect. We began to collect water and throw it over him, eventually soaking his whole coat. Ten minutes later, a recheck of the temperature revealed a drop of a mere .2 degrees so we let him soak for a while longer before deciding that getting him down off the mountain might actually be the better option.

Off we went again, quickly accepting, but never adjusting to what felt like some form of ritual torture. We experimented with different methods of carrying and walking but realized that our options for alleviating the difficulties involved in carrying his huge bulk were sorely limited. We tried to make light of it by making jokes about the patient and the outcome of the afternoon. Dad said that the next time I invited him on a hike he would ask which dogs were coming first! All the while we eagerly anticipated the arrival of our rescuers who would undoubtedly arrive around the corner at any moment like knights in shining armour. After another hour of intense physical distress and disturbingly little progress, we had begun to question whether or not our confidence in them was sound. All the while, the one who was in the best position was Indy, prone, spent, out of it. We envied him.

Two hours later, we had descended a considerable distance down what had become the pathway from hell. We had navigated steep and difficult areas of loose rock and been up to our ankles in mud that had left us with damp and dirty feet. I had developed a huge blister on the back of my foot. Dad had fallen once but miraculously managed to ensure that Indy was not dropped. The dog's temperature remained the same but he was slowly becoming more aware. This brought more movement and a determined desire to hang his head over the side of stretcher to watch the pathway ahead, making the bearing of his palanquin even harder for the slaves. Help was nowhere to be seen and we felt pretty fed up.

Finally, around the corner ahead of us came Tristan, at the gallop. He had run up the mountain and assured us that we were not far from the parking lot. Sharon was not far behind him. Grabbing hold of a handle, it was remarkable to see the difference just one person could make, but it was a further ten minutes before we reached Sharon (never the fastest climber) who was immediately more worried about my seventy six year old father who, she thought, looked in worse condition than the dog. After he had reassured her that appearances can be deceptive, the story of their late arrival came out:

Before setting out, both she and Shannon had tried to look up the day use area I had named on the internet, but found no trace of it. Instead, there was a reference to a mountain with the same name twenty miles to the south of our location. When they arrived at the end of the range road where I had said to turn right, they decided that I must have been mistaken in my directions due to the stress I was under, and therefore turned left since that way led to the other place. When they arrived at this location, there wasn't even a signposted day use area, so after a long and futile search, they decided to go back to where I had originally asked them to come to. And there, sure enough, was the big sign for the day use area and our car parked in the lot!

It also transpired that Shannon was unwell. Even so, she had immediately agreed to bring Sharon in her car (as we only have the one vehicle) but now, only Sharon and Tristan were up to making the ascent. Now, Sharon joined in the carrying and the four of us struggled on for another five minutes before sending her off to get the car and bring it to the trailhead.

Ultimately, we arrived back at the road at 7:30 pm, after just over two and a half hours of descent. But the trauma was not quite over. It was Shannon's car that awaited us on the highway, not ours. Tristan, waiting for nearly three hours on his own in the car had had the air conditioning on without the engine running. Our car battery was flat as a pancake. So we loaded the limp, wet Leonberger into the back of Shannon's estate car, Sharon, Tristan and Dad piled in, and I went to wait in our SUV for roadside assistance in the form of Scott.

As soon as they got back in cell range, Shannon phoned Scott and he drove straight out, despite an exhausting day at work, to give me a jump start. No wonder I refer to them as our 'best in the world neighbours' at the beginning of 'Some Dogs' and this book!

It was 10:15 pm by the time I made it home and I was overjoyed to see that Indy was up and about, walking (albeit rather crazily) and drinking a little. But he wasn't out of the woods yet.

Miracles Can Happen

The next morning, Indy seemed much stronger, but although he drank, he refused to take any food. Later that day Sharon and I drove to the vet's clinic to return the stretcher (which we had washed overnight) and offer our thanks. Although we reassured Ingrid that everything seemed fine, she was not so sure. She explained that even though his collapse appeared to have been caused by heatstroke, there may be residual damage to Indy's organs and we needed to keep a close eye on him. She gave us two litre IV bags to get some more fluids into him and demonstrated how to insert the needle under his skin. Later, I sat with him as the liquids dripped through the tube. He was very co-operative despite the discomfort the needle must have caused.

By that evening, Indy seemed OK but still refused to eat. So when I awoke on Saturday to find him listless and staring, we instantly agreed that Sharon would not attend the hike and instead, seek an emergency appointment with Ingrid.

It was quite difficult for me to explain to the assembled group why Sharon would not be attending. A big lump formed in my throat as I explained what had happened to Indy. Many of the participants already knew and literally loved him. Tracey was there and I noticed how distraught she was, fighting to hold back her own tears.

The hike for me was something of a nightmare. There I was, revisiting the scenes of this disturbing event, whilst still being massively unsure of whether or not he would survive the ordeal. For once, time seemed to pass very slowly. Alarmingly, I was constantly told by Michael that I should get in touch with Sharon. So when we had completed the meditations and channelling and I had returned the group to a place where they could easily find their way back to the parking lot, I requested their permission to leave the hike early and once more hurried down the mountainside.

Another mad dash to the point of cell reception and a phone call revealed the truth: Ingrid had conducted tests and to her great relief, Indy's kidneys, which were highly likely to have been damaged by his

317

experience, were actually fine. However, his liver was, quite literally, cooked. The saving grace in this was that the liver is a self-regenerating organ. It just needed a little bit of help. For this, she prescribed liquid milk thistle (to be accompanied by beef burgers!) to try and tempt him to eat. I spent the rest of the afternoon going from one drug store to another, until I eventually found it a mere twelve minutes from where we live. As you may imagine, the beef burgers were somewhat easier.

By the time I returned home, Sharon had thoroughly researched milk thistle and found it to be something of a 'miracle cure'. It was heralded as being very effective for humans with liver issues and although dogs weren't mentioned, if Ingrid thought that it might work with Indy, then that was good enough for us.

Initially we added it to the beef burgers, but he wouldn't eat them and they got devoured by a voracious pack of Huskies. Then we tried it in his water, but that got left on the side. So eventually we resorted to squirting the liquid into his mouth, which he wasn't happy with at all. I guess I expected a 'miracle cure' to produce something miraculous and instantaneous, but I was to be disappointed. Sunday dawned with precious little improvement, so we dosed Indy again. By evening he was still lethargic and he now hadn't eaten since the previous Wednesday. Panic started to set in.

In spite of my difficulties in channelling clearly for myself when under stress, I plaintively requested Michael's assistance. He was very reassuring. "Do not have any concerns. This is neither an elective nor an assumed illness. He will make a full recovery."

What are elective and assumed illnesses?

I am regularly asked about health issues in one-to-one channellings. Individuals are reminded that the human body is a perfectly functioning organism. For many reasons it may experience minor ailments such as colds, headaches, muscle strains etc., but these are of small consequence. If it becomes majorly dis-eased, this is for one of two reasons.

Either the individual who has the dis-ease has elected to have it before they ever incarnated; or they have assumed the illness during their lifetime for some reason.

Choosing to have a dis-ease, especially a terminal one, may seem like a really dumb choice. After all, who would want to be bothered by the ravages an illness may bring to the body?

However, the experience of having an illness may be of great benefit to the individual, or members of their family who are affected by it. For ourselves, coming to terms with, accepting and even embracing physical difficulties can provide huge leaps forward in our personal learning. For others, coping with the emotions provoked by illness in others can also provide tremendous opportunity for development. Although the circumstances at the time may seem painful in so many ways, in the long run, an elective illness is always a good thing.

An assumed illness is somewhat different. The term refers to dis-ease that we acquire during our lifetime because of what we create in our own bodies. To understand this, it is first necessary to recognize that our minds have the ability to control every aspect of our physical being. Mostly, this is achieved on an automatic basis. But the body can be a self-healing organism if we are able to harness the ability of our minds to create whatever is required within our body. Unfortunately, by the same token, our minds can also create the imbalance of dis-ease.

When we are born into a lifetime, we do so in recognition of the state of being that we are meant to deliver ourselves against. In other words, we decide that we will be a particular way. If an old soul then lives out their life in contradiction of these expectations, as a consequence, they may 'assume' a dis-ease. This will be for one of two very specific purposes, either to draw them up to a realisation of what they are doing by creating a very impactful signpost; or to give them an opportunity to restore the mastery that is within their capability by healing themselves.

This is perhaps best illustrated by the story of a lady Sharon and I knew some years ago. She had lived a very successful life but freely admitted that she was mercenary and cut-throat in her approach to business. She contracted cancer and conventional medicine was having little effect. She sought assistance from various alternative healthcare practitioners, including Sharon, and was miraculously cured. She became fascinated by how this was possible and sought answers that were to prove awakening for her. She was quite transformed. However, after a couple of years she found the prospect of the material benefits of her old world too seductive to resist and she quickly reverted to her old ways. In all respects, her former self returned and perhaps unsurprisingly, so did the cancer.

Fortunately, I knew exactly what those terms meant, so I was greatly comforted.

Monday showed little improvement and we went to get more IV fluids. Ingrid had begun to be very concerned by now and tried to prepare us for the worst.

On Tuesday it was as if nothing had ever happened. Indy was up early, demanding his food. We mixed in the milk thistle and he ate ravenously. From this point on there was no looking back.

Our joy that day was to be marred by the arrival at our gate of the MD peace officer who had been dealing with our case from the outset. He had always been courteous, his manner formal but understanding and as benign as may be expected from someone who performs that role. Today he was aggressive and hostile, demanding to know why the dogs were still here. He related how the MD had just cleared out another home where the owner had similar numbers of dogs and things had turned 'real nasty'. I knew exactly what he meant by 'real nasty'. It was another way of saying that the dogs were put to sleep. He asserted that we had better get rid of ours or things would turn 'real nasty'. He speculated that perhaps animal welfare services should get involved, implying that our dogs weren't well looked after, and that things could turn 'real nasty' (although at my insistence, he took back his words when he saw the obviously excellent condition of the dogs who had come to greet him at the gate). When I talked of trying to get a job in the Maritimes that would resolve our location issue, he questioned what a man without a job was doing with so many dogs. In general he seemed to be doing his best to infer that we were little better than dog hoarders. "Why don't you just hand them over to a rescue?" he demanded. My protestations that we were in essence a rescue fell on deaf ears. He scoffed when I said that the dogs were a part of our family. He went away issuing the dire warning that something would have to be done and that things were going to get 'real nasty'.

Clearly somebody had been on his tail about resolving this case which still remained open, perhaps letting him know that if he didn't do something, things were going to get 'real nasty'.

Operation Noah's Ark

A few weeks later, things started to get 'real nasty'. We knew what would happen because our first response after the peace officer's visit had been to ask the MD for more time. In refusing, they explained that we would now get a letter stating what steps we had to take in order to comply with the outcome of the hearing.

What we didn't expect was that a 'Stop Notice' would be physically stuck to our front gate. It was there for the entire world to see, as if we were being pilloried. It was humiliating.

Amongst the legal double speak, it said:

You are hereby ordered to: <u>Immediately reduce the number of dogs to three (3) adult dogs as permitted by the Land Use Bylaw</u> to bring the operation into compliance with the Land Use Bylaw and Municipal Government Act.

You have no later than 12:00pm (Noon) on the 11th day of October, 2010 to comply with this Stop Order.

The significance of the date, some two weeks hence, was not lost upon us and seemed a cruel choice. It was Canadian Thanksgiving.

At the bottom it said **'No person shall remove this without the authority of the Municipal District of XXX'** (yet when we acknowledged its posting and requested permission from the MD to remove it, they chose to ignore us).

It is difficult to describe the feelings that the notice evoked. We had known full well that it was coming, but to see it plastered on our gate in black and white was like a blow to the solar plexus, leaving us with mounting feelings of nausea. Prior to its arrival, we had chosen to ignore its inevitability; not because we were in denial, but because making it a part of our current reality would merely have served to prolong the discomfiture it would cause without need. Now we had to face it.

The horror of the implications of the notice hit Sharon like a steam train. It was as if she now descended into a dark pit of despair. It wasn't so much the enormous difficulty that finding twenty two homes presented, as the knowledge of how awful losing even one of our dogs would be for us. The prospect was too dreadful to imagine and for hours, she wandered around like a speechless ghost, her eyes perpetually full of tears, a shell of her usual self.

Throughout the day that we had discovered the notice, nothing got done. It was not possible for me to discuss what we would do with Sharon since the enormity of the problems seemed to overwhelm her. I was very grateful that by the evening, Michael was ready to intervene, and even more grateful that Sharon was only too willing to listen.

"You are allowing fear to take hold within your vibration. It unbalances you and your perspective. You have no reason to have any concern. All of your dogs will be taken care of. Irrespective of what comes to pass, you will get them all back."

The effect of these simple words upon Sharon was almost miraculous in the way they galvanised her. Immediately we began to plan a Noah's Ark like campaign of placing the dogs in temporary homes. The idea was quite simple, we would spread them out amongst the homes of friends who had the ability to not only look after them, but would cherish their presence.

Within half an hour, we had identified several potential Ark sites, but although we knew of many likely locations, the acquiescence of the owners still had to be sought! So that night we sent out a distress email to all of those who could possibly help and within twenty four hours, offers of assistance started to flow in.

Now we came to a more onerous decision. Which three would we keep?

Those of you who have read the book 'Sophie's Choice' will understand how this felt to us. Although our circumstances were nothing to rival the hideousness of that character's choice, it felt a bit that way. So many of our charges came from horrendous backgrounds and had come to trust us so totally that letting them go would feel like a further betrayal to them. How would the avatars that had come to us with a specific purpose to fulfill cope with being moved from their base of activity? All this was to say nothing of our personal emotional attachments to them as our pets and members of our extended family.

Our debate quickly foundered on rocks of sentimentality and pain, so we tried to inject detachment and practicality into it. After that, it was almost obvious. The three biggest dogs ate the most food, took up the most space and might well be the most intimidating for others to have in their households. The three happened to be Indy, Kachina and Poppy. Indy was the avatar that held the light for the whole property and it would not be a good idea to move him on anyway. Kachina was totally bonded to Indy and being separated from him would undoubtedly lead to escape attempts and her permanent loss. Worse still was that her being a wolf could lead to all sorts of complications. She simply wouldn't fit in anyone's house, wouldn't accept new owners, would panic and who knows what would ensue. Poppy would drive anyone crazy with her need to protect. This would inevitably lead to barking. These three had to stay.

For the rest, we expanded upon the criteria for home selection. Our biggest concern was that a dog would escape from its 'Ark'. We knew full well that they could all demonstrate tremendous determination in their desire to be where they wanted to go. The thought of any of them wandering unfamiliar streets in search of their home was agonising. Availability of safe containment and a fosterers familiarity with the wiles of canines was a principal consideration. Second, but not far behind, was the need to find homes where the dogs would be truly valued for what they were and receive something like the same degree of affection and acceptance that they get here. Fortunately, we knew many people who felt the same way about our dogs as we do.

Proximity was also something of an issue for us. We wanted to place the dogs within reasonable travelling distance of our home so that we could visit with them as often as time permitted. The offers that we had provided places for single dogs, pairs or even one group of three; but several were as far as three hours away and from our perspective, were very much less than ideal. There were also a couple of offers to house all of the dogs together. Whilst at first glance these seemed ideal and quite exciting, the accommodations in which they would be housed could have proved disastrous since they offered neither heat nor light, nor human companionship.

Overall, we received offers that would have enabled us to house all of the dogs twice over. Unfortunately, many, though very well intended, were not suitable. This did not prevent us from being profoundly grateful to all those who made the kind offers and we realized how privileged we were to have so many supporters.

Of course our criteria, whilst very protective of the dogs and certainly for their highest good, almost made a rod for our own backs. So it was no real surprise that with only just over a week before the 'Stop Notice' came into effect, we had only managed to find places for twelve of them. With these, we were very comfortable. Regrettably, the remaining ten were the Huskberger puppies and Timba and Lara's family. In anyone's book, they would probably qualify as the most demanding amongst our dogs, if only because of their very high energy levels. Also, Huskies are so pack orientated that to split them up into singles would have undoubtedly caused much heartache for them and difficulty for any potential fosterer.

Many people who knew of our plight asked a question that seemed obvious to them. "Why don't you put them in kennels?" It goes without saying that these people knew neither of the full extent of our personal financial plight, nor of the vast expense involved in kennelling so many dogs. We were also acutely aware of how stressful kennelling could be for dogs, and were still haunted with the remembrance of how Dougal would actually lose his ability to wag his tail when kennelled, so convinced was he that he had been abandoned. Although this was not to be his plight on this occasion, we feared the reaction of ten animals who had never known anything other than utter freedom.

Nevertheless, when our friend Fawna suggested that we contact StoneHaven kennels, which was a mere twenty minute drive from our home, we did not dismiss the idea. She explained that it had recently been taken over by an old school friend of hers called Cheryl who had herself been extensively involved in dog rescue. Perhaps she may look sympathetically on our plight?

Sharon immediately made contact and after a long and enjoyable phone conversation, excitedly announced that Cheryl was prepared to look after all of the dogs for a few weeks at least. From the call, Sharon was able to discern that Cheryl was indeed empathic to our situation, as well as being fully conversant with the difficulties of dealing with MDs. Ironically, she had heard of the book (although she had not actually read it) and had not dismissed us as nutcases! It wasn't ideal, but we reasoned that the Huskies were resilient, and even more importantly, Cheryl promised that she would give them all as much exercise as possible. The deciding factor came when Michael confirmed that it would be a safe place for them. As far as we were concerned, there could be no better endorsement of a kennel than his. We joked that the Queen will endorse suppliers to the monarchy with a royal warrant, entitling the holders to display a crest that denotes 'By Appointment to Her Majesty Queen Elizabeth'. That would have been of less worth to us than Michael giving StoneHaven the OK!

The only problem was that it wasn't free. Although Cheryl was enormously kind and magnanimous, allowing all ten to stay at StoneHaven for a very low price, even that was more than we could afford. Curiously enough, this caused me no concern at all and although Sharon was momentarily a little panicked, Michael was reassuring that all would be well.

Later that afternoon Sharon spoke with Tracey who, throughout the turmoil of trying to rehome the dogs, had been a tower of strength to us. In our darkest moments she would arrive full of cheer and encouragement, freely giving of her time, money and wine(!), and asking nothing in return. She had been a real blessing to us and demonstrated in such a concrete form what true friendship meant. And now she became our angel. As soon as she got off the phone with Sharon, she telephoned Cheryl at StoneHaven and paid in advance for the dog's first week there. Not only that, she gave her commitment that she would pay for their entire stay, for as long as it took. We were humbled.

All of the dogs now had Arks. We could rest easy in the knowledge that all of them would be safe. All we had to do was put them on board. And that would be the easy part, wouldn't it?

The Nightmare Diaries

If I had believed that the hard part was over, I was foolish and deceiving myself.

The anticipation of giving the dogs away bore little resemblance to the agonies that actually doing it created.

It occurred to me that the experiences would best be described when they were raw and in the moment. So these 'diaries' were written last thing at night on each of the days that we surrendered the dogs to their respective Arks.

If you find the chapter title slightly melodramatic, then I haven't managed to convey just how much the dogs mean to us and how much a part of our lives they are. From our perspective, these days were truly nightmarish.

8th October, 2010

It began today. With a lurking sense of dread and horrible inevitability, the day has arrived on which we must begin taking the dogs to their foster homes. First to go will be Tasha and Emily.

I spend the morning grooming Emily (yes, it really does take that long, in spite of the fact that she is our smallest dog!) and she misbehaves as usual. She hates grooming. Nevertheless, a rather smart PBGV is now ready to go and spend an unknown amount of time with Susan Palliser.

The routine of the grooming masks the sickness in the pit of my stomach. At least she'll be happy with Wexford and Jock. I think.

Sharon spends the afternoon at the vet with last minute preparations for other dogs. She returns tense and upset. The vet on duty – not our usual kind and sensitive Ingrid – is aggressive and unsympathetic to what's happening to us. Sharon comes home with a bill for more than double what we'd expected or are able to 'cope' with. She forced

Sharon to have jabs for the dogs that are not required by the kennel and not necessary. I'm furious.

We load Tasha and Emily in the back of the SUV. They think they're going for a walk and so are very excited. Our first stop is Angie and Diego's. How ironic that Tasha is coming to them in this manner, almost exactly a year after Duke arrived. This fact is not lost upon Natalia, their youngest. She immediately starts to call them both Duke. Tasha is delighted to see Ruby and the 'real' Duke and they play wildly together. Diego goes out to buy wine since they're dry and he can tell that we need a drink. We discuss our situation while the girls play with the dogs. Tasha seems really happy. The wine helps.

Time is getting on and there's still Emily to deliver. We quietly slip out while Tasha plays with the other dogs in the back yard. We're not sure if she knows we're going. It's easier for us this way.

A mere ten minutes later and we're at Susan's. Emily is very excited. She's been here before and knows the routine. She can't wait to see her friends and be with dogs smaller than herself. It's tough being the smallest dog in a large pack.

Susan orders in takeaway. Superb Indian food. The rich flavours assuage the pain of what is to come. Temporarily.

The time draws near for us to depart. It's already 10:30pm. Susan suggests we take Emily and Jock for a walk. I can't bear to go, so I let the women take them while I keep Wexford company. He's asleep and oblivious.

When they return, I go to fetch the car, parked a short distance away. Emily follows me to the door and cries. She stands up on her hind legs and puts her front paws on my thighs. She knows. I blot out the angst and walk out into the cool evening. It clears my head but only a little.

A few minutes later I'm back. I walk in the front door and Emily rushes to greet me, crying again. It's too much and I'm fighting back tears now. We try to be cheerful as we bid Susan goodbye with our heartfelt thanks. She tries to be cheery too. It won't be for long. As I hug her I can barely supress a sob and I can't look at Emily. How did she know? How does she feel? I glance at her as we get in the car and then I speed off. I pull out at a junction and don't even see the car to my left. The driver's not pleased and tailgates me for a while. I don't care.

The car ride home is silent. Forty minutes of non-conversation, punctuated by my noisy use of tissues. I didn't expect Emily to get to me like this. Is Sharon being more stoic than me or does she hide it better? The tears make starbursts of the car headlights coming in the opposite direction. It would be quite pretty apart from the fact that it makes it hard to see.

When we arrive home it's nearly midnight. Twenty three dogs are there to greet us. Do they know two are missing? Do they have any hint that it might be their turn soon? Let's pretend everything's normal for now.

9th October, 2010

Inara is like a dog possessed this morning. She runs around wildly with no apparent reason. Sharon thinks that she's looking for Tasha as they normally play together at this time. I'm inclined to agree. She seems lost without her. Not so normal after all...

Susan rings first thing to tell us that Emily cried rather pitifully after we left. Thank god I didn't know or I'd have turned the car around. However, Susan let her sleep on her bed and that seemed to console her. This morning she took Emily for a long walk with Jock and she was like a pig in clover. At least she's happy.

As I'm feeding the dogs I look around for Tasha who's unusually quiet this morning. Oh yes. She's not here. Then a few seconds later I reserve Emily's portion for her, knowing that she prefers to eat separately. I catch the error and give her bone to another of the dogs. I'm struck again by the sadness of her absence.

Angie rings later to let us know that Tasha is fine and doesn't seem to have noticed we've gone! She stole Duke's food this morning and is tiring him out with her constant demands for play. Valeria and Natalia are lavishing affection upon her. I hope Ruby doesn't get forgotten. Another sigh of relief for us.

Grim reality returns as we have to take Daisy to her foster home. I'm a little worried about this one. The home is great, well fenced with lots of room. The people are lovely. But the memory of Daisy's agonized howl when we first rescued her still haunts me. I drive slowly and we agree that we won't necessarily leave her there.

Daisy trots into the house happily enough and we sit and have coffee while she explores. She ignores the incumbent Dachshund and spends a little too long sitting by my side staring up at me with pleading eyes. I can't take my eyes off her. I feel she knows. I *know* she knows.

Our friends are so nice and so understanding. As we leave, we promise to return with Daisy before the deadline. As I open the car door for Daisy she leaps in gratefully and I know I'm not telling the truth. She's not coming back here. It's not the people or the house. They're perfect. It's her. I can't leave her with strangers. We need somewhere for her where she won't feel abandoned and still has familiar things around her. Fortunately Sharon agrees. We'll have to think again on this one.

We call in at Belcourt Pet Spa on the way back with some advertising materials I've produced for them. Michael and I chat about the business. It's a good distraction. Murray comes out and asks how things are. I'm elusive in my reply but he's not fooled. He goes out to talk to Sharon who's remained in the car with Daisy and the others who've come with us.

When he returns I know that Sharon hasn't told him how I feel. I haven't told her. Maybe it's obvious. Maybe I'm laughing and smiling too much. But Murray reads my agony like a book anyway. He reminds me that everything is happening for a reason and that there's a light at the end of the tunnel. Then he tells me to explain to the dogs what's happening and let them know it's only temporary. It's too much to handle and I start sobbing in the store like a big baby. He understands and gives me a much needed hug. I think he's upset to see me this way. Me too.

We spend the afternoon driving, looking for possible needles in the haystack of where we might, with a minor miracle, find a suitable place for us to live. There are so many imponderables. So many chickens before so many eggs. So much that depends upon the free will of others. It's probably a waste of time but it's better than doing nothing and it's a glorious day. Indy and Molly are in the back and Dougal and Daisy on the rear seat. I feel the need to keep Daisy close for as long as we can.

The journey is fruitless and we don't get back until late. Susan rings again. Emily is good. So are the twenty three we still have with us. We can pretend a little bit longer. But I know that tomorrow isn't going to be quite like this.

10th October, 2010

Today is spent getting ready for our guests who are coming for Thanksgiving. Of course, they're not so much coming to celebrate with us as help us remove the remaining dogs from the house by midday. Not exactly a cause for celebration. As a precursor, more depart today, but not until late afternoon. Small blessings...

I work outside while Sharon and Tristan work inside. The dogs follow me around and are generally unhelpful but a great distraction. Their antics give me some comfort and watching their games of chase is a good sop. But inevitably, the time comes when I must take today's foster fur kids away. Just before I do so, I come downstairs to check my emails. I'm intercepted by Kaiti who follows me. It's unheard of that she's even up and about, let alone showing this much interest in what's going on. Of course, she knows. As I type replies she sits under the desk and demands affection. I can't remember the last time she was this fussy.

A few minutes later I load her and Pippa into the back of the SUV. Our first and second ever dogs, and here I am, taking them away. Do they feel betrayed? Following Murray's advice, I've explained the situation to them. It's a mercifully short drive to their temporary lodgings. The lady of the house doesn't seem too keen on them being there even though she's agreed to it; but her husband is enthusiastic. We lead them indoors and bring in their bedding, bowls and food. Then I have to rush out again to pick up their third refugee.

When I arrive back at home a sorry sight meets my eyes. Sweet Pea is terrified. She senses something bad is about to happen and her eyes are as big as saucers. Sharon's been outside with her, trying to reassure her and give her some comfort. But as soon as the car arrives, she tries to run away. Her back legs aren't up to it and she doesn't get very far. Then she does her 'hundred pounds heavier' magic and I can barely lift her into the back.

She cries all the way there. I open the tailgate to find a quivering wreck. As I lift her out there's a terrible smell. I dismiss it as nerves. I put her down on the grass at the fosterer's backyard and she feels better. She seems to like the flat ground and the grass. She wanders around for a while and I wonder what that persistent smell is. The hosts come out to see her. Kaiti and Pippa join them. At first, Kaiti thinks she's encountering a strange new dog and gets all antsy. Then she realizes it's 'the one from home' and all is OK.

The three of them roam around the new grounds, having a ball sniffing at the new stuff. But that smell's still troubling me. Eventually Sweet Pea over exerts herself and inevitably collapses. As I go to help her up, I realize that in her fright, she opened her bowls all over my the leg of my pants as I took her out of the car. Not a pleasant experience for either of us!

I hang around explaining their many quirks and the lady begins to warm to them. Kaiti and Pippa go inside but Sweet Pea is still thinking about it. Eventually we have to give her some help as there is a miniature bridge between their yard and the house. It's nothing for a dog in normal shape, but for Sweep, it's literally a bridge too far. Once indoors, she settles down. That is to say, she flops. Kati's already asleep on her bed and Pippa's pestering the lady for attention. Nothing new there then.

As I drive home I'm not too upset. I'm confident about this one and the people are close enough to us to allow for easy visitation. I congratulate myself on not getting upset today. I'm reassured because Kaiti understood totally (she's fully conscious) and Pippa's a prostitute for affection. As for Sweep... today is worse for Sharon.

This evening Colleen stops by with wine and cheese. She and Sharon drink the red and I drink the white. All of it. It helps. Then Colleen departs with another dog and I maintain a stiff upper lip. No problem there. But three hours later, I get an email telling me how sad the dog seems and I'm in floods of tears again.

Nineteen remain and the worst nightmare of all is still to come.

11th October, 2010 (Canadian Thanksgiving)

I wake up surrounded by nineteen dogs. It's just how it was when I finished writing 'Some Dogs'. How ironic. By midday there can only be three left.

Early morning phone calls reassure us that all seems to be well with the evacuees. Emily has started to cry at infrequent intervals, but Susan gives her chews to keep her happy. The noise making could be a ruse by Emily. She's crafty.

Friends come to help us take the dogs away. The process is long and drawn out and painful. The tension mounts and becomes palpable. The dogs are only too aware that something is very wrong. I avoid their gazes. With every step she takes, Sharon is pursued or blocked by canines seeking reassurance.

A final convoy sets out with fifteen minutes to go. Sharon goes with them in our car. I'm the one left in the house. I await the visitation from the bylaw officer. He will confirm that we have complied with the stop order and it will be removed from our gateway. The pillorying will have ended. Part of me is relieved that I am left behind. I don't have to face the many scenes of letting dogs go. I don't want to shed any more tears. My eyes hurt too much. I don't even say goodbye to them. I've already spoken with each one 'privately'.

An eerie silence descends. Indy goes into some kind of depression. He flops on the front porch with his head between his outstretched front legs. Kachina searches the compound endlessly, more curious than upset perhaps. But the effect is most profound upon Poppy. Suddenly there is no pack. Nothing to protect. No purpose. She mopes around the house, quieter than I have ever seen her, her head hanging.

I begin to prepare our Thanksgiving dinner with the copious amounts of food our friends have brought over. I leave the front door wide open. The dogs wander in and out and I know that when the officer arrives, they'll alert me to his presence. I mentally rehearse things I'm going to say, mixed in with permutations of things I'd like to say. But I'll not get the chance to say anything. He doesn't show up. What a cruel trick to play. What a way to make a Thanksgiving go well.

So I begin to ponder just exactly what we have to be thankful for today. So much pain, so much hardship, so much stress, so much anguish, has filled our lives. But the funny thing is, none of that matters. The list of what we have to be thankful for far outweighs anything that has gone before.

We have a marriage that has survived a period of difficulty that has tested it as if in fire. It is still strong. It has been for twenty three years.

We have neighbours and friends who are incomparable in their support, generosity and kindness. They are unfailing in their encouragement, and financial support. Without them, we would have foundered many months ago.

I have parents who do not judge and give without asking for return. They have never let us down and pulled us out of the worst scrapes imaginable, often to their own cost.

And we share our lives with twenty five wonderful souls, many of whom are angelic beings. They infuse us with their amazing energies and lavish their unquestioning and unending love upon us.

We have a lot to be thankful for.

The party that has delivered the dogs to their foster locations returns. The mood is surprisingly cheery. The dogs have, for the most part, responded well to their temporary change in circumstance. It seems that those little chats worked.

We sit down to our Thanksgiving dinner. We are surrounded by our friends and there is much merrymaking. The remaining three dogs mill around us quietly. It's as if their whole personas have become muted. I'm in awe that Sharon is so cheerful when my heart is so heavy.

Of course, not everything is always quite what it appears to be. Our guests leave and Sharon retires to our bedroom. She has a complete meltdown behind closed doors and sobs her heart out.

I go to the basement to sit here and type this. It's difficult to see through the mist of tears. We are no longer surrounded by our dogs. There are only three left. Twenty two cannot be with us. I feel a hollowness inside. Numb. Bereft.

The rains have started to pour and all the Arks with our precious cargoes have sailed away from us.

Footnote

It seems a great pity to end the book on this sad note but it is what it is!

Although it is a little while since I wrote 'The Nightmare Diaries', our prospects of finding a place where we can go with all of the dogs where they will be safe, protected and accepted, seem slim.

I am no closer to getting a job. Whenever I arrive at a point where the chances of an offer seem high, something changes the minds of the employers. I know it's the etheric. I have agreed to what I must do, and that doesn't seem to involve a return to full time employment.

The wheels on the wagon keep turning thanks to Tracey. We have depleted all of my sainted parent's capital and only survive thanks to her.

This rollercoaster has had us experiencing despair, despondency, heartache, sadness, grief, anguish and fear. Yet these are all emotions which we may master. We can choose how we feel about all situations that we face and it is part of our journey and the lessons that we learn to see circumstances for what they are.

Experiencing any of the above serves no real purpose for us. It adds no value and changes nothing. So we've allowed ourselves what were perhaps necessary moments of self-pitying indulgence and we've gone through all of those feelings listed.

Now it is time to gain mastery over them and see the situation as it really is and do what is necessary to restore it to how it was meant to be.

On occasions we catch ourselves wondering if we will ever get the dogs back. When we do so, we see the thought for what it is. Stupid.

Of course we will.

We know this because an Archangel told us so.

WOULD YOU LIKE TO HELP?

Archangel Michael has always maintained that the messages within these books need to be spread more widely.

We cannot do this alone. Although 'Some Dogs' has certainly proved to be a local bestseller, Michael is still adamant that we seek to ensure global distribution for the story because of the learning it imparts.

The most effective way of ensuring that this happens is to create awareness through viral marketing. In other words, through word of mouth.

If you have enjoyed reading of our continuing adventures and would like to help spread the information as Michael has requested, may we please ask that you do the following?

Tell anyone and everyone about the book.

Tell them how much you enjoyed it.

Recommend that they read it too!

Write a review on Amazon, even if you didn't get your copy from there.

In this manner, we are confident that it will quickly and easily spread all over the world.

BUT, please *don't* lend anyone your copy; ask that they buy their own.

(When I wrote this in the first book, the owner of one 'Angel' store read it and refused to stock 'Some Dogs'. They believed it was contrary to 'pay it forward' principles. It's a shame they didn't read the rest of the story, then they might have realized that we needed the money raised by the book to look after the avatars.)

We are still hopeful of raising enough money to start the Avatar sanctuary that is mentioned in 'Some Dogs'. Clearly, our personal circumstances have overtaken us somewhat, but we will get there!

As we stated before, the more copies that are sold, the closer we come to ensuring that as many of these amazing beings as possible are given the opportunity to fulfill their promise of service if they fall upon hard times.

And by promoting awareness of all that is revealed here, we may even manage to change the world for the better along the way.

Thank you in advance for your help and kindness. It is truly appreciated.

If you would like to know more about our story, see more pictures of the dogs and find out other ways in which you can help. Please visit our website at:

www.somedogsareangels.com

You can also get regular updates on what's happening to us and see other pictures and videos on our Facebook 'Some Dogs Are Angels' fan page.

Made in the USA
Charleston, SC
18 October 2011